Translating Human Rights in Education

English Abstract

Legally backed by the United Nations Convention on the Rights of Persons with Disabilities (UN CRPD), inclusive education has gained momentum as a global human rights paradigm in recent years. But how does Article 24 of the convention actually influence the development of inclusive school systems within state parties? The book probes current meanings of inclusive education in two contrasting state parties to the UN CRPD: Nigeria, whose school system overtly excludes disabled children, and Germany, where this group primarily learns in special schools. The paradox of disability segregation being maintained despite rhetorical and legal support for inclusive education counters long-held views on the fundamental differences in reform processes in contrasting world regions. In both countries, policy actors aim to realize the right to inclusive education by segregating students with disabilities into special education settings. In Nigeria, the demand for special education arises from the glaring lack of such a system, but in Germany, conversely, from its extraordinary long-term institutionalization. This act of diverging from the principles embodied in Article 24 is based on the steadfast and shared belief that school systems that place students in special education has an innate advantage in realizing the right to education for persons with disabilities. Accordingly, inclusion emerges as an evolutionary and linear process of educational expansion that depends on institutionalized special education, not a right of persons with disabilities to be realized in local schools on an equal basis with others. Based on this result, the book reveals that the crucial factor undermining the realization of Article 24 of the UN CRPD is the discursive-institutional power of special education to corroborate each nation's progress in providing "Education for All," or the lack of it—both nationally and internationally. Based on this result, the book proposes a refined human rights model of disability in education that shifts the analytical focus toward the global politics of formal mass schooling as a space where discrimination is sustained.

German Abstract

Artikel 24 der UN-Behindertenrechtskonvention (UN-BRK) etabliert inklusive Bildung als globale Menschenrechtsnorm. Doch wie beeinflusst Artikel 24 UN-

BRK die Entwicklung inklusiver Schulsysteme? Diese Frage wird im Buch basierend auf der Rekonstruktion bildungspolitischer Diskurse in Nigeria und Deutschland untersucht—zwei Vertragsstaaten, deren Schulsysteme gleichermaßen, wenn auch höchst unterschiedlich, durch das Recht auf inklusive Bildung herausgefordert sind. Diese Analyse zeigt, dass trotz rhetorischer und rechtlicher Unterstützung inklusiver Bildung die Segregation von behinderten Kindern aufrechterhalten wird. In Nigeria erwächst die Forderung nach einem sonderpädagogischen Fördersystem aus dessen gänzlichem Fehlen, in Deutschland hingegen aus seiner außerordentlich langen Institutionalisierung. Dieser Akt der Abkehr von den in Artikel 24 verankerten Prinzipien beruht auf der festen und gemeinsamen Überzeugung, dass Schulsysteme, die Schüler:innen in Sonderschulen unterbringen, einen Vorteil bei der Verwirklichung des Rechts auf Bildung für Menschen mit Behinderungen besitzen. Dementsprechend wird Inklusion integriert in einen evolutionären und linearen Prozess der Bildungsexpansion, der von institutionalisierter Sonderpädagogik abhängt, und wird damit nicht zu einem Recht von Menschen mit Behinderungen, das in wohnortnahen Schulen verwirklicht wird. Auf der Grundlage dieses Ergebnisses zeigt das Buch schließlich, dass der entscheidende Faktor, der die Verwirklichung von Artikel 24 UN-BRK untergräbt, die diskursiv-institutionelle Macht der Sonderpädagogik ist, den erreichten oder ausbleibenden Fortschritt eines Landes bei der Realisierung einer "Bildung für Alle" zu belegen—sowohl national als auch international. Auf der Grundlage dieses Ergebnisses schlägt das Buch ein menschenrechtliches Modell von Behinderung in der Bildung vor, das den analytischen Fokus verlagert auf die globale Politik der formalen Massenschulbildung als einen Raum, in dem Diskriminierung aufrechterhalten wird.

TRANSLATING HUMAN RIGHTS IN EDUCATION

The Influence of Article 24 UN CRPD in Nigeria and Germany

Julia Biermann

University of Michigan Press
Ann Arbor

For questions or permissions, please contact um.press.perms@umich.edu

Published in the United States of America by the
University of Michigan Press
Manufactured in the United States of America
Printed on acid-free paper
First published May 2022

A CIP catalog record for this book is available from the British Library.

Library of Congress Cataloging-in-Publication data has been applied for.

https://doi.org/10.3998/mpub.12000946

ISBN 978-0-472-07528-7 (hardcover : alk. paper)
ISBN 978-0-472-05528-9 (paper : alk. paper)
ISBN 978-0-472-90270-5 (OA e-book)

The University of Michigan Press's open access publishing program is made possible
thanks to additional funding from the University of Michigan Office of the Provost and the
generous support of contributing libraries.

Dissertation, Humboldt-Universität zu Berlin, Faculty of Humanities and Social Sciences,
2018

.

To Malte

Contents

Digital materials related to this title can be found on the Fulcrum platform via the following citable URL: https://doi.org/10.3998/mpub.12000946

Figures

Tables

Acknowledgments

This work is based on my doctoral thesis titled "Comparing Article 24 UN CRPD's Influence on Inclusive Education in Nigeria and Germany: Institutional Change in Educational Discourse," submitted to the Faculty of Humanities and Social Sciences, Humboldt-Universität zu Berlin (day of Defense: 2 May 2018).

This book would not have been possible without the support I received from numerous people over the last decade.

From the first rough ideas through the dissertation process to the final manuscript, Prof. Dr. Lisa Pfahl and Prof. Dr. Justin J.W. Powell have been a constant source of support, encouragement, and inspiration. I'm very grateful to both. I would also like to extend my gratitude to Prof. Dr. Vera Moser for her support as chair of the doctoral commission.

My deepest thanks goes to all interviewees and supporters in Nigeria and Germany. Their help has been invaluable in learning about inclusive education change on the ground.

For the dissertation, I received a doctoral scholarship from the Friedrich Naumann Foundation for Freedom. In addition, financial support to prepare the book manuscript came from the Faculty of Education and the Institute for Educational Science at the University of Innsbruck. For both, I am very grateful.

For their important feedback and critical comments at different stages of my research, I would also like to thank all participants of the doctoral colloquia at the University of Bremen and Humboldt-Universität zu Berlin as well as the members of research workshops at the University of Innsbruck and the Academic Network for Inclusive Education: International and Comparative Perspectives.

My deepest gratitude goes to Malte for his unrelenting support, foresight, and courage. Everything is nothing without you.

Abbreviations

BMAS	Bundesministerium für Arbeit und Soziales (Federal Ministry of Labour and Social Affairs)
BMZ	Bundesministerium für wirtschaftliche Zusammenarbeit und Entwicklung (Federal Ministry for Economic Cooperation and Development)
BuReg	Bundesregierung (Federal Government)
CESCR	International Covenant on Economic, Social and Cultural Rights
CRPD	Committee on the Rights of Persons with Disabilities
CSACEFA	Civil Society Action Coalition on Education for All
CSO	Civil Society Organization
DGB	Deutscher Gewerkschaftsbund (German Trade Union Confederation)
DIMR	Deutsches Institut für Menschenrechte (German Institute for Human Rights)
DPhV	Deutscher Philologenverband (German Philologists' Association)
DPO	Disabled Persons Organization
EFA	Education for All
ESSPIN	Education Sector Support Programme in Nigeria
FME	Federal Ministry of Education
FMWA	Federal Ministry of Women Affairs
FRN	Federal Republic of Nigeria
GPE	Global Partnership for Education

IOM   International Organization of Migration
JONAPWD Joint National Organization of Persons with Disabilities
KMK   Kultusministerkonferenz (Standing Conference of the
               Ministers of Education and Cultural Affairs of the Länder
               in the Federal Republic of Germany)
MDGs   Millennium Development Goals
NAP   National Action Plan
NBS   National Bureau of Statistics
NESSE   Network of Experts in Social Sciences of Education and
               Training
NGO   Non-governmental Organization
NPC   National Planning Commission
NPE   National Policy on Education
NPoC   National Population Commission
OHCHR   Office of the High Commissioner of Human Rights
PISA   Program for International Student Assessment
SDGs   Sustainable Development Goals
UBE   Universal Basic Education
UBEC   Universal Basic Education Commission
UIS   UNESCO Institute of Statistics
UN   United Nations
UN CRPD United Nations Convention on the Rights of Persons with
               Disabilities
UNESCO   United Nations Educational, Scientific and Cultural
               Organization
UNGA   United Nations General Assembly
UNHRC   United Nations Human Rights Council
UNICEF   United Nations Children's Fund
UPE   Universal Primary Education

ONE

Introduction

Translating Human Rights in Education

On 13 December 2006, the United Nations General Assembly adopted the Convention on the Rights of Persons with Disabilities (UN CRPD) by Resolution 61/106 (UNGA 2006). The UN CRPD is the most recent human rights treaty, for the first time explicitly acknowledging that persons with disabilities are holders of human rights, rather than objects of charity or medical interventions (Heyer 2015). This human rights approach to disability has far-reaching consequences for the provision of public goods, including education (Della Fina 2017; Heyer 2021). In line with Article 24 of the UN CRPD, 184 state parties (as of October 2021) are required by international law to ensure inclusive education systems in order to realize the right to education of persons with disabilities (UN 2021). The UN Committee on the Rights of Persons with Disabilities defines in its 2016 General Comment on Article 24 that these are systems that must not discriminate against children and youth on the basis of disability, but rather ensure equal opportunities and participation for all in local schools (CRPD 2016). Inclusive education systems are hence characterized by a "broad availability of educational places for learners with disabilities at all levels throughout the community," places that are, in addition, "accessible to everyone, without discrimination" (CRPD 2016, paras. 21, 22). The importance of inclusive education as a human right is further strengthened with the Sustainable Development Goals (SDGs). Specifically, SDG 4 suggests countries "ensure inclusive and equitable quality education and promote lifelong learning opportunities for all" by 2030 (UNGA 2015).

The global scope of this reform challenge becomes obvious considering the divergent ways in which school systems currently cater for the education of children with disabilities (Richardson and Powell 2011; Köpfer, Powell, and Zahnd 2021). In low-income countries of the global South, universal access to primary education remains—despite some achievements in recent years (UN 2015)—a goal yet to be achieved. The number of out-of-school children remains particularly high in sub-Saharan Africa; this region accounts for over half of the global out-of-school population (UIS 2015, 11). In this context, the realization of inclusive education as a human right is challenged by the widespread reality of outright exclusion from formal schooling, which in particular affects disabled children and youth (UNICEF 2013; WHO and World Bank 2011). In high-income countries of the global North, on the other hand, patterns of disability-based inequalities persist even though they long ago established systems of mass schooling. These inequalities are linked to the institutionalization of special education systems (Powell [2011] 2016; Ryan 2020). Independent of the modes of classification and organization, many special education systems continue to exhibit an overrepresentation of male students, socially disadvantaged children, and ethnic minorities (Berhanu and Dyson 2012; Gabel et al. 2009; Powell and Wagner 2014). In this context, the realization of inclusive education is challenged by the widespread persistence of segregation and separation in schooling (Pfahl and Powell 2011; Beco 2016). These varying educational provisions point out two things: first, the global reality of nonparticipation in mainstream education based on disability and, second, the wide range of challenges to realize equal educational opportunities for all.

Almost all countries worldwide are therefore confronted with the same reform mandate—to ensure inclusive education systems—but are challenged by it in very different ways. How do state parties cope with the normative claims of Article 24 considering their divergent educational realities? Which conditions provide the country-specific contexts of schooling for the realization of inclusive education? And, eventually, what contributions does a human rights treaty make in changing contrasting school systems? Analyzing the effects of Article 24 simultaneously in Nigeria and Germany—two state parties at different ends of the global spectrum of mass schooling—, this book uncovers the complex interplay between international pressures to guarantee human rights and national pathways in education in the most populous countries of Africa and Europe. It provides a deeper understanding of the processes at the global/local nexus that interfere with the enforcement of disabled children's human rights in education—and this despite a global increase in policies, activism, and research on the topic since passage of the UN CRPD a decade and a half ago.

Contextual Understandings of Article 24 UN CRPD

In different world regions, research on inclusive education is concerned with practical challenges of equalizing access and participation at the levels of schools and classrooms (Agunloye 2012; Naraian 2017; Lütje-Klose et al. 2017). Other research additionally points out the critical roles of political will, institutional discrimination, and professional power for and against inclusive education (Lang 2009; Pfahl and Powell 2009; Slee 2013). Neither approach, despite highlighting contextual challenges, engages with what stands between the human right to inclusive education and its realization: the varying and context-specific understandings of Article 24 UN CRPD. These understandings are generated in discourses—regulated practices of knowledge production (Foucault [1969] 2002, 49–50, 201)—in which the global reform challenge is negotiated against the background of national policy frameworks and local realities of schooling.

So far, the contextual appropriation of Article 24 has not yet been the focus of research. Article 24 is primarily used as an argumentative bedrock to legitimize research on inclusive education, and to advocate for reforms, respectively (Werning et al. 2016; Umeasiegbu and Harley 2014; Ziemen et al. 2011). What remains underexplored, though, is the actual contribution of Article 24's human rights ideas for the systematic transformation of diverse school systems, because this requires extensive fieldwork and in-depth comparative research. One vital space where global and local ideas link up are the discourses that translate Article 24 into educational change on the ground. These discourses determine if and how human rights prevail against the institutional forces that so far maintain disability-based discrimination in education systems across the globe. This book focuses on the blend of global and local ideas in federal policy discourses on inclusive education and, in addition, reveals their institutional effects. To underscore global variance, a comparative case study design is applied to reconstruct the translation of Article 24's human rights paradigm in state parties with highly contrasting school systems: Nigeria, which has the world's highest total number of out-of-school children and where most disabled and disadvantaged children have no access to formal education at all (FME 2015; Mizunoya, Mitra, and Yamasaki 2016, 17, 22; Omoeva et al. 2013, 63);

and Germany, which has "one of the world's most differentiated special educational systems," where children with disabilities primarily learn in special schools (Powell [2011] 2016, 151; KMK 2018). The main research question is this: how does the UN CRPD's Article 24 influence the development of inclusive school systems in Nigeria and Germany? Answering this question, the book is the first to systematically compare the translation of the human right to inclusive education into educational change in the global North *and* the global South. This comparison goes beyond a mere analysis of the legal ratification of a human rights treaty. It reveals the processes that determine how human rights ideas and norms gain traction in the first place, and what consequences their implementation in contrasting national contexts has for the systemic inequities experienced by children and youth with disabilities.

Historical Evolution of Inclusive Education as a Human Right

Codified in Article 24 of the UN CRPD, the human right to inclusive education represents the pinnacle of a decade-long struggle to systematically strengthen a human rights approach to disability in education. The framing of "education rights as rights of inclusion" is, as Heyer specifies, a reaction to "the history of purposive exclusion and marginalization of students with disabilities" (2021, 46).

The 1948 Universal Declaration of Human Rights (UNGA 1948), even though guaranteeing everyone the right to education, did not refer to disability, nor did the 1966 International Covenant on Economic, Social and Cultural Rights (UNGA 1966). Primarily perceived as objects of rehabilitation, persons with disabilities were at that time positioned outside the realm of human rights (Heyer 2015, 24–26). The 1975 Declaration on the Rights of Disabled Persons contributed to the recognition of the right to education of persons with disabilities (UNGA 1975, para. 6). Given the strong focus on disability prevention and rehabilitation, however, the document's "equality promises were subject to caveats," as Degener and Begg point out (2019, 46). Integration of persons with disabilities into mainstream society, for example, was promoted only "as far as possible" (UNGA 1975, pt. preamble). Gradually, this focus started to broaden with the 1981 International Year of the Disabled Persons (UNGA 1976). Backed by the year's theme of "full participation," disability rights groups in Germany, for example, staged a so-called cripple tribunal to highlight the human rights violations disabled persons face when segregated in "special" kindergartens, schools, homes, and workplaces (Daniels 1983; Köbsell 2006). The first human rights treaty recognizing the right to education of disabled children was the 1989 UN Convention on the Rights of the Child (UNGA 1989). In Article 23, the treaty declares that state parties must recognize disabled children's special needs and ensure that they have "effective access to and receive education" (UNGA 1989, para. 3).

Eventually, the Standard Rules on the Equalization of Opportunities for Persons with Disabilities (UNGA 1993)—which concluded the 1982–93 Decade of Disabled Persons—outlined steps to be taken in order to increase access and participation. Specifically, state parties were called "to recognize the principle of equal primary, secondary and tertiary educational opportunities for children, youth and adults with disabilities, in integrated settings" (UNGA 1993, rule 6, preamble). This way, segregation was deemed an exemption, but remained legitimate when needs cannot yet be adequately met in the general school system (UNGA 1993, rule 6, para. 8). Taking into account structural barriers, the Standard Rules thus reflect a growing conviction that disabled children should receive the support they need not only in segregated settings, but also in general education.

A year later, in 1994, the Salamanca Statement—outcome document of the World Conference on Special Needs Education—strengthened this approach. Deploying the concept of inclusive education for the first time internationally, the statement's vision was that "schools should accommodate all children regardless of their physical, intellectual, social, emotional, linguistic or other conditions" (World Conference on Special Needs Education 1994, 6). Shifting from segregation to inclusion, the Salamanca Statement suggests that countries strive to overcome the structural-organizational divide between regular and special education via integration; that is, to meet the needs of disabled children in mainstream schools (Kiuppis 2016, 28–29). Over the next decade, the concept of inclusion broadened again, focusing not only on placement and special education within mainstream schools, but on "the issues of *access to*, as well as of *participation* and *achievement* in education for various groups" (Kiuppis 2016, 30). At the 2000 World Education Forum in Dakar (Senegal), for example, the international community agreed on six Education for All (EFA) goals to be met, inter alia, by the development of "'inclusive' education systems which explicitly identify, target and respond flexibly to the needs and circumstances of the poorest and the most marginalized" (World Education Forum 2000, para. 52).

In 2006, the right to education of persons with disabilities was eventually codified into international law with adoption of the UN CRPD (UNGA 2006). Even though all former human rights conventions referred to the right to education for all, Article 24 of the UN CRPD is the first to regulate in a legally binding way that its realization depends on the development of inclusive school systems. In this way, the right to education evolved into a right to inclusive education (Beco 2014; Della Fina 2017; Heyer 2021). Its specifics will be detailed in the following chapter. For now, it is important to point out that the realization of inclusion poses a systematic reform challenge that calls for transformations in and of education to overcome—as the United Nations Office of the High Commissioner for Human Rights states—"discriminatory approaches" that "exclude, segregate and integrate on the basis of the existence of an impairment" (OHCHR 2013, para. 5). In this way, human rights law acknowledges that disabling environments and attitudes are fundamental factors that impede equal access and participation of persons with disabilities and must therefore fundamentally change.

Though it sets universal standards, Article 24 must be appropriated in each ratifying state in order to realize the associated claims in education (see Merry 2006, 222). These two aspects—universalism and relativism—point to the two main strands of criticism directed at human rights. They refer to the concept's philosophical foundations, with biases inherited from European and North American political thought, that is, the universalization of claims that, grounded in particular Western narratives, reimpose global hierarchies (see Mutua 2001; Santos 2009); or human rights criticism targets a perceived "implementation gap," that is, the selective domestic application of codified rights even by those states that drafted, adopted, and ratified the respective conventions (Hamelink 2012; Hafner-Burton and Tsutsui 2005). However, others also point out the unintended consequences and transformative powers of international human rights, referring, for instance, to the 1960s civil rights movement in the United States (Hall 2005) or the global disability rights movement (Degener 1995; Bickenbach 2009).

Explicitly addressing this tension between universal standards and their domestication, this book highlights the ways in which human rights are appropriated, defended, or redefined by actors that use them. Therefore, I take up the proposal of Sally Engle Merry, who has analyzed the mobilization of global ideas for local change: "To translate human rights into the vernacular is not to change their fundamental meanings. Instead, the legal basis of human rights and the institutions through which they are implemented retain their grounding in local structures and understandings" (2006, 219). Interested in how Article 24 effects educational change on the ground, I accordingly uncover the complex interplay between international pressures and national pathways in human rights translations.

Institutional Change in Educational Discourse

In the tradition of a social-constructivist approach to reality (Berger and Luckmann [1966] 1984), the translational model of educational change assumes that the development of inclusive school systems depends on the knowledge (re)produced in discourses on inclusive education (Keller 2011). Within these discourses, global ideas blend with context-specific norms and standards for the education of disabled children. It is with this knowledge that the institutional logics of school systems can be challenged, disrupted, or confirmed—furthering or preventing their transformation (cf. Thornton and Ocasio 2008). To reconstruct this knowledge, I refer to discursive institutionalism (Schmidt 2008) and analyze the coordinative policy discourses on inclusive education among federal policy actors in Nigeria and Germany, that is, the group of state and civil society actors who, in accordance with Article 33 UN CRPD, assume responsibility for implementing the international human rights treaty into domestic law and for developing a national action plan. The debates accompanying these processes are an important and strategic space to analyze the contextual appropriation of human rights ideas, norms and standards. Federal policy actors mediate between Article 24 and school systems as they negotiate and coordinate positions on inclusive education change. In setting the frame for reforms, these negotiations influence whether disability-based exclusions and segregation in schooling are overcome—or sustained.

For this analysis, I gathered over one hundred policy documents and conducted thirty expert interviews during extensive research trips in Nigeria and Germany. Based on this information, I first reconstruct the country-specific discourses on inclusive education to show how human rights ideas blend with institutionalized ideas about the education of disabled children in these two contrasting contexts. Second, I reveal the impact of these discourses on educational change in each case by theoretically explaining the relation between discourses and the institutional environments they are embedded in. To this end, I trace the institutional processes that facilitate the discursive blend of global and local ideas and standards regarding the education of disabled children (see George and Bennett 2005). With this design, I combine a sociology-of-knowledge approach to discourse (Keller 2011) and grounded theory (Charmaz 2014) with sociological institutionalism, in particular organizational and discursive institutionalism (Schmidt 2008; Czarniawska and Sevón 2005a; Meyer and Rowan 1977).

Based on this discursive-institutional lens, I aim to use the terms "children with disabilities" and "children with special needs" in an institutional, not a medical or clinical, sense. Hence, I refer with these terms to the group of children for whom regular education settings are unavailable und inaccessible. I thus take the position that disability-based exclusion and segregation come into existence as children are denied access to or participation in regular schools on the basis of a recognized impairment, disadvantage, or difficulty (Powell 2007, 2013).

The comparative analysis reveals that the discursive translations of Article 24 into educational change in Nigeria and Germany paradoxically highlight the need for an institutionalized special education system in order to realize the right to inclusive education: in Nigeria, because of the lack of special education, and in Germany because of special education's high level of professionalization and differentiation. I refer to this intersection as the "special educationalization of inclusion," understood to be the logic of change that similarly instructs policy reforms in both school systems. Accordingly, the realization of inclusive education in Nigeria focuses on the expansion of a special education system, and in Germany on special education's retention, albeit within general schools. In each case, this logic of change reflects the different ways in which special education is currently provided: in Nigeria not at all, and in Germany in a highly professionalized, segregated system. These provisions are considered by policy actors to be the relevant contextual particularity that in each case eventually requires the decoupling of institutional changes from the requirements of Article 24.

Thus, the different educational provisions for children with and without disabilities characterizing each school system are taken into account. However, the pursuit of context-appropriate reforms also contributes to reform agendas that generate a paradox: realizing the right to inclusive education with the help of special education systems that segregate children between and within schools on the basis of disability. Based on the promise of special education to provide needed additional resources (outside of regular classrooms), ability-selective schooling remains uncontested in translations of the human rights paradigm entailed in Article 24 of the UN CRPD. Even more, its contribution to inclusion is radically reinterpreted—not as a barrier, but as its ultimate enabler.

Outline

The book focuses on the translation of Article 24's human rights package into educational change in Nigeria and Germany. These translations determine how the convention influences the development of inclusive schooling in contrasting systems; they mediate between the global reform challenge and national pathways in education.

Chapter 2 provides the conceptual and theoretical base of the comparative analysis. It first delineates Article 24's normative and regulative content and conceptualizes the human rights paradigm of inclusive education as a "program of change." Second, it portrays the challenges of realizing inclusive education in different world regions and applies the regulative, normative, and cultural-cognitive dimensions of institutions to school systems as the "object of change" addressed by Article 24. Third, the chapter develops a translational model of institutional change, in which I combine neoinstitutional theory and discourse analysis to reconstruct and explain translations. With translations, the analytical interest pertains to the powerful dynamics that instruct the fusion of global human rights ideas and standards with contextual norms and approaches to the education of disabled children.

Chapters 3 and 4 present the Nigerian and German case studies, respectively. I portray the historical developments and current characteristics of each school system, present the data corpora compiled for the empirical analysis and detail the discourses and their institutional effects. For Nigeria, chapter 3 delineates that in negotiating positions on inclusive education, federal policy actors draw on questions about the realization of universal basic education to achieve the developmental goal of Education for All. Yet their positions are also shaped by the demand for a special education system for children with disabilities. In these negotiations, Nigerian policy actors confront the educational exclusion of a vast number of children and generate a discourse mediated by the understanding that the development of an inclusive school system is about institutionalizing a special education system. This understanding builds upon shared expectations about children's inability to succeed in regular education and the Nigerian school system's incapacity to provide special education. Both factors contribute to a change of the exclusionary logic into one of segregation/ separation.

For Germany, chapter 4 shows that federal policy actors frame inclusive education in relation to the school system's entrenched segregated structures, thus extending earlier controversies about the legitimacy of special schools. In defending or criticizing special schools, policy actors generate a discourse that is mediated by the understanding that the development of an inclusive school system is about the retention of special education professionalism, yet shifting it outside of special schools. This understanding builds upon shared expectations about children's inability to succeed in regular education and the German school system's extensive capacity to provide special education. These debates emphasize that interschool segregation in special schools would be supplemented with intraschool separation in special classes.

Chapter 5 compares the two cases on discursive as well as institutional levels. Despite crucial differences, the cross-case analysis demonstrates that the translations of Article 24 rely similarly on the "special educationalization of inclusion" and reveals the institutional processes involved in the generation of this logic of change. Both discourses make a special education system their point of reference to express practical problems and contextual particularities relevant for the development of an inclusive school system. I identify the elements of institutionalized translations, including the institutional mechanism of a paradoxical solution, the discursive strategy of decoupling to comply, as well as the ability-capacity-expectations that together constitute an institutional myth about the inevitability of ability selection in education. Conjointly, these elements similarly generate the "special educationalization of inclusion" in order to demonstrate the contextual appropriateness of reform processes in Nigeria and Germany. Revealing the institutional conditions of Article 24's travel in this way provides a deeper understanding of the influence the human rights paradigm of inclusive education has actually had on educational change in these contrasting school systems. This analysis reveals that contextual particularities, considered to be an invariable part in the development of inclusive school systems, are also a factor contributing to the reinterpretation of the human rights reform agenda in a global South and North context of education.

Chapter 6 summarizes the processes and barriers of institutional change in the context of Article 24—and reflects on their numerous implications. Finally, I argue that the discursive-institutional power of special education systems to define and corroborate educational progress—or the lack of it— is a crucial factor contributing to the nonimplementation of Article 24. To counter translations of Article 24 that foster, and do not challenge, ability selection in the name of the human right to inclusive education, I develop a human rights model of disability in education. This model confronts universalizing assumptions about the realization of inclusion as a space in which discrimination is sustained. These assumptions are entailed in the ability-selective and progression-based rationalities that drive the "special educationalization of inclusion" and thus subvert the radical worldwide change the UN CRPD calls for.

TWO

The Translation of Article 24 UN CRPD

Institutional Change in Educational Discourse

The influence Article 24 UN CRPD exerts on the development of inclusive school systems in state parties depends on the translation of its universal ideas into specific educational changes in local contexts. In general, research on such translations is interested in the transposition and transformation of ideas when they travel across levels and between contexts (Diane Stone 2012, 487–89). The analytical focus is therefore not only on the dissemination of policies but primarily on the interactions between actors that facilitate the circulation of their ideas (Lendvai and Stubbs 2007, 174).

An important body of work on the translation of human rights investigates the mobilization of global ideas for local change. Sally Engle Merry and Peggy Levitt, for example, traced the adaption of women's rights ideas by non-governmental organizations (NGOs) in Peru, China, India, and the United States, revealing that global value packages rely on local ideologies, images, and narratives to become meaningful for actors on the ground (Merry 2006; Levitt and Merry 2009; Merry and Levitt 2017). They term this process "vernacularization," highlighting that human rights need to be "remade in the vernacular"—that is, "translated into local terms and situated within local contexts of power and meaning"—in order to become effective (Merry 2006, 1). In this process, human rights "become resources in local struggles" vested with the power "to change the way people think and act" (Merry 2006, 137), a power that, in turn, hinges on the universal claim of human rights. The translation of human rights ideas can thus contribute to a heightened rights consciousness among marginalized groups and, in addition, carve out political spaces for the assertion of these rights (Merry 2006, 219). This aspect is particularly evident in Lynette Chua's study on the LGBT movement in Myanmar. It reveals that human rights practices—the "mode in which human rights are made sense of and put into action" (Chua 2018, 134)—provided activists with an alternative way of life that allowed them to transform their grievances and, eventually, themselves. These practices, though meaningful, can also be flawed, driving both community mobilization and social discord. Parsing the vernacularization of women's rights in South Korea, Cheng (2011) also elucidated the contradictory effects of human rights. While the attempt to localize women's human rights could challenge traditional ideals of womanhood, these ideals were nonetheless reconfirmed in the same process. While these vernacularization studies have investigated how activists adjust global human rights to local contexts, they have not yet engaged with the rights of disabled persons.

Focusing on the intermediary space of disability rights that opens between the global and the local, this book adds a complementary perspective to these works. In a comparative manner, it engages with the discourses on inclusive education in Nigeria and Germany that link human rights ideas with already existing ideas about the education of disabled children enshrined in the context-specific rules, norms, and beliefs about schooling. In this way, I expand previous work in two respects. First, I not only focus on activists in NGOs but look equally at civil society and state actors. This decision is based on the UN CRPD itself, as Article 33 stipulates that state parties must actively involve disabled persons organizations (DPOs) in the process of implementation and monitoring. This requirement, of course, does not render disability rights activism outside of these processes redundant. However, the active involvement of persons with disabilities and their representing organizations in these processes provides a new space for political participation of activists and their coordination with political decision-makers. This space, however, has not yet been the focus of vernacularization studies, one reason being the disparity between "human rights as law and mobilizing these ideas for social movements" (Merry 2006, 458). Given the international disability movement's slogan "Nothing about us without us" (Charlton 1998), this distinction, however, becomes fuzzy in the appropriation of disability rights enshrined in the UN CRPD. Therefore, it will be the focus of this book.

Second, I expand previous works by focusing not only on the appropriation of human rights within organizations but also on their institutional sources and effects. In this way, I can show *how* human rights ideas are appropriated and, in addition, explain *why* they undergo changes when applied in different institutional contexts of schooling. Why do some human rights ideas gain traction and others not? Why are some local aspects emphasized in this process and others not? In addition to revealing the substantive meaning human rights gain in different contexts, answering these questions allows me to uncover the underlying discursive-institutional processes that orient the local appropriation of global ideas.

To study these dynamics empirically, I now conceptualize three aspects constitutive for human rights translations: the global rights package, the local institutional realities against with its appropriation takes place, and the channel through which global norms and local ideas are linked (Levitt and Merry 2009, 446).

The Global Human Rights Package:
The Provisions of Article 24 UN CRPD

Article 24 entails a global rights package. It obligates state parties to recognize the right to education of persons with disabilities and, in order to realize it, ensure inclusive education system at all levels. According to the High Commissioner for Human Rights, this provision implies, in turn, that an inclusive education system is "the only means to ensure the right to education to all students, including persons with disabilities" (OHCHR 2013, para. 6).

But what does an inclusive education system look like? The UN CRPD itself neither defines inclusive education nor delineates features of an inclusive education system (Della Fina 2017, 452). This is partly due to the controversies that accompanied the drafting of Article 24. Stretching over three days (2–4 August 2005), longer than the time devoted to any other convention article, the deliberations were overshadowed by fierce debates (UN 2005). These centered on whether inclusive education entails a right to attend special education schools or, on the contrary, the state's obligation to abolish them (Degener 2017, 52). The question was not decided; instead, as a compromise, the right to inclusive education in general was enshrined (Degener 2009, 214; 2017, 52). Accordingly, ambiguities remained that were, however, clarified by the Committee on the Rights of Persons with Disabilities—a body established by Article 34 UN CRPD that comprises eighteen independent experts monitoring the implementation of the convention.

In 2016, after an extensive consultation process involving DPOs as well as state actors from around the globe, the committee adopted a General Comment on Article 24 (CRPD 2016). The document details the normative provisions of Article 24 and specifies resulting state party obligations. In doing so, the right to education is expanded into a right to inclusive education. This expansion not only occurs on a linguistic level—even though, as Della Fina notes, the UN CRPD "is the first legally binding instrument to contain an explicit reference to inclusive education" (2017, 451)—but particularly takes place at the programmatic level, foregrounding, in the words of Beco, the duty "to abolish the various mechanisms that exclude disabled people from society" (2018, 400).

According to the General Comment on Article 24, inclusive education is "a fundamental right of all learners," that is, individuals, and not their parents (CRPD 2016, para. 10, lit. a). Its realization, the document specifies, depends on "a process of continuing and proactive commitment to eliminating barriers" that restrict access and participation (CRPD 2016, para. 10, lit. d; also OHCHR 2013, para. 7). These barriers can be found in different aspects of educational institutions, such as physical infrastructure and communication, but also in the wider community, including social, financial, and attitudinal barriers as well as laws and policies (CRPD 2016, para. 13). Realizing inclusive education, hence, requires "a transformation in culture, policy and practice in all formal and informal educational environments to accommodate the differing requirements and identities of individual students" (CRPD 2016, para. 9; also OHCHR 2013, para. 7). In other words, the problem the UN CRPD's Article 24 addresses with the development of inclusive school systems is the barriers impeding equal access and participation in education.

At the structural-organizational level of school systems, these barriers are entailed in learning environments that exclude or segregate children on the basis of disability. The General Comment on Article 24 clearly states that exclusion (the denial or prevention of access to any form of education) and segregation (the isolation of students with disabilities in separate environments) are not compatible with the right to inclusive education (CRPD 2016, para. 11). This evaluation also applies to the integration of disabled children, which is based on the understanding that they will be placed in mainstream educational institutions and expected to "adjust to the standardized requirements of such institutions" (CRPD 2016, para. 11; also OHCHR 2013, para. 4). Inclusion, in contrast, requires encompassing changes to "provide all students of the relevant age range with an equitable and participatory learning experience and the environment that best corresponds to their requirements and preferences" (CRPD 2016, para. 11; also OHCHR 2013, para. 4). To this end, a "broad availability of educational places for learners with disabilities at all levels throughout the community" is demanded (CRPD 2016, para. 21). These places, in addition, "must be accessible to everyone, without discrimination" (CRPD 2016, para. 22). In 2007, the Special Rapporteur on Disability of the Commission for Social Development emphasized that for persons with disabilities "the real gap in the area of education lies between availability and accessibility" (Special Rapporteur on Disability 2007, para. 34). Education is available when a sufficient number of functioning schools exists in a community to provide quality compulsory education to all children, and accessible when no group or individual is denied access (CRPD 2016, paras. 21, 22; Tomasevski 2004, i). In this respect, the ultimate goal of Article 24 is to make all schools available and accessible for all, including children and youth with disabilities.[1]

This vision is based on two foundational human rights principles: the norms of nondiscrimination and equal opportunity (see also Article 3 lit. b, e, and 5(2) UN CRPD). Both principles determine and reinforce each other: Discrimination—that is, according to Article 2 of the UN CRPD any distinction, exclusion, or restriction on the basis of disability that impairs the recognition, enjoyment, or exercise of all human rights—impedes equal opportunities; in turn, equal opportunities presuppose the absence of discrimination (CRPD 2016, para. 13; also Dörschner 2014, 54–55; Degener 2012, 411–12).

Against this background, state parties are called on to reform their education systems by immediately ensuring the nonexclusion of children with disabilities from education as well as the provision of reasonable accommodation (CRPD 2016, para. 41, lit. a, b). As an individualized support measure, reasonable accommodation targets the modification and adjustment of educational environments in order to ensure that persons with disabilities can "enjoy and exercise" their right to education on an equal basis with others. A denial of reasonable accommodation, conversely, constitutes a "discrimination on the ground of disability" (CRPD 2016, para. 41, lit. b; also OHCHR 2013, paras. 41–44). At the structural-organizational level, these obligations amount to two responsibilities. First, state parties are encouraged to introduce a "no-rejection clause" into education law, championed by the High Commissioner for Human Rights as "an anti-discrimination measure" to prevent denial of access to "mainstream schools on the basis of disability" (OHCHR 2013, paras. 26, 71).[2] Second, state parties are prompted to progressively overcome the segregated systems of regular and special education (OHCHR 2013, para. 26). According to the

General Comment on Article 24, an inclusive education system is "not compatible with sustaining two systems of education: a mainstream education system and a special/segregated education system" (CRPD 2016, para. 40). Ultimately, this view is confirmed in several concluding observations to state party reports on implementation of the UN CRPD issued by the Committee on the Rights of Persons with Disabilities. To foster inclusion, the experts, for example, recommended Germany to scale down its "segregated special-needs schools," where most impaired, disabled or disadvantaged students are placed (CRPD 2015a, para. 45). The 2020 Education for All Global Monitoring Report takes up this understanding, declaring that the "key tenet of inclusion is ensuring that the diversity of the school-aged population is represented in every classroom," a goal that "is undermined by the existence of special schools" (UNESCO 2020, 76).

In conclusion, Article 24 entails a global reform mandate: that is, to develop inclusive school systems in order to realize the right to education for persons with disabilities. This aim provides a universal blueprint for educational change in state parties. In addition, Article 24 entails a global reform agenda—an outline of goals, problems, and solutions to be considered by state parties aiming to comply with the reform mandate. Barriers to and in education are the problem Article 24 addresses with the development of inclusive school systems. At the structural-organizational level of school systems, these barriers pertain to the unavailability and inaccessibility of schools for children on the basis of disability. To reduce barriers, state parties are legally obliged to overcome ability-related exclusions from and segregation within education. Applying the norms of equal

TABLE 1. Article 24 UN CRPD as a "Program of Change"

Human rights paradigm of inclusive education	
Ideational dimensions	*Content of Article 24 UN CRPD*
Reform mandate	
Cause of change	Human right to inclusive education
Aim of change	Development of inclusive education systems at all levels
Value of change	Realization of the right to education for all children
Reform agenda	
Problem to be solved	Barriers to and in education
Solution to be applied	Overcoming of exclusion and segregation
Goal to be achieved	All schools available and accessible to all children
Norms to be applied	Equal opportunity and nondiscrimination

Source: Based on Schmidt 2008, 306; 2015, 173.

opportunity and nondiscrimination, state parties must therefore pursue the goal of making all schools available and accessible to all children. Together, the reform mandate and the reform agenda form the human rights paradigm of inclusive education—the distinct set of global ideas reflecting the human rights base for educational change in state parties.

Constituted by shared ideas about the educational rights of persons with disabilities, Article 24's "program of change" offers state parties a tableau for the transformation of their school systems. In a human rights language, it problematizes the organizational structures that exclude or segregate children based on a disability. In doing so, Article 24 shifts the focus to institutional barriers that impede access and participation. This paradigm shift to disability in education provides distinctive impulses for the change of school systems around the world. Whether the global reform mandate and agenda actually instruct educational changes in state parties is an empirical question to be addressed later in the book. To do so, I first delineate the institutional challenges of realizing inclusive education to illuminate the diversity of historically shaped sociopolitical contexts in which Article 24's global value package is adopted by state parties.

Local Realities of Schooling: Institutional Challenges for Realizing Article 24 UN CRPD

Across the globe, formal school systems aspire to provide for the education of all children (Richardson and Powell 2011). However, severe challenges remain, as disabled children are, according to the 2011 World Report on Disability, "less likely to start school and have lower rates of staying and being promoted in school" (WHO and World Bank 2011, 206). Likewise, the 2010 Education for All Global Monitoring Report, issued by the United Nations Educational, Scientific and Cultural Organization (UNESCO), uncovers that disability is one of the "most potent factors in educational marginalization" around the world (UNESCO 2010, 181). This fact was recently confirmed in the 2020 report reminding us that disabled children "are among the hardest to reach" in any education system (UNESCO 2020, 71).

In low-income countries of the global South, one of the main barriers disabled children and youth face is the widespread reality of outright exclusion from formal education. The number of out-of-school children remains particularly high in sub-Saharan Africa. This region accounts for more than thirty million such children, more than half of the global out-of-school population; a number that has increased slightly over the last decade (UNESCO 2020, 213; Omoeva et al. 2013, 15). In many countries, like Zimbabwe, more disabled children are out of than in formal primary education (UNESCO 2020, 72). In Nigeria, the country that accounts for the highest total number of out-of-school children, half of all disabled children are excluded from schooling (Mizunoya, Mitra, and Yamasaki 2016, 22). Even in countries that have almost realized universal access to primary education, such as South Africa, the share of disabled children among the out-of-school population remains high (Mizunoya, Mitra, and Yamasaki 2016, 22). In its observations on South Africa's first state party report, the UN Committee on the Rights of Persons with Disabilities expressed its concern about the "high number of students with disabilities . . . , who still remain largely outside the school system," as well as "the continuing growth in special education schools as opposed to inclusive education" (CRPD 2018a, para. 40, lit. a). Struggling to achieve Education for All, low-income countries overall have very limited capacities to provide for the education of disabled children. Summarizing the discussions held at the Second African Network of Evidence-to-Action on Disability Symposium in 2009, Tsitisi Chataika and colleagues report that the lack of "human, financial and physical resources and infrastructure were identified as major constraints to inclusion in African countries" (2012, 393). In addition to a lack of resources, social stigmatization impedes access and participation of disabled and impaired children and youth (Mostert 2016). Yet the absence of institutionalized support systems could, theoretically, also constitute an advantage for the realization of inclusive education. Why? Because it entails "the potential to 'leapfrog' over some of the expensive and exclusionary practices developed in special education," as Miles and Ahuja point out (2007, 142). Richardson and Powell, in addition, remind us that "although they may lag 'behind' western countries . . . , the countries of Latin America, Asia, and Africa exemplify alternative strategies in educational integration as well as alternative images of inclusion that hearken back to different values of independence, the formation and guarantee of capabilities, and strategies to secure well-being in local contexts" (2011, 122).

Even though special systems have been crucial to overcome the outright exclusion of disabled children in many high-income countries of the global North, they prove to contain "barriers to inclusion" (Powell [2011] 2016). Based on a comparative study of special education in the United States and Germany, Justin Powell highlights that disabled students "remain largely in the tracks or school types that too often lower expectations and stigmatize participants and offer less valuable credentials" ([2011] 2016, 49). Specifying the historical expansion of special education further, Sally Tomlinson reveals those institutional arrangements for previously excluded groups "offered only a minimal education mainly through the labels of disability or special educational needs" (2017, 2). In Europe, for example, the school systems of Germany and Belgium rely heavily on special schools; they organize education "along ability lines" in hierarchical structures (NESSE 2012, 19, 72) and therefore have some of the highest rates of segregation on the continent (UNESCO 2020, 77; European Agency 2017, 27, 51).[3] But even when countries have turned away from segregated special schools, they have not necessarily reached the goal of inclusion. Following an anticlassification approach, Sweden, for example, has one of the lowest rates of children diagnosed with special needs; however, most of them learn in special classes (NESSE 2012, 16; Biermann and Powell 2014). The Committee on the Rights of Persons with Disabilities accordingly expressed its concern that in Sweden "schools can refuse admission to certain pupils with disabilities on the grounds of organizational and economic hardship" (CRPD 2014a, para. 47).

Independent of the modes of organization and classification, special education systems exhibit an overrepresentation of male students, socially disadvantaged children, and ethnic minorities (Powell and Wagner 2014; Harry 2014; Berhanu and Dyson 2012; Gabel et al. 2009). As early as 1982, Sally Tomlinson challenged the common view that children from lower classes are prone to have special education needs. From a sociological standpoint, she instead argued that special education is "more a legitimation of low social status than the treatment of an educational need" ([1982] 2014, 19). Delineating the "techniques of disability" mediated by special education, Lisa Pfahl could moreover show that discourses of special education not only sustain professional attitudes, but also negatively affect the self-image of students (Pfahl 2011; Pfahl and Powell 2011). For these reasons, special education systems are criticized for constraining learning opportunities and therefore negatively impacting life chances.

Given these realities of education, school systems in the global South and the global North entail barriers that impede equal access and participation. For that reason, they are equally, yet differently, challenged by the provisions of Article 24. This fact is sustained when looking at the issues commonly raised by the Committee on the Rights of Persons with Disabilities in its observations on state party reports. In several cases, it reprimanded states for the continued practice of segregating disabled students in special schools or classes as counteracting the principle of inclusive education in mainstream schools, for example in Gabon (CRPD 2015b, para. 52), India (CRPD 2019a, para. 50), Kenya (CRPD 2015c, para. 43), Russia (CRPD 2018b, para. 48), and the United Kingdom (CRPD 2017, para. 52). With respect to countries that have scaled down segregation or introduced inclusive education policies, the committee is concerned about the continued placement of disabled students outside regular classrooms, for example in Spain (CRPD 2019b, para. 45), Australia (CRPD 2013, para. 45), and South Korea (CRPD 2014b, para. 45).

To grasp the intricacies of this systematic global reform challenge analytically, I now conceptualize school systems as Article 24's "object of change." To this end, I use the integrated model of institutions developed by the sociologist W. Richard Scott (2008) und utilized by Justin J. W. Powell ([2011] 2016) for the comparative analysis of special education systems. Providing an analytical heuristic, this model allows us to theoretically distinguish the institutional dimensions of schooling challenged by the human rights paradigm of inclusive education.

The cultural-cognitive pillar of an institution entails shared understandings that not only order the social world but also confer meaning to it (Scott 2008, 51, 57). Culturally prevailing educational ideals and disability paradigms, in this way, affect how disability is approached in education. In stratified school systems, this approach is often based on beliefs in "natural and innate ability" (Powell [2011] 2016, 42). Disability, in turn, functions as a marker of difference, indicating individual, within-person deficits that education systems need to compensate for (42). Building on a medical or clinical approach to disability, this view is challenged within the field of disability studies for neglecting the social factors that foster disablement (Campbell 2009; Wolbring 2008). Cognitively, a deficit-focused view on disability is based on expectations about abilities required to succeed in formal education settings. The distinction between students possessing or lacking these abilities hence depends on the assessment that something that is expected to be possible is not—for example, a child being able to access a school building or meeting the requirements set by the curriculum without adjustments or additional support (Weisser 2005, 21; 2007, 240). Manufacturing inability, this ableist paradigm eventually legitimizes the call for special education experts capable of providing specialized support (Tomlinson 2017, 6).

Institutionally, this call reflects binding expectations about "legitimate means to pursue valued ends" (Scott 2008, 55). Special education practices designate appropriate ways to include disabled children and youth in mass schooling. In other words, the organization and professionalization of special education influence who can access and participate in which educational setting under what conditions. Special education professionals are "gatekeepers" who, as Powell and Pfahl point out, "utilize standardized measures of academic performance and behavioral norms to select diverse pupils' bodies into supposedly homogenous groups at status passages, especially to legitimately selection processes between grades or school types" (2019, 392). This practice of dealing with ability-related differences in schooling has long been criticized from a disability studies perspective for creating and maintaining structural and social barriers to equal participation (Barton and Tomlinson 2014; Gabel 2005; Barton 1988; Tomlinson 2012, [1982] 2014).

Eventually, the UN CRPD establishes the mandate to remove these barriers in international law. In this way, legal reform pressures emanate from the treaty, affecting the regulative pillar of schooling—the "rule-setting, monitoring, and sanctioning activities" that "constrain and regularize" behavior (Scott 2008, 52). To reflect the UN CRPD principles, state parties are called to reform policies and adapt laws, in particular regarding the provision of appropriate support in local schools. In addition, they are required to report to the UN Committee on the Rights of Persons with Disabilities about progress in realizing the right to inclusive education.

The "object of change" delineates the institutional dimension of Article 24's reform challenge. It focuses on the institutional pillars of school systems, which impose educational barriers based on disability. To overcome these barriers, state parties to the UN CRPD must initiate a process of change targeting the rules, norms, and beliefs affecting schooling. Together, these three institutional pillars of schooling maintain and sustain educational disability—that is, according to Powell, the continuous process of becoming disabled in schooling through an official special-needs classification and education in spatially segregated stigmatizing facilities, albeit to varying degrees in different education systems (2007, 321; [2011] 2016, 40). When state parties want to comply with Article 24's "program of

TABLE 2. The Institution of Schooling as Article 24 UN CRPD's "Object of Change"

Pillar	Cultural-cognitive	Normative	Regulative
Definition	Beliefs: socially supported shared understandings	Norms: morally governed binding expectations	Rules: legally sanctioned regulative rules
Adaptation	Educational disability paradigms	Organization and professionalization of (special) education	(Inclusive) education laws and policies

Source: Adapted from Scott 2008, 51, and Powell [2011] 2016, 42.

change," they are required to decrease educational disability. How policy actors encounter this arduous task on the ground is an empirical question touching upon the translation of human rights into institutional change, a process that is discursive by nature.

Linking the Global and the Local: Translation as Discourse

The notion of translation as discourse points to the powerful and conflictual nature of negotiations about the relation between Article 24's "program of change" and school systems as its "object of change."[4] These negotiations are discursive, because they are "conducted above all with words and ideas" (Deborah Stone 2012, 36). Facilitated by the communicative interaction of policy actors, it is within discourses that global ideas are contextually appropriated. Vivien Schmidt, who brought a discursive perspective to institutional theory, accordingly, argues that "discursive processes alone help to explain why certain ideas succeed and others fail" (2008, 309). In an institutional sense, translation as discourse is therefore not an operation "performed on languages," but through language (Wæraas and Nielsen 2016, 237).

With translation as discourse, the analytical interest pertains to the powerful dynamics that instruct the discursive fusion of global expectations with local realities of schooling in state parties to the UN CRPD. Foregrounding the complexities of travel, this perspective avoids falling prey to the optimistic but erroneous assumption that the ratification of a human rights treaty also implies its domestic implementation, or that implementation processes necessarily comply with the entailed human rights paradigm (see, e.g., Blanck, Edelstein, and Powell 2013). Instead of regretting this fact, this book utilizes the circumstance that Article 24 can be read, interpreted, and used in different ways when it is put into practice by policy actors in state parties. What happens when global and contextual ideas are juxtaposed? To empirically study Article 24's influence on educational change means to explore how the "program of change" and the "object of change" come together in discourses that, in turn, hold the two together.

A Translational Model of Institutional Change

The translational model of institutional change assumes that institutional change depends on the knowledge policy actors (re)produce in discourses.[5] Berger and Luckmann, central founding figures of the sociology of knowl-

Article 24 UN CRPD
Program of Change

Translation

Discursive Space

Institution of Schooling
Object of Change

Figure 1. Translation as discourse

edge, define knowledge as the "certainty that phenomena are real and that they possess specific characteristics" ([1966] 1984, 13). In other words, knowledge entails the symbolic orders that affirm what adequate and appropriate descriptions and perceptions of the world are (Keller 2008, 235). Over time, meaningful knowledge solidifies into institutions and becomes objectified in rules, norms, and beliefs "that, together with associated activities and resources, provide stability and meaning to social life" (Scott 2008, 48). This way, meanings produced in and through communicative interactions become a facticity outside of them, empowering and controlling future actions (Berger and Luckmann [1966] 1984, 77; Meyer and Rowan 1977, 341; Jepperson 1991, 145). All of this occurs in and through discourses—regulated practices of knowledge production within and through which the world can be known (Foucault [1969] 2002, 49–50,

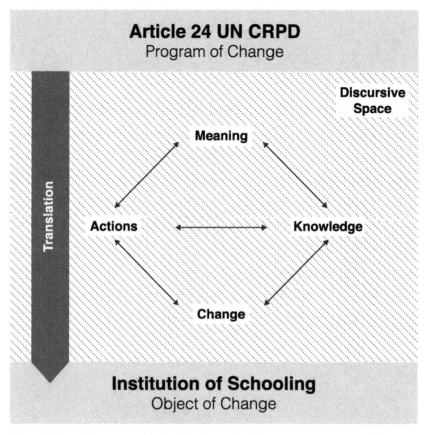

Figure 2. Translational model of institutional change

201). Discourses and institutions therefore maintain and reinforce each other; discourses legitimize institutions and institutions shape discourses.

In debating inclusive education, state and civil society policy actors negotiate positions that determine what Article 24's "program of change" means for their countries' school systems. They discursively align global ideas with institutionalized knowledge about schooling, confer meaning to Article 24, and, eventually, determine the scope and extent of change. The thus (re)produced knowledge is what links human rights to their realization in state parties.

Based on this model, I understand discourses as facilitating institutional work. The knowledge policy actors reproduce discursively is what can challenge, disrupt, or confirm the rules, norms, and beliefs that stabilize school systems as institutions (Lawrence, Suddaby, and Leca 2009, 1). In this way, discourses translate global policy ideas into local knowledge, actions, and, over time, institutions.[6]

Reconstructing Translations

The reconstruction of human rights translations as discourse is driven by the role the global values package of Article 24 plays in the institutional change of school systems. Finding an answer requires two analytical exercises: first, to reconstruct discourses on inclusive education and, second, to reveal their institutional effects.

Discourses consist of a complex set of statements that form the objects they speak about (Foucault [1969] 2002, 54). These statements can, however, not simply be made; they must follow certain rules to be recognized and regarded as true (Nola 1998, 120). These rules are shaped as actors argue, and eventually determine, which of the competing interpretations of the social world gains legitimacy for a specific time and place. The resulting knowledge reflects a historically situated power constellation, which is captured in the notion of "power/knowledge" (Foucault 1980). In other words, discourses (re)produce knowledge that is socially considered as true by following institutionalized rules, norms, and beliefs that order the world (Keller et al. 2005). What follows is that discourses must be distinguished according to the objects they form, not the topics they debate (Foucault [1969] 2002, 82–83).

To elucidate Article 24's influence on institutional change empirically, it is therefore not sufficient to reveal how the document is debated. Rather, it is necessary to reveal in which discourses this happens, what objects these discourses form, and how these affect the institutions of schooling. For that reason, translations are analyzed as coordinative policy discourses on inclusive education, in which the UN CRPD is situated as an event (see Schmidt 2008; Keller 2013a). Following a sociology-of-knowledge approach to discourse (Keller 2011), this practically means reconstructing knowledge that policy actors (re)produce in Nigeria and Germany by revealing where, why, and by whom inclusive education is debated, and what role Article 24 plays in and for these debates (see Münch 2016).[7] In their totality, these statements provide an understanding of what the development of inclusive school systems is all about in each country. This reconstruction will reveal the knowledge through which policy actors appropriate Article 24 in a specific institutional context by linking the global values package to local norms, beliefs, and rules that sustain the institution of schooling.

The most curious question is this: why does inclusive education become a concern for policy actors in the first place? To answer it, the analytical focus is on institutional carriers, that is, the vehicles that transport ideas to different levels, across places, and through time (Scott 2008, 79). As "modes of transmission" (Scott 2008, 80), carriers allow us to observe how human rights ideas about inclusive education are transported into the discursive space of translations and juxtaposed with institutionalized ideas about schooling. Affecting why and how inclusive education becomes a topic of discourses, institutional carriers determine which ideas evolve into exogenous or endogenous reform pressures and thus trigger institutional changes.

Theoretically, Article 24 is predestined to function as a symbolic carrier conveying the "program of change" through the rules and norms of international law. This information may, however, be challenged by or compete with other symbolic carriers. For example, the educational disability paradigms entrenched in classifications of special educational needs may perpetuate taken-for-granted understandings of "good" schooling for disabled children. Relational systems, in addition, can carry institutional ideas through networks. (Scott 2003, 882; 2008, 79) Specifically, the organization of policy actors in special interest groups or professional associations can influence which and how ideas are carried into discourses. As Levitt and Merry (2009, 458) have shown, it makes a difference whether human rights are used in social movements or taken up as international law by politicians and lawyers.[8]

How do the resulting discourses affect the institutional change of school systems? To answer this question, the focus is on the educational changes proposed.[9] The extent to which discourses can perpetuate change depends on the institutional pillars addressed and affected by them. Institutional changes can range from "surface inclusion" at the level of mere symbolic politics, to "structural modifications" relating to the organization of education, to "deep culture" revisions of the constitutive schemata of schooling (Corbett and Slee 2016, 409.0/484). In this way, discourses may eventually contribute to changing the institutional logics on which school systems operate: outright exclusion, segregation in special schools, separation in special classes, integration (incompletely joint education of children with and without disabilities), or inclusion (joint teaching of all children) (CRPD 2016).

Focusing on the fusion of global and institutionalized ideas, this theoretical framework allows us to reconstruct how policy actors make sense of the human rights paradigm of inclusive education in considering the contextual particularities of their respective school systems. In this way

TABLE 3. Framework for the Reconstruction of Translations

Institutional pillars of schooling		
Cultural-cognitive	*Normative*	*Regulative*
Institutional effects <u>on</u> discourses		
	Symbolic systems	
Institutional carriers	Educational paradigms	Structural, organizational and professional norms	Educational policies and laws, including Article 24 UN CRPD
	Relational systems	
	Models of formal schooling instructing the perception of school systems	Authority systems deciding about dis/ability and special needs	Governance systems enforcing the UN CRPD implementation
Institutional effects <u>of</u> discourses		
Extent of change	"Deep culture" revisions of the constitutive schemata of schooling	"Structural modifications" of the organization	"Surface inclusion" of symbolic politics

Source: Powell [2011] 2016, 42; 2009, 214; Scott 2008, 52-57, 79-82.; 2003, 882; Corbett and Slee 2016, 409.0/484.

this book goes beyond a mere analysis of the obvious processes related to the implementation of Article 24. It reveals the institutional processes that determine how its "program of change" gains traction to influence the development of inclusive school systems.

Explaining Translations

Understand the power of translations in institutional change requires a second analytical step, that is, examining the relation between discourses and the institutional environments they are embedded in. Translations are not a single measure of Article 24's influence. Instead, this influence is determined by the institutional processes that link Article 24 to the institutional realities of schooling through discourses (see Schneider and Jannig 2006, 92–93). To understand translations in their complexity therefore requires explicating the relevance of institutional environments in and for discourses. This means I do not singularize Article 24 as *the* cause for the development of school systems, but instead map the institutional paths of translations that bring forth, or hamper, this influence (see George and Bennett 2005, 25).

To theoretically grasp the relation between discourses and their institutional environments, I transfer key assumptions of organizational institutionalism from the organizational to the ideational level of translations. Organizational institutionalism assumes that organizations model their structures and practices based on environmental expectations (Meyer and Rowan 1977; Meyer, Scott, and Deal 1992, 54). In turn, formal structures and practices of organizations are manifestations of social beliefs about what efficient and effective organizations are (Meyer and Rowan 1977, 341). Put another way, it is crucially important for the survival of organizations that it is believed that their structures and practices are effective and appropriate to practical demands—yet organizations do not need to prove this (Meyer and Rowan 1977, 349). In this way, myths about what "constitutes a proper organization" are generated that more and more organizations need to comply with to gain legitimacy (Meyer and Rowan 1977, 347; Meyer and Scott 1983, 200–201). As a result, organizations become similar to each other (Boxenbaum and Jonsson 2008, 78). The similarity between organizations—their isomorphy—is the result of institutional pressures institutionalized in their environments.[10] In dealing with these environmental expectations, organizations can be exposed to conflicting and competing demands though. To balance these pressures, organizations tend to comply with environmental expectations only on a ceremonial level while varying their activities on the inside "in response to practical considerations" (Meyer and Rowan 1977, 357).

The explanatory value of organizational institutionalism is to show that legitimacy is not an "empirical property" of organizations (Deephouse and Suchman 2008, 49). Instead, legitimacy must be positioned as an "explanatory concept" to understand the isomorphic relation between organizations and the environments they are institutionalized in (49). This relation is determined by the way organizations deal with expectations that have created an institutional myth about what an efficient and rational organization should look like (cf. Meyer 1994). To explain human rights translation, our theoretical concern, however, cannot pertain to isomorphic changes of organizations, but must be their institutional work as policy actors in discourses.

Accordingly, I understand that policy actors grouped in organizations, who together generate discourses on inclusive education change, are responsive to their institutional environments. In the case of translations, this environment comprises Article 24 at the international level as well as the institutional rules, norms, and beliefs of school systems on national levels. Both—program and object of change—entail expectations about appropriate ways to educate disabled children, which policy actors need to balance in negotiating the development of an inclusive school system. To explain translations, the crucial task is therefore to reconstruct how the "program of change" and "object of change" are linked in the discursive space of translations. This relation determines what institutional changes emerge as contextually appropriate in the respective country context.

To reveal how the program and the object of change interact in the discursive space of translations requires to examine which institutional processes contribute to the discursive juxtaposition of global and local ideas. Will Article 24's reform mandate and agenda be adopted or rejected? Which aspects emerge as contextually relevant for the development of inclusive schooling in discourses? How do the discursively constructed processes of change become aligned with the human rights specified by Article 24?

For this examination, we should bear in mind that school systems worldwide are interconnected, as more and more international organizations, especially from within the UN system, are involved in educational agenda setting, policymaking, and monitoring (Martens and Knodel 2014; Wiseman, Pilton, and Lowe 2010; Chabott 2003). International paradigms provide a common reference point for policy actors around the globe. Vested with homogenizing pressures, they can "become an inescapable form of reassurance" for change (Ball 1998, 128) that may be "mobilized at particular moments of protracted policy conflict to generate reform pressure and build policy coalitions" (Steiner-Khamsi 2014, 157). In this context, translations of Article 24 may prove to be not the result of a globalized education agenda, but their driver (Artiles and Dyson 2005; Arthur, McNess, and Crossley 2016). The result could be school systems that become increasingly similar to each other (Meyer et al. 1997).

However, global policy paradigms also have the potential to "narrow the discursive space of possibilities" for change "in the educational contexts to which [they] move" (Beech 2009, 349), or may even induce unintended consequences (Beech 2011). Translations of Article 24 could therefore contribute to processes of change that aim to develop inclusive school systems but do not meet the related human rights standards (Jakobi, Teltemann, and Windzio 2010). This could then be considered an instance of decoupling between programs and processes of change, a knowledge politics in the form of "'policy bilingualism,' where one set of reforms is advanced . . . while another—sometimes diametrically opposed—set of reforms is promoted" (Steiner-Khamsi 2010, 332). Policy bilingualism is especially prevalent when educational reforms are supported by international donors, who "provide funding *under the condition* that a specific reform package—presented as 'best practices'—is imported and implemented" (Steiner-Khamsi 2010, 331; also Steiner-Khamsi and Stolpe 2006). Steiner-Khamsi, accordingly, argues that educational reforms in "developing countries" can therefore look like "those in developed countries," but can eventually be traced to "global speak" (2010, 331). This way, a Western model of schooling is strengthened that generates, stabilizes, and validates expectations about appropriate ways to school children with and without disabilities, expectations that have the potential to reinforce power-related global hierarchies (Meyer and Ramirez 2000; Adick 2003; Brock-Utne 2000). If and how these processes play out in translations of Article 24 is an empirical question I am going to answer based on case studies conducted in Nigeria and Germany.

THREE

Nigeria

*Inclusive Education as a Strategy of Education
for All by Special Education*

The translation of Article 24 UN CRPD's human rights paradigm into educational change in Nigeria is confronted with the pivotal and endemic reality of exclusion. In 2010, more than eight million children were excluded from basic education; this number is not only the world's highest but also rising (UNICEF 2015, 2017; UIS 2021). The most potent risk for exclusion is disability; half of all disabled children have no access to schooling, in contrast to every fifth nondisabled child (Mizunoya, Mitra, and Yamasaki 2016, 22). But even when children with disabilities have gained access to (special) schools, their learning is restricted due to severe lacks in capacity and quality (Obiakor, Eskay, and Afolayan 2012). Currently, the formalized Nigerian education system is not capable of providing and maintaining meaningful access to education for all. What difference does the human rights paradigm of inclusive education make in realizing equal access and participation? This is the central question of this case study. To answer it, I first delineate the historical development and current characteristic of Nigeria's school systems and then reconstruct the federal policy discourse on inclusive education.

Setting the Scene: The Formal School System—
Policy Development and Current Realities

The institutionalization of a formal education system—which is supplemented by an indigenous and Islamic education system—is characterized

31

by the attempt to adapt Western education to divergent local conditions and make its institutions accessible to all children and youth. In this process, formal schooling was converted from being a means of colonization to one of self-determination, and eventually morphed into a force for socioeconomic development. Despite this evolution, the overarching educational challenge has not changed fundamentally in Nigeria over the decades: it is to confront the historically created and politically perpetuated divisive character of a school system that is not capable of fulfilling the hopes it has created.

Critical Historical Junctures

Historically, the advent of Nigeria's exclusionary school system dates back to the arrival of missionaries in the 1840s. In opposition to traditional and Islamic education, they introduced Western education, including special education, through the foundation of Christian schools (Omenka 1989, 15–20).[1] Aiming at evangelization, missionary education was restricted to primary education and limited to training that qualified for work in the colonial government or European businesses (Fafunwa [1974] 2018, 92; Falola and Heaton 2008, 127). In addition, it mainly spread in the southern part of what is today known as Nigeria, though not rapidly. In his essay *The Education of a British-Protected Child*, the acclaimed novelist Chinua Achebe reports that missionaries needed thirty-five years to advance the seven miles from the Niger River town of Onitsha in 1857 to his hometown of Ogidi in 1892 ([1993] 2010, 7). The strongest opposition that missionaries faced emerged in the northern part of the country, with its centuries-long tradition of Islamic education (Fafunwa [1974] 2018, 70–72; Abdurrahman and Canham 1978).[2] After having left the field of education to missionaries for decades, the British colonial government imposed its first regulations in 1882 (Thakur and Ezenne 1980, 15). That year it passed an educational ordinance based on the 1844 British Education Act, which set out rules for examinations, teacher certificates, and financial support for British West African territories (Fafunwa [1974] 2018, 94; Fabunmi 2005, 2). The colonial government began to operate its own schools from 1900 onward, when the separately administered Protectorates of Northern and Southern Nigeria were established. To aid their colonial enterprise, these schools educated clerks and teachers, primarily in the South (Thakur and Ezenne 1980, 16; Niven 1967, 283).[3]

After amalgamation of both protectorates into a single Colony of Nigeria in 1914, the British introduced the first colonial education policy, the

1925 Memorandum on Education in British Colonial Territories. With this policy, the colonial government reacted to the 1922 Phelps-Stokes report on education in Africa, which highlighted the poor quality of education offered by "indifferent" colonizers and "short-sighted" missionaries (Fafunwa [1974] 2018, 125; also Fabunmi 2005, 3). To improve education and curb substandard schools, the 1925 memorandum was supplemented by an educational ordinance in 1926 requiring, inter alia, teacher registration and the approval of new schools by the Board of Education (Fafunwa [1974] 2018, 126; Adesina 1988, 22, 25). To unify the northern and southern education systems, the colonial government in addition set out a long-term plan for educational expansion (Fafunwa [1974] 2018, 131–33).[4] This plan, however, never materialized, as the 1930s global economic crisis and World War II left the colonial government without resources (Thakur and Ezenne 1980, 17–18; Fafunwa [1974] 2018, 129–30). In this environment, critiques of the colonial regime and its education system heightened in the late 1940s and early 1950s, such that Nigerians increasingly demanded political self-rule and self-administered schools (Fafunwa [1974] 2018, 130; Falola 2009, 133). Clouded by ethnic politics, the fight for self-determination eventually led to the formation of Northern, Western, and Eastern Regions.

The 1950s, according to A. Babs Fafunwa—the first Nigerian professor of education (Oyelade 2017)—then "witnessed the most phenomenal expansion in the history of Nigerian education" (Fafunwa [1974] 2018, 166). All three regions introduced universal primary education (UPE) programs in line with the 1952 Educational Ordinance (Ejiogu 1986, 59). The Western Region, in particular, recorded considerable success. In 1954, 61 percent of all five- to fourteen-year-old children were enrolled in schools, an unprecedented increase from 35 percent the previous year (Fafunwa [1974] 2018, 168). Even though the number of children in primary schools also increased in the north, UPE could not be fully realized for several reasons, including a lack of resources and conviction concerning the value of Western education (Fafunwa [1974] 2018, 174–75). In the Eastern Region, the program's implementation was not successful, as political upheaval led to an insufficient number of trained teachers (Fafunwa [1974] 2018, 171). During that period, special schools were founded by faith-based or philanthropic organizations in the South. The Sudan United Missionaries, for example, opened a school for blind children and youth in 1953 in Gindiri (Plateau) and the Catholic mission opened the Pacelli School for the Blind in Lagos in 1962; the latter is to this day a flagship special school (Andzayi 2003, 25–26; Abang 1992, 41). The Methodist mission founded a school for deaf pupils in 1956 in Lagos. In light of these developments, Nigeria was confronted with a highly divergent education system when it gained independence from British colonial rule in 1960.

The educational situation deteriorated in the years following independence due to fierce political upheavals and rivalry, a civil war from 1967 to 1970, and, subsequently, the establishment of successive military governments with intermittent phases of democratic rule (Falola 1999). Given these disruptions, the federal government tried to foster national unity via educational expansion from the late 1960s onward. To this end, it began to take over all schools to increase access to education for all (Agunloye 2012, 18–19). Second, the government started developing a common national basis for education in form of a National Policy on Education (NPE). To prepare such a policy, a National Curriculum Conference took place in 1969, which, A. Babs Fafunwa reports, was unique in that it was not "a conference of experts and professionals but of the people" who "review[ed] old and identif[ied] new national goals for Nigerian education" ([1974] 2018, 210). Passed in 1977, the NPE became the cornerstone of Nigeria's federal education policy, and a revised version remains in place until today. Eventually, the federal government launched a nationwide UPE program in 1976 and guaranteed the right to education for every Nigerian citizen in the 1979 constitution (Garuba 1996, 77). In this period, the institutionalization of special education was also advanced, notably through the establishment of a special education department within the Federal Ministry of Education in 1975. In addition, the Federal Advanced Teachers College for Special Education in Oyo was founded in 1977, as well as the National Teachers College for Special Education in Ibadan. Furthermore, a degree program in special education was introduced at the University of Jos (Garuba 1996, 77; also Thakur and Ezenne 1980, 53–54).

Due to an economic crisis triggered by the oil-price slump in the late 1980s—resulting in drastic cuts in government spending—and accelerating population growth, enrollment rates, which had risen until then, plummeted, and the education system came close to collapse (FME 2003, 11–12; Obidi 2005, 190–91). To counteract this development, the then military government introduced a nine-year universal basic education (UBE) program in 1990, parallel to the adoption of the World Declaration on Education for All (FME 2003, 12; Obanya 2001). This program, however, failed to halt the education system's persistent decline.

With beginning of the new millennium and under restored civilian rule, the quest for educational expansion was renewed under the umbrella of international development frameworks. These included UNESCO's

Education for All (EFA) initiative as well as the UN's Millennium Development Goals (MDGs) (FME 2008, iv).

Taking up both frameworks, the government revitalized the pledge to educational expansion by introducing another UBE scheme in 1999 (FME 2003, 37), which became law in 2004 with the Compulsory Free Universal Basic Education Act (FRN 2004a). In the years following, this law was substantiated by several other policy documents, including, for example, the 2004 National Policy on Education (FRN 2004b), revised in 2013 (FRN 2013a),[5] the 2005 Nigeria Education Sector Diagnosis (FME 2005), and the 2012 Four-Year Strategic Plan for the Development of the Education Sector (FME 2012a). In addition, Nigeria has become a signatory to a vast number of UN conventions, including those on the rights of the child and persons with disabilities (UN 2021). More recently, and with a particular focus on disability-based exclusions from basic education, it is reported that the government initiated a National Policy on Special Needs Education in 2015 and released a Draft National Policy on Inclusive Education in 2016–17 (Akogun, Njobdi, and Adebukola 2018, 15; UNESCO 2020, 40).

The importance of education for the country's socioeconomic development was eventually addressed in domestic development plans, such as the National Economic Empowerment and Development Strategy (NPC 2004) and the Vision 20:2020 (NPC 2009); the latter demanding educational reforms to transform Nigeria into one of the twenty largest economies in the world by 2020. Both documents stipulate educational expansion to allow more Nigerians to complete primary education, progress into secondary education, and participate in tertiary education or vocational training. This goal is reiterated in the most recent document, the Economic Recovery and Growth Plan for 2017–2020 (FRN 2017a).

The ubiquitous presence of international development partners adds an additional layer to an already highly saturated, not easily comprehensible policy framework. For the field of education, there are several specific development frameworks such as UNESCO's National Education Support Strategy for Nigeria 2006–2015 (UNESCO 2008). In addition, the United Nations Children's Fund (UNICEF) supports universal basic educational change with specific programs (UNICEF Nigeria 2021). Despite these combined efforts, Nigeria did not achieve its goal of universal primary education by 2015 (FME 2015; FRN 2015). Nevertheless, the expansion of education through the universalization of schooling is still pursued. Since 2016, these efforts take place under the UN's Sustainable Development Goals (SDGs), succeeding the 2015 expired MDGs (FRN 2017b).

TABLE 4. Historical Development of the Formal School System in Nigeria

Year	National Policy Development
	Pre-1950s: Advent of a formal system of Western education
1840s	Foundation of the first formal primary schools offering Western education by missionaries in the Lagos area
1850	*Start of British colonization*
1882–1952	Formalization of the education system by the colonial authorities
1914	*Amalgamation of the Protectorates of Northern and Southern Nigeria into one colony, the Protectorate of Nigeria*
	1950s–1990s: First wave of educational expansion
1950s	Introduction of Universal Primary Education Programmes in the Western, Eastern, and Northern Regions
1960	*Nigeria gains independence*
1960s–1990s	*Successive military governments with intermittent phases of democratic rule*
1976	National Policy on Education
1990	Basic Education Programme responding to the World Declaration on Education for All (EFA)
	Post-2000s: Renewed commitment to "Education for All"
Since 1999	*Fourth Republic / return to civilian rule*
1999	Universal Basic Education Scheme
2000	Millennium Development Goals (MDGs) and EFA Goals
2004	Universal Basic Education Act
2007	Signing of the UN CRPD
2010	Ratification of the UN CRPD, Adoption of the Vision 20:2020
2015	MDG Endpoint Report and EFA National Review, National Policy on Special Needs Education
2016	National Policy on Inclusive Education, Sustainable Development Goals

Current Characteristics

At present, Nigeria accounts for the highest total number of out-of-school children in the world. In 2010, more than eight million children of primary school age had no access to basic education, that is, about one-third of all six- to eleven-year-olds (UIS 2021; Omoeva et al. 2013, 67).[6] Over the course of the last few years, this number increased further given the deteriorating security situation due to the ongoing Boko Haram insurgency in the country's north, preventing hundreds of thousands of additional children from attending schools (UNICEF 2015, 2017). In 2021, UNICEF Nigeria reported on its website that "one in every five of the world's out-of-school children is in Nigeria" (UNICEF Nigeria 2021).

In 2015, on average, one-fourth of all children in primary education age had never attended a primary school (NPopC and RTI International

2016a, 17, 28). However, the percentage of children who actually attend primary schools increased slightly, from 51 percent in 1990 to 68 percent in 2015 (NPopC and RTI International 2016b, 5). When children get access to schools, they usually stay, as dropout rates in primary education remain relatively low, at about 1 percent for grades 1 to 5, increasing to about 3 percent in grade 6 (NPopC and RTI International 2016b, 8). For that reason, the number of children who completed six years of primary education rose from 73 percent in 1993 to 82 percent in 2015 (FRN 2015, 5). Nonetheless, access to basic education for all children remains a goal yet to be achieved.

If we dissect the data, a certain pattern becomes apparent: exclusion from basic education in schools is hugely tied to socioeconomic status, place of residence, and gender, all of which intersect with disability. The 2015 Nigeria Education Data Survey revealed that 63 percent of the poorest children between the ages of five and six never attended a school, compared to only 2 percent from the richest households (NPopC and RTI International 2016a, 15). This information is furthermore characterized by a staggering regional divide, as primary school attendance in the south is twice as frequent as in the northeast and northwest regions (NPopC and RTI International 2016b, 4). In addition, the National Bureau of Statistics reports that "the ratio of Nigerian male students to Nigerian female students . . . averaged at 4.5:1" in the early 2010s (NBS 2015, 7). In fact, UNESCO estimates that for girls from the poorest backgrounds a full cycle of primary education will not be achieved until 2086, while this goal had already become true for boys from the richest households in 1998 (UNESCO 2014, 2, 10).[7]

The three dominant reasons for school abstention are a long distance from schools, the requirement for children to work, and high costs (NPopC and RTI International 2016a, 28). Meanwhile, the three prevailing reasons for dropouts are monetary costs, the need for labor, and poor school quality (NPopC and RTI International 2016a, 29). Given the dilapidated character of public schools, private schools become a viable alternative for more and more families (Dixon 2013; Ukpor, Ubi, and Okon 2012; World Bank 2015, 65). While Nigeria's elite turn to high-cost international schools, the poor turn to often unapproved or unregistered low-cost private schools (Härmä 2013), as well as private Islamic schools (Adelani 2014).[8] Given these realities, Nigeria is one of the most unequal countries regarding access to formal education by region, gender, and wealth: most excluded children are poor, live in rural areas in the northern regions, and are girls.

Disability, however, constitutes the most potent risk for educational exclusion for all children and youth. The government acknowledges in its National Action Plan for the Implementation of UBE that this is because most children with disabilities are "invisible to the system," resulting also in a lack of data (FRN n.d., 41). When information is available, it is often inconsistent given the different conceptualizations of disability, the lack of official special-needs diagnostics, and the challenges of admitting to having a child with disabilities in a stigmatizing context without support services. The 2015 National Report of the Nigeria Education Data Survey, for example, accounts for a disabled school population of 0.7 percent and finds that disability is responsible for less than 1 percent of school abstentions and less than 4 percent of dropouts, respectively (NPopC and RTI International 2016a, A 37–38). A meta-analysis of various censuses, in contrast, reports a disability prevalence rate of 0.4 percent for children of primary and secondary school age, but estimates that half of them are out of schools (Mizunoya, Mitra, and Yamasaki 2016, 17, 22). With 50 percent, the rate of disabled out-of-school children accounted for is significantly higher than the one for nondisabled school-age children, which stands at 18.5 percent (Mizunoya, Mitra, and Yamasaki 2016, 22).

Regarding enrollment, the Federal Ministry of Education reports in 2008 that less than 3 percent of disabled children, who make up 7 percent of the total population, attended primary schools and less than 2 percent secondary schools (FME 2008, 61). If enrolled, children are often confronted with low-quality education, as special schools lack materials and qualified personnel (FRN n.d., 41; IOM 2014, 42). Given the overall lack of public educational provisions for disabled children, private special-needs schools are often the only place families can turn to in order to receive any form of education for their disabled children (Ajuwon 2012; Obiakor, Eskay, and Afolayan 2012, 34). Mostly founded and maintained by churches, philanthropic organizations, or parents, private special schools typically cater for students with sensory impairments and intellectual/cognitive disabilities (Nkechi 2013; Obiakor and Offor 2011; Abang 1992). For these reasons, most persons with disabilities have never received any form of formal education or at low levels (FMWA 2011, 171, 183; N. Smith 2011; Nkechi 2013).

In sum, these current characteristics of schooling in Nigeria underline the institutional reality of exclusion. Disabled or disadvantaged children are largely excluded from a formal school system that exacerbates educational barriers to schooling by enhancing the importance of socioeconomic capital, gender, and place of residence.

Getting Started: Reconstructing the Nigerian Discourse on Inclusive Education

Against the background of the exclusionary reality of education, how is Article 24 UN CRPD's "program of change" now translated into educational change? How does its reform mandate—to ensure an inclusive school system—and its agenda—to make all schools accessible and available for all—connect with contextual ideas about education already in place? And with what effect on the rules, norms, and beliefs that facilitate the institution of schooling? To answer these questions, I now turn to my empirical work: the reconstruction of the Nigerian discourse on inclusive education that took place on the federal level between 2004 and 2015. The focus is on the federal policy level as the Nigerian school system operates under the umbrella of the 2004 Universal Basic Education (UBE) Act.[9] In terms of translation, the key question is therefore how Article 24's global human rights package is negotiated in relation to the national commitment to UBE. The study's endpoint is 2015, as the MDGs expired that year. Accordingly, progress toward UBE was evaluated at the national and international levels. As of 2015, the UN CRPD—even though ratified—was not yet domesticated; the domestication finally occurred in 2019 with passage of the Discrimination against Persons with Disabilities (Prohibition) Act (FRN 2018; Ewang 2019; Onogu 2016).

The Nigerian case study concerns an individual instance of Article 24's translations. To reconstruct this translation, I follow a sociology-of-knowledge approach to discourse (Keller 2011) and analyze the knowledge that policy actors (re)produce about inclusive education when they "engage one another in a 'coordinative' discourse about policy construction" (Schmidt 2008, 310). This analysis is based on data I collected in the capital, Abuja, in 2012 and 2013. There I got in contact with federal policy actors, including representatives from federal ministries, civil society organizations (CSOs), and international development partners. These policy actors are integral to the translation of global human rights ideas, because they are "involved in the creation, elaboration, and justification of policy and programmatic ideas" (Schmidt 2008, 31). In this process, they "convey ideas from one context to another, adapting and reframing them from the way they attach to a source context to one that resonates with the new location" (Levitt and Merry 2009, 448).

Two groups of policy actors are distinguished. First is the group of state actors, who have a "monopoly on the legitimate use of force to implement rights effectively" (Wolfsteller 2017, 230). This is primarily the federal government, including its ministries and commissions, which are tasked to initiate the development of an inclusive school system at the national level, and account for this process at the international level. The second group includes civil society actors, for example, disabled persons' organizations (DPOs) and rights groups, who need to be involved in the UN CRPD implementation process, as required by Articles 4(3) and 33(3) UN CRPD.

In the policy field of education, key state actors include the Federal Ministry of Education and the Universal Basic Education Commission, an agency set up by the federal government to coordinate the implementation of UBE across Nigerian states (UBEC 2021). Their activities are monitored and supplemented by nonstate actors, such as the Civil Society Action Coalition on Education for All, a network of six hundred civil society organizations established in the run-up to the World Education Summit in Dakar in April 2000 (CSACEFA n.d.). In addition, an array of international organizations are involved in the implementation of UBE. UNICEF, for example, supports the government in monitoring and developing plans that tackle the high number of out-of-school children (UNICEF Nigeria 2021). Besides, the UK-funded Education Sector Support Programme in Nigeria, for example, supported the government in planning, financing, and delivering basic education between 2008 and 2017 (ESSPIN 2017).

In the policy field of disability, key state actors were the Federal Ministry of Woman Affairs and Social Development, responsible for policies aiming at persons with disabilities (FMWA 2011). Key nonstate actors were the Joint National Organization of Persons with Disabilities, the Nigerian umbrella organization of persons with disabilities (JONAPWD 2015), and individual DPOs advocating for the rights of persons with disabilities. Due to the UN CRPD's nondomestication at the time of data collection, I could not identify policy actors responsible for the implementation of the human rights treaty.

With this selection, I do not assume that policy actors can influence policymaking or debates to the same extent; indeed, state actors and international organizations are more powerful than civil society or disabled persons organizations. However, it is important to juxtapose their views because in confronting the problem of inclusive education, this wide range of policy actors negotiates Article 24's human rights paradigm in a coordinative policy discourse; they therefore form an organizational field that constitutes the discursive space of translations (Benzecry and Krause 2010, 419; Scott 1994, 71).

The data I gathered consist of policy documents produced by various actors paired with expert interviews covering the years 2004 to 2015. Both data sources are characterized by a dynamic connection between words, meanings, and policy actions (Prior 2008, 479). While documents—written texts produced by organizations (Salheiser 2014, 813)—foreground policy actors' codified knowledge, interviews—written texts that result from a communicative action produced by the researcher (Helfferich 2014, 559)—access tacit knowledge thus offering a deeper insight into the negotiation of change. For this study, I was particularly interested in official and publicly available publications of policy actors such as positions papers, action plans, mission statements, and leaflets. In containing organizational positions, these documents are artifacts of communicative practices carrying policy actors' approaches to inclusive education. Since important documents were published in the years following 2015, I include these in the analysis as well, such as the 2016 Draft Policy on Inclusive Education (FME 2016) and the 2018 Discrimination against Persons with Disabilities (Prohibition) Act (FRN 2018). In addition, I conducted interviews with representatives of organizations that are involved in policy debates. In total, I gathered almost sixty documents and conducted almost thirty interviews. Out of this corpus, I selected forty-three documents and nine interviews for an in-depth analysis, an overview of which is available in the appendix.[10] In topically dealing with inclusive education, Article 24, and/or disability-based exclusions in education, these data entail the discourse fragments that I analyzed through grounded-theory-based and content-driven qualitative analysis (Charmaz 2014; Keller 2011). In this process, I abstracted from the original data to reveal the overarching knowledge formation driving the Nigerian discourse on inclusive education at the federal policy level. In presenting the results, I will, however, quote from some original data to illustrate the points made.

Negotiating Inclusive Education Change: The Nigerian UBE Implementation Discourse

In Nigeria, the topic of inclusive education emerges within a discourse about the implementation of UBE. The UBE Act provides the base for policy actors to advocate for the development of an inclusive education system in order to overcome the exclusion of millions of children and youth, including those with disabilities (FRN 2004a). The UBE Act not only answers to the 1999 constitution's obligation to ensure "equal and adequate educational opportunities at all levels" (Constitution of the Federal Republic of Nigeria 1999, Chapter II [18]), it also implements the 1999 Universal Basic Education Scheme initiated to meet the goal of universal primary education. This way, the UBE Act exerts coercive and normative pressures.

Providing the context of discourse production, the UBE Act conveys information about the legal obligation to "provide free, compulsory and universal basic education for every child" (FRN 2004a, para. 2(1)), that is according to the 2004 National Policy on Education (NPE), a nine-year cycle of six years of primary and three years of junior secondary education (FRN 2004b, para. 15). With the revised NPE of 2013, the basic education cycle was extended by one year to a total of ten years of schooling (FRN 2013a, para. 10).[11] Indeed, the UBE Act constitutes a historical turning point, renewing the government's commitment to educational expansion under the umbrella of the EFA development goal (UNICEF and FME 2012, 3). Most documents analyzed were composed in reaction or relation to the implementation of UBE, and most interviews referenced the UBE Act as core legislation designed to realize an inclusive school system. The legal obligation to UBE thus generates and frames an implementation discourse in which the development of an inclusive school system is negotiated.

Ideationally, the negotiations of the UBE mandate bring forth a cascading structure of change in which the institutionalization of an inclusive school system aids the implementation of UBE to serve the country's overall socioeconomic development, not the realization of the UN CRPD. In this way, the discourse reverts to international education policy discussions of the 1990s, importantly the 1994 Salamanca Statement (World Conference on Special Needs Education 1994). This document coined inclusive education as a concept and strategy to realize the right to education for marginalized and excluded children in the pursuit of EFA.

With this cascade, policy actors across the organizational field strive to implement UBE by confronting the perennial problem of exclusion with the development of an inclusive school system, that is, a system that provides different forms of special education to excluded "special groups."

Special groups in education encompass several dimensions of inequality, which relate to the inability to access and participate in formal schools. This inability, in turn, constitutes these groups' special educational needs. According to the UBE Act, special groups are "nomads and migrants, girl-child [sic] and women, almajiri, street children and disabled groups" (FRN 2004a, para. 15). The 2004 NPE eventually distinguishes between three

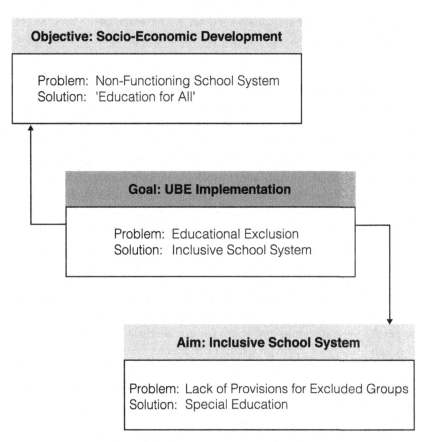

Figure 3. Cascade of Change I

groups with special needs; namely "The Disabled," "The Disadvantaged," and "The Gifted and Talented" (FRN 2004b, para. 94). The group of disabled persons includes those with visual, hearing, physical, health, speech, and language impairments or intellectual, learning, and multiple disabilities, as well as emotional and behavioral disorders. The group of disadvantaged children and youth includes nomads and other groups, who "due to their lifestyles and means of livelihood are unable to access conventional educational provisions" (FRN 2004b, para. 94). To the group of gifted and talented belong "people (children and adults) who have/possess very high IQ and are naturally endowed with special traits . . . [and are] insufficiently challenged by regular schools" (FRN 2004b, para. 94). Conversely, only one group emerges as not special and freed from the notion of exceptionality: able-bodied, urban, school-aged males of average talent living in the country's south. In fact, it is this group that has so far reached the highest attendance rates in basic education, as already shown.

In order to meet the special needs of these groups, the government promotes different special education programs (e.g., FME 2015; FRN 2013b, paras. 114–20; FMWA 2011; FME 2007). For disabled and gifted children, this special-needs education provides basic education with the help of special teachers, materials, and equipment in special schools or classrooms (FRN n.d., 40–41). Disadvantaged children, on the other hand, should be reached through nomadic or integrated Koranic education as well as mass literacy programs. Nomadic education delivers six years of basic education to nomad pastoralists, migrant fishermen, and farmers in mobile or permanent nomadic schools or via radio (FME 2015, 54–61).[12] Integrated Koranic education introduces basic subjects such as math and English alongside the traditional study of the Koran to almajirais—boys that study the Koran and earn their own livelihood through begging—in Islamiyyah, Model Tsangaya, or Model Almajirai schools (FRN n.d., 41–42; FME 2015, 61–63). In addition, mass literacy programs target "difficult to reach" illiterate adults and youth to provide basic literacy, for example through literacy-by-radio programs or in literacy centers (FME 2015, 84–85). In sum, these provisions reveal that the notion of special groups in education links impairment, disadvantage, and difficulty with the need for special education.

From a discourse perspective, it is important to note that a distinction is made at the policy level between special groups in education and forms of special education. Special groups in education are those vulnerable to exclusion from basic education in formal schools; disabled children are one of those groups. Special education, on the other hand, is a form of basic education outside regular formal schools, including special-needs, nomadic, adult, and nonformal education (see FME 2007, 15–16). Dis-

TABLE 5. Special Groups and Forms of Special Education in Nigeria

Universal basic education for excluded groups	
Special groups	Forms of special education
Disabled children	Special-needs education
Gifted and talented children	Special-needs education
Disadvantaged children	Nomadic education, integrated Koranic education, adult and nonformal education

ability, in this context, functions as an umbrella term for impairment-based limitations that hinder children in regular school settings; no references are made to sociocultural perceptions of disability as factors that may also contribute to exclusions. The 2016 Draft Policy on Inclusive Education reconfirms this view by distinguishing between impairment, "Loss or limitation of physical, mental or sensory function on a long term and/or permanent basis," and disability, "a condition where a person cannot function optimally without an aid either in a long term or in a permanent basis" (FME 2016, 6). Overcoming a sole focus on medical conditions, this distinction nonetheless confirms the understanding that disability is a problem encountered in the performance of basic activities that cannot be compensated with basic technical aids. We will see later what effects this has on the understanding of inclusive education.

Even though disability-based special-needs education is addressed in policy papers, there is hardly any opportunity for diagnosis, or an official statement of special educational needs given the lack of resources. The Federal Ministry of Education reports, though, that under the EFA framework one facility was established "to screen, assess and place children with special needs in schools," the National Diagnostic and Assessment Centre for Special Children in Abuja (FME 2015, 137). Effectively, the notion of exclusion-related special needs has therefore little or no immediate impact on placement or financial, educational, or assistive support for disabled children. However, the broad approach to special educational needs and student's inability to access UBE is vital for the discourse on inclusive education, as it generates several subdiscourses. Each of these focuses on a particular special group: nomads and their nomadic education, almajirais and integrated Koranic education, disabled children and their special-needs education, as well as illiterate adults and youth targeted by adult and nonformal education.[13] With these subdiscourses, the Nigerian discourse perpetuates a broader understanding of inclusion that targets several marginalized groups. The ultimate aim is to integrate the autonomous Islamic and traditional education systems and the largely unregulated special-needs education sector into the formal UBE system.

Following the explicit wording of the UN CRPD's Article 24, I focus from now on the subdiscourse concerned with overcoming educational exclusion based on disability. To reconstruct its phenomenal structure, I am going to combine the typified assumptions of federal policy actors about inclusive education into a specific form—a "process of change"—and identify its goal, scope, and dimensions (see Keller 2011, 58). The process of change, in sum, displays the typified assumptions of federal policy actors

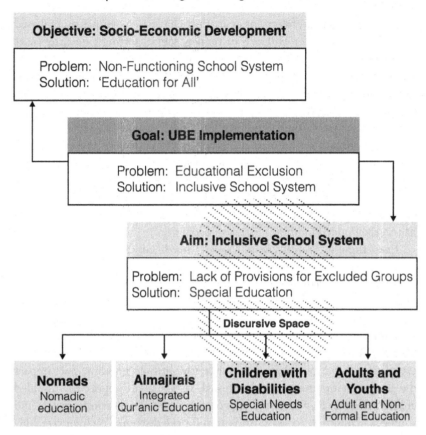

Figure 4. Cascade of Change II

about the development of an inclusive school system for children with disabilities in Nigeria.

Goal of Change

Policy actors across the spectrum—state, nonstate, and international organizations—share the understanding that the development of an inclusive school system is a tool for educational expansion in order to include disabled children in UBE. This understanding is reached as policy actors actively reflect on the global norm of inclusive education, in particular the reform agenda "all schools for all" and, eventually, determine its current unattainability in the Nigerian context.

One state actor, for example, recognized that "the world is going inclusive" implying that "every school should be able to accommodate every child . . . and every child should be free to go to every school" (N9: 105–12). This vision, however, seems nonviable for the interviewee given the lack of provisions for disabled children. Instead of "put[ing] them in the classroom," a representative of a CSO similarly argues, disabled children would need a "specialized program" to be included in education (N_1: 343–46). In foregrounding the need for special educational provisions, these policy actors do not outrightly reject the global goal of "all schools for all." However, they conclude that the joint instruction of children with and without disabilities in regular schools is currently impracticable. Even more, they relegate this goal to a later stage of educational progression. In other words, the underlying conviction policy actors share is that the overcoming of disability-based exclusion requires, first of all, the provision of special education, which can only be transferred into regular schools after being institutionalized. In this way, the absence of a segregated special education system becomes the main barrier to inclusion, not an institutional advantage. This anticipated evolutionary process of inclusive education change is best summarized in the metaphor of "moving up the inclusive education ladder," which a representative of an international organization introduced.

So, for us on the inclusive education ladder, you find some are still not thinking about it at all. They completely neglected them. But you find people who are on the second ladder, they are already thinking about it. Because they are thinking about it, they've established special schools. But you can find people who have moved up from special schools to doing an integrated system, integrated unit[s] still in the normal schools. So that is how the ladder will be moving until when you have a system where in the same classroom you find all these different types of children, living with visual impairment, living with hearing impairment, children from poor homes. All of them will now be in the same classroom. They would learn together, and they will have teachers with capacity to be able to teach them and meet their needs. So, in terms of the inclusion ladder, that is where we are going. (N_3: 237–47)

Progression-oriented, the inclusive education ladder frames institutional change as an evolutionary process of educational expansion, which depends on the provision of special-needs education. This distinct form of education must initially be provided in segregated special schools, can then

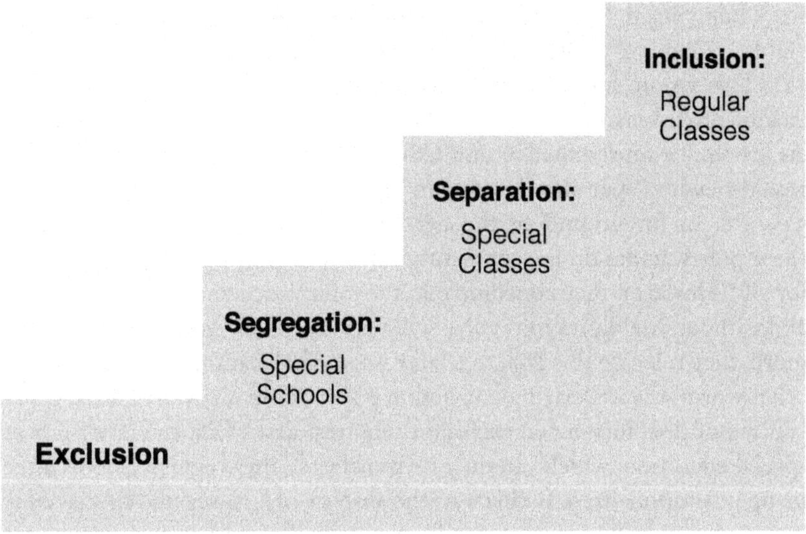

Figure 5. Inclusive education ladder

be transferred to separated special classes, and ultimately can be located in regular classrooms. In this logic, segregation and separation are stages of inclusion that need to be reached and surpassed to eventually realize inclusive education as joint learning.

Based on this succession of goals, the inclusion of children with disabilities in the Nigerian school system follows an apparently universal chronology of "moving up the inclusive ladder." The goal policy actors therefore pursue with the development of an inclusive school system in the context of UBE is "educational expansion through special education." Achieving this goal then provides the base upon which joint learning could be pursued at a later stage.

Scope of Change

In advocating for "educational expansion by special-needs education," policy actors argumentatively approach inclusive education change from two different angles.

One group, mostly state, nonstate, and international actors in the policy field of education, primarily argue against the background of international development goals (e.g., ESSPIN 2013; UNICEF and FME 2012; CSACEFA 2010). They tend to foreground the need for educational expansion for all, which then also means providing for disabled children. This view is substantiated by national development frameworks such as the Vision 20:2020, the domestic plan to transform the country into one of the twenty largest economies in the world by 2020. Identifying education "as a human right and critical element in human development," this document aims "to ensure that all boys and girls, irrespective of ethnicity, gender or disability, complete a full course of basic education" (NPC 2009, 35). In line with this vision, the representative of an international development organization elaborates: "We are going beyond disability alone. We are thinking more of a bigger scope of inclusive education" because, in addition to disabled children, "girls, children in [the] fishing community, children in [the] nomadic community, housemaids" are excluded from schooling (N_3: 394–98). The essence of this argument is that the development of an inclusive system is the institutional precondition to overcoming exclusion and thus achieving the overall developmental objective of EFA. In this way, the cascade of change is read top-down.

Another group, mostly nonstate and civil society actors in the policy field of disability, approach the development of an inclusive school system primarily from the angle of education and disability (e.g., JONAPWD 2012; Special Interest Group for Persons with Disability 2009; Guar and Ivom 2010). They tend to foreground the need for special-needs education to realize disabled children's right to basic education. The essence of their argument is that an inclusive system requires special educational provisions for disabled persons. In this way, the cascade of change is read bottom-up.

Despite these two different approaches, the groups' positions ultimately reinforce each other and thus bring forth one line of argumentation, which defines the scope of inclusive education change as realizing the right to basic education for children with disabilities. Analytically, policy actors therefore form a discourse coalition, even though they hardly collaborate with each other in real life. This is because debates pertaining to educational expansion primarily take place in the policy field of education and are mostly independent from debates about special provisions for children with disabilities in the policy field of disability.

Dimensions of Change

In arguing for the realization of the disabled child's right to basic education, policy actors across the spectrum develop complementary ideas about the transformation of education. First and foremost, they identify the lack of special provisions as the main barrier to realize UBE and are, more

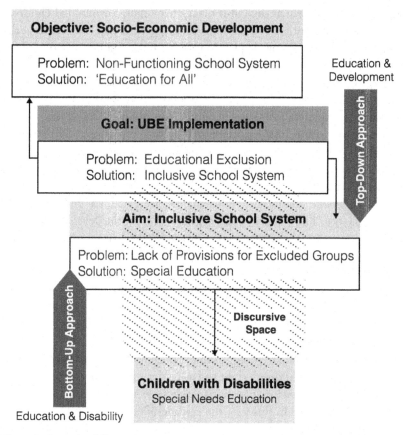

Figure 6. Cascade of Change III

broadly, concerned with legal protections against discrimination on the basis of disability.

Access to Special Educational Provisions in Regular and Special Schools

One of the most perennial problems identified as contributing to the continued exclusion of disabled children is the lack of appropriate schools. In fact, in its report issued in preparation for the Vision 20:2020 development framework, the Working Group on Education determined that "90% of primary schools lack adequate facilities let alone facilities to cater for those with special needs" (National Technical Working Group on Education Sector 2009, 24). Hence, the dilapidated infrastructure and lack of resources is identified as a crucial barrier for disabled children to access schools or participate in a meaningful way in education.

To tackle this problem, state and nonstate actors envision an inclusive education system. DPOs, in this respect, demand, via the Vision 20:2020 Special Interest Group for Persons with Disability, access to a "single educational system that will cater for the needs of all learners within an inclusive environment with various placement options" (Special Interest Group for Persons with Disability 2009, 33). Over the last several years, the federal government in fact has reiterated its promise to establish such a system. The 2004 National Policy on Education (NPE), for example, stipulates that "all necessary facilities that would ensure easy access to education shall be provided" (FRN 2004b, para. 96, lit. c). These facilities comprise "inclusive education or integration of special classes or unit into ordinary/public schools under the UBE scheme" as well as "special education equipment and material" and "special training and re-training of the personnel" (FRN 2004b, para. 96, lit. c).[14] These guidelines eventually became law with the 2018 Disability Act mandating that "all public schools, whether primary, secondary or tertiary shall be run to be inclusive of and accessible to persons with disabilities" (FRN 2018, para. 18; similarly The Senate 2013, para. 23). To this end, all schools are required to have "at least a trained personnel to cater for the educational development of persons with disabilities" as well as "special facilities for the effective education of persons with disabilities" (FRN 2018, para. 18; similarly The Senate 2013, para. 23).[15] These planned measures corroborate the idea that an inclusive school system is one that provides for the special-needs education of disabled children in regular as well as special schools and classrooms. The Federal Ministry of Education, likewise, outlines in the 2015 EFA Review Report that the aim of its "Support for Special Needs Education Programme" is "promoting inclusive education and increas[ing] access to basic education for children with special needs" (FME 2015, 137).

On what basis is it then decided who gets access to which setting? The following data reveal two crucial factors determining access to regular or special schools: first, the severity of a child's disability and, second, the schools' special education capacity. The 2013 NPE introduces educationally relevant degrees of disability. Even though stating that "persons with special needs shall be provided with inclusive education services in schools which normal persons attend," this vision is restricted (FRN 2013a, para. 118). In fact, the following sentence determines that "special needs persons who cannot benefit from inclusive education, special classes and units shall remain in special schools" (para. 118). The 2016 Draft Policy on Inclusive Education adopted a broader approach to the need for "removing barriers and involving all learners who otherwise would have been excluded through marginalization and segregation" (FME 2016, 8). Despite that,

the document maintains the key role of special schools not only in educating disabled children (alongside nondisabled peers) but also in becoming resource centers for regular schools and their teachers (FME 2016,
19). The distinction between children regarded as able to participate in
regular education and those regarded as incapable can also be found in a
report by the Global Partnership for Education—a global fund partnering
donors, civil society, and the private sector (GPE 2021). In assessing Nigeria's education plans, the network's appraisal reiterates that "all schools are
expected, in the spirit of 'inclusive' education, to accommodate children
with special needs, unless the nature of the disability is severe" (GPE 2013,
20). Even though distinguishing levels of disability, these documents do
not explicitly determine which impairments would allow or prevent access
to regular schools and classrooms. Nonetheless, these discourse statements
reveal that children's impairments are hierarchically organized on the policy level, the precondition for allowing for the ability-based placement of
children in different school types in the first place.

Even though an inclusive system with several placement options is
politically intended, children with disabilities hardly participate in UBE.
The representative of a DPO highlights the lack of provisions, such as
sign language interpreters or material in Braille, resulting in the fact that
"the school is not inclusive" (N_8: 385–89). Ultimately, this interviewee
underlines the inaccessibility of regular schools. Aiming primarily at able-
bodied children, they neither acknowledge nor meet the needs of disabled
children and youth.

To increase the accessibility of regular schools, the Federal Ministry
of Education issued an Implementation Plan for Special Needs Education
Strategy stipulating that "each school should cater for at least 50 students
with special needs" (FME n.d., 4). To meet this requirement, schools are
expected "to carve out two additional classrooms for 15 students with special needs per class," some of whom are expected to "move from special
classrooms to the integrated classrooms" over time (FME n.d., 4). In addition, schools shall build ramps, adapt toilets, and widen doors for wheel-
chair users, as well as "operate mixed ability classes, where children with
special needs will receive education along-side their peers, catering for up
to 20 students" (FME n.d., 4). Besides adjustments to schools' physical
infrastructure, the government promotes the provision of assistive devices
to make classrooms more inclusive. The Federal Ministry of Education,
for example, encourages teachers in its 2010 Training Manual on Adaptation and Implementation of Inclusive Education to "allow students to
tape lectures," "to find a note taker," and to provide "alternative ways of

completing assignments" (FME 2010). The essence of these proposals is to make existing regular schools more accessible by establishing special classrooms for disabled children *and* providing special equipment for them. Eventually though, these proposals disclose that most disabled children are not expected to benefit from regular education, as participation in regular classrooms depends on two conditions: the nonsevere nature of a child's disability and the provision of assistive devices to compensate limitations.

Eventually, policy actors across the organizational field advocate for special education provisions in special schools to realize the right to education for all disabled children. These provisions are hardly available in the notoriously resource-strapped Nigerian school system. The federal government, in its National Action Plan for Implementation of the UBE Programme, in fact concedes that "the number of special needs schools is insufficient to handle children with special needs which cannot be met by conventional schools" (FRN n.d., 41). Indeed, the document only accounts for 302 special-needs schools, two-thirds of which are owned by state governments and one-tenth by the federal government, while the rest are governed by private actors, including NGOs and faith-based organizations (FRN n.d., 41). In light of that shortfall, the Federal Ministry of Education asserts in a 2012 report the goal of "Establishing Additional Schools for Children with Special Needs and Equipping them Adequately with Trained Personnel and relevant Equipment" (FME 2012b, 25). The unavailability of special schools is not the only identified barrier to education; even more critical is the lack of teachers and learning materials. Again, the federal government states:

> There is a shortage of appropriate learning materials in special needs schools. Teachers are also, in many cases, unfamiliar with special methodologies needed for working with children with special needs. . . . On paper, teachers in special needs schools are suitably qualified. However, . . . their qualifications sometimes count for little. (FRN n.d., 41)

This analysis underlines the extent of undersupply hampering any educational prospect for disabled children. UNESCO observes that the "teaching-learning materials available to them [teachers in special schools] are inadequate," urging the government to equip "special schools adequately" (UNESCO 2008, 27). Moreover, DPOs demand "opportunity to capacity training of specialized teachers and institutions to ensure the education of Persons With Disability are of a higher and comparable standards" (Special Interest Group for Persons with Disability 2009, 33). As a "turn-around strategy," the group calls for the "establishment of more COEs [colleges of education] (Special)" to train more specialist teachers (Special Interest Group for Persons with Disability 2009, 39). The 2018 Disability Act stipulates that the "education of special education person-nel shall be highly subsidised" (FRN 2018, para. 19).[16] In making these comments, state, nonstate, and international policy actors alike call for the professionalization of teacher training in special education as well as the establishment of adequately equipped special schools. In other words, they aim for the institutionalization of a special education system—the epitome of inclusion in UBE.

Legal Protection against Discrimination

Nonstate policy actors, in particular DPOs, relate the continued exclusion of disabled people from public goods and services, including education, to missing antidiscrimination legislation. Over the years, the so-called Dis-ability Bill with a Commission was debated in the National Assembly and even passed several times (House of Representatives 2008; The Senate 2013). However, the bill did not win the president's assent until 2019, for reasons unknown to DPO representatives at the time the interviews were conducted.

It's more than ten years that we've been trying to get the govern-ment to sign the disability bill in Nigeria, but it has never been suc-cessful, we keep on trying. (N_4: 48–50)

Since 1993, there's been an attempt to make a legislation that would enhance the lives of persons with disabilities in Nigeria. But it looks like it's always meeting a brick wall. (N_6: 115–16)

In short, the legislative process surrounding the disability bill was for DPOs not always fully transparent. The same is true for the processes surrounding the ratification of the UN CRPD. One DPO representative reports that "it has come to our surprise that the government has ratified the UN Convention," as "the disability community was not involved in the process of the ratification" but is, instead, "very much focused on this dis-ability bill" (N_4: 43–46). In making this comment, the interviewee priori-tizes the disability bill while meeting the UN CRPD with skepticism. Even more, the convention is pushed to the sidelines as another DPO representative declares that the organization hasn't made use of the UN CRPD in its advocacy work yet "because it's not been domesticated, it's just paper" (N_5: 131–32).[17] In addition, Nigeria had as of 2021 neither issued its first state party report to the UN Committee on the Rights of Persons with Disabilities nor specified the formalities of the national monitoring process (see NHRC n.d.). The disability community therefore doubts that the ratification of the convention is a genuine commitment to disability rights and their realization on the ground. Rather, they regard the ratification as a symbolic act of state actors directed toward the international community, as the following quotations illustrate:

> Some just copy it and sign with their mouth, not because they want to see the rights of the disabled being met, but just for signing sake. (N_4: 65–66)

> They sign it not fully grasping the intricacy, the issues that are really involved. . . . They rushed to sign it, I must say. It's a rush to sign it because they've not really studied the issues that are involved. (N_8: 294–96)

The essence of these actors' statements is the decoupling of international commitments and national actions. The UN CRPD is therefore seen as just another example of an internationally produced document added to the already highly saturated Nigerian policy space without any consequence; for that reason, direct references to the human rights treaty are rare. In support of this point, I note that the federal government repeatedly emphasized its commitment to legal change on the international stage. In 2009, for example, it declared in a report for the UN Human Rights Council that legislators in the National Assembly "work towards the speedy passage of the [Disability] Bill" (FRN 2009, para. 61). But as early as 2007, in its 10 Year Strategic Plan, the Federal Ministry of Education specified that a policy goal, in the context of special-needs education, was to "monitor implementation of the Disability Act and develop special programme[s] to support implementation" (FME 2007, 13).

As mentioned earlier, the bill eventually became law in January 2019 (Ewang 2019). A core provision of the Discrimination against Persons with Disabilities (Prohibition) Act is the establishment of a National Commission for People with Disabilities; indeed, twenty out of fifty-eight sections deal exclusively with the commission's functions and powers.[18] It is vested with an array of responsibilities. These range from the formulation and implementation of educational and social policies for persons with disabilities to ensuring the "monitoring, evaluation and realization of government policy objectives" (FRN 2018, para. 38, lit. a, h). The commission is also responsible for issuing "insignia of identification with persons with disabilities," receiving "complaints of persons with disabilities on the violation of their rights," as well as procuring "assistive devices for all disability types" (FRN 2018, para. 38, lit. l, n, r). Most responsibilities, though, refer to education.

The commission is tasked to "collect data and records on special education of persons with disabilities" and to "facilitate the procurement of scholarship awards for persons with disabilities up to university level" (FRN 2018, para. 38, lit. f, i). In addition, it has to "ensure that all facilities in each community all over the Federation shall be built or modified, where and when feasible, to accommodate the special need of persons with disabilities" (FRN 2018, para. 38, lit. g). Eventually, the commission must also "establish and promote inclusive schools, vocational and rehabilitation centres for the development of persons with disabilities" (FRN 2018, para. 38, lit. j). This vast array of far-reaching functions first of all emphasizes the need for material and financial support as well as assistive devices to enable access and participation in education. More importantly though, the all-encompassing responsibilities reveal the need for organizational representation in order for disabled persons to become visible in the political, and eventually social, sphere as a group discriminated against, as the following comment reveals:

> We are not standing on our own. . . . We can't really fight for ourselves . . . so we were canvassing for our own commission, an organization by us, run by us. (N_8: 214–18)

In making this point, the interviewee declares the commission to be the ultimate symbol of empowerment, as it promises self-representation as well as autonomy.

The quest for a commission, in fact, hints at the intricacies of political access and participation in Nigeria. The Nigerian political space is characterized by an abundance of commissions with exclusive powers and functions. In the field of education, we find, for example, the National Commission for Nomadic Education, the National Commission for Mass Literacy, Adult and Non-Formal Education, and the Universal Basic Education Commission. Currently, the National Assembly is debating the establishment of dozens of new commissions, including a National Commission for the Eradication of Child Destitution (Establishment) Bill (PLAC n.d.a). In the negotiations over the disability bill, the establishment of a

National Commission for Persons with Disabilities was the most controversial point. This became obvious during a public hearing in the Senate in March 2013. After legislators pointed out the difficulties involved in setting up a commission, the disability community got up and collective chanted for several minutes, "Nothing about us without us." They used the prominent slogan of the international disability rights community to demand organizational representation for and by persons with disabilities. Why? The answer is that organizational representation is a necessity if a group is to participate in the Nigerian political space. Whether this achievement also contributes to social inclusion, that is equal access and participation in other areas of social life such as education is to be seen. After all, the inclusion of disabled persons faces a specific challenge: to make it a special interest, not of the commission alone, but of the wider society.

To summarize, the process of change envisaged in the UBE implementation discourse calls for several changes to realize an inclusive education system in Nigeria. These include modified organizational-professional practices of special-needs education, as well as new legislation and altered perceptions of disability. These changes affect the norms, rules, and beliefs of schooling and threaten the premises of an exclusionary school system. However, they also reinforce a special education system that segregates or separates children into special schools or classes on the basis of disability. In this way, the institutional path of Nigeria's school system is about to be amended, changing its exclusionary logic into a logic of interschool segregation coupled with intraschool separation.

Speaker and Subject Positions

In advocating for the development of an inclusive school system, policy actors speak from the position of "facilitators of change," that is, the legitimate place from which discourse statements can be formulated (cf. Keller 2011, 55). In this role, they aim to create demand and supply for the inclusion of disabled children in the UBE system.

From the perspective of a state actor, the creation of demand and supply implies two efforts: first, to "sensitize" other state actors about the global educational trend of inclusive education; and, second, to encourage persons with disabilities to demand according changes.

> We have seen that the world now has moved away from . . . special schools. The world is into inclusive education. So, okay, let's sensitize them [to] that. . . . Then for persons with disabilities . . . We

realize that they don't really know what the struggle is all about, you understand, because we have to really sensitize them. They have to take the bull by the head. (N_7: 92–93, 100–103)

In short, the state actor tries to encourage the supply of special provisions for persons with disabilities by demanding them from other state actors and, most notably, DPOs themselves. Indeed, a DPO representative sees the empowerment of persons with disabilities as a crucial task. However, the interviewee details the constrains the organization faces in trying to do so.

What we should be doing really is empowering persons with disability in the country. . . . But, unfortunately, that aspect has not been fully met because of financial constraints. . . . We need partnerships [for] our activities, supporters to build, to carry out, those activities. (N_5: 27–30, 274–75)

This actor's point is that the creation of demand and supply hinges on financial support from international organizations. Their resources are crucial to enable political participation. This line of reasoning is taken up by the representative of an international organization who remarks that its intentions are to remind the government of its duty to realize EFA, to increase the capacity of civil society organizations to demand UBE, and to raise the interest of other international organizations in the topic.

A lot of our own role is . . . supporting government to doing what they should do, and also supporting communities to also create demand to ask for some of these things, . . . supporting the associations themselves, association[s] of people living with disability, supporting the CSOs to create a lot of these, a lot of these demands and international organizations who are in the country, how can they support this demand. . . . how can they support the education sector, particularly this inclusive education? (N_3: 137–38, 352–60)

Basically, the interviewee is detailing the complex task of creating a demand for inclusion, that is, to encourage more domestic and international actors to advocate for UBE by providing special education for disabled children.

As "facilitators of change," all policy actors foreground their knowledge about disabled children's right to education when speaking about

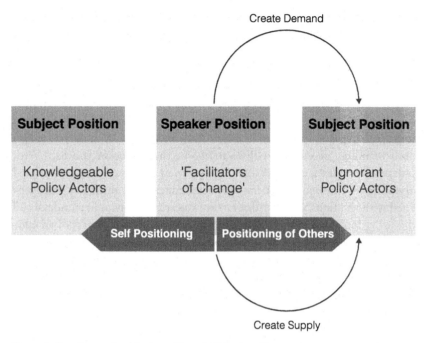

Figure 7. Speaker and subject positions in Nigerian discourse

the development of an inclusive school system. This knowledge is what enables them to advocate for inclusive education change in the first place. All speakers in the subdiscourse therefore position themselves as "knowledgeable" and thus in opposition to "ignorant actors." In referencing different levels of knowledge, speakers hint at—but never explicate—the role of traditional understandings of disability and impairment in the exclusion of children.

Interpretative Frame

As "facilitators of change," policy actors across the organizational spectrum share ideas about appropriate ways of dealing with disabled children in schooling. These ideas are based on knowledge about disabled children's special needs and the school system's inadequate capacity to provide special education. (Re)produced discursively, this knowledge frames the development of an inclusive school system as a process of expanding special education. This interpretative frame—defined as a "fundamental meaning and action-generating schemata" (Keller 2011, 57)—is what links the ideas entailed in the global rights package of Article 24 to preexisting ideas and institutions of disabled children's education (see Levitt and Merry 2009, 451–52).

Knowledge about the special needs of disabled children in education is based on the conviction that impairments impede regular education. These ideas were first advanced with the introduction of a Western model of schooling in the wake of colonialism. Christian missionaries founded impairment-based special schools and thus introduced a hitherto foreign understanding of educational disability in the Nigerian context. With independence from colonial rule in 1960, an understanding of educational disability as an impairment-based special educational need was strengthened with the first National Policy on Education. This policy understood the provision of special-needs education to be an essential part of an educational expansion project aiming to provide education for all Nigerians. Given the successive failures to institutionalize such a system, the notions of special educational needs and the need for special education were revived once again with the renewed commitment to EFA under the umbrella of internationally set development goals. In this context, educational changes again focused on the inclusion of marginalized groups in education, and depended on policy actors' awareness of the special educational needs of disabled children requiring special-needs education.

Within the discourse, these ideas emerge when policy actors identify the lack of special education provisions as the main barrier for realizing the right to education for disabled children. Talking about the special needs of disabled children eventually proves that actors truly advocate for the inclusion of disabled children in UBE.

Knowledge about the limited capacity to provide special education builds on ideas about educational progress achieved in other world regions. These ideas are based on the "inclusive education ladder," which proposes successive goals in the development of an inclusive education system—first the overcoming of exclusion through "educational expansion by special education," and later inclusive education as joint learning. This knowledge is articulated when comparisons are made between the Nigerian and other school systems. One civil society actor, for example, explains the arduous process of creating demand and supply for special-needs education with the fact of Nigeria's being a "developing country."

It's a developing country, that's all I can say. . . . It's still in the grass-roots. . . . Government is starting to make her attempt, but it's the implementation that is the big thing. (N_1: 375–77)

In classifying Nigeria as a developing country, the interviewee promotes a hierarchy between school systems that have already overcome exclusion and those still struggling to do so. This hierarchy is reified by international education policies, in which EFA is formulated as a developmental objective to accelerate countries' socioeconomic progress, as well as the involvement of a vast number of international development organizations in Nigeria. The hierarchy of school systems perpetuates the idea of succeeding inclusive education goals: first, inclusion in education and, later, inclusive education as joint learning.

Considering disabled children's inability to profit from regular education and the Nigerian school system's incapacity to provide for their special-needs education, the development of an inclusive school system can only become a discursive concern of institutionalizing a special education system.

Wrapping Up: The Nigerian Story about Inclusive Education Change

Having reconstructed the interpretative repertoire that makes up the UBE implementation subdiscourse, I now summarize the empirical results in a story about the development of an inclusive school system in Nigeria (see Keller 2011, 59). As an interim result, this story entails the distinct set of ideas with which Article 24's "program of change" is translated into educational change.

According to this story, the development of an inclusive school system is closely linked to the implementation of UBE to realize the right to basic education for all children, including those with disabilities. For this "special group," policy actors identify the lack of special education provisions as the main problem impeding access to and participation in basic education. Therefore, policy actors agree that in striving for inclusive education change, the goal is educational expansion by special-needs education. The joint instruction of all children in one school and classroom, on the other hand, is relegated to a later stage of educational progression once disabled children are included in the school system. To achieve the goal of educational expansion, policy actors focus on resources to support children with disabilities. These include special teachers and learning materials as well as assistive devices, primarily provided in special schools or classes, but potentially also in regular classrooms if children can succeed there. In addition, DPOs push for the adoption of a Disability Bill with a Commission to provide an organizational platform for self-representation

TABLE 6. The Story of Inclusive Education Change in Nigeria

Ideational dimensions	Content
Cause for change	Implementation of UBE to achieve the development objective of EFA
Aim of change	Development of an inclusive school system
Value of change	Realization of the right to basic education
Problem to be solved	Lack of special educational provisions for disabled children
Goal to be achieved	"Educational expansion by special-needs education"
Solution to be applied	*Resources* Special education provisions, including assistive devices, special teachers, learning materials and schools or classes
	Law Antidiscrimination legislation
Norms to be applied	Educational progress
Role taken	"Facilitators of change"

and dedicated resources. In advocating for these changes, policy actors see themselves as facilitators of change who need to create demand for and supply of special-needs education among policy actors "ignorant" of the right to basic education for children with disabilities. Considering practical and contextual reasons, the development of an inclusive school system depends on the institutionalization of a special education system, the ultimate expression of educational progression toward EFA.

With this story, the Nigerian discourse responds to global as well as institutionalized ideas about the education of disabled children. Global ideas pertain to the reform mandate that requires states to ensure an inclusive school system, which policy actors acknowledge as the aim of an educational change. The reform mandate, however, is not directly linked to Article 24 but to its historical precursors, which framed inclusive education as a key strategy to realize EFA. For practical and contextual reasons, policy actors reject the reform agenda of "all schools for all children" for the time being. The inability of disabled children to profit from regular education, and the current incapacities to provide special-needs education, are seen as requiring, first, to overcome the outright exclusion of disabled children and not joint learning. To advocate for their inclusion, policy actors thus utilize institutionalized ideas about the legal and normative obligation to UBE by making the development of an inclusive school system the tool of its implementation. The Nigerian translation of Article

24 UN CRPD thus reframes the global values package of inclusive education in local terms of pending educational progress. The reform mandate is accepted as a tool to include children with disabilities in formal schooling in order to realize their right to universal basic education. Yet the agenda of inclusive education as joint learning of all in local schools is rejected. Even though the equation of inclusive education with EFA resembles the fundamental human rights idea of removing barriers for all learners, the translation simultaneously promotes inclusion and disability-based segregation.

In sum, the Nigerian case study reveals an indirect translation of the UN CRPD's Article 24; ideas and norms are taken up but not linked to the human rights treaty but to the global framework for EFA. In other words, information pertaining to inclusive education changes is primarily conveyed via the UBE Act and the international EFA agenda. To take a case in point, the 2016 Draft Policy on Inclusive Education enumerates several policies promoting inclusive education—beginning with the Universal Declaration of Human Rights, the Convention on the Rights of the Child, the Salamanca Statement, and Sustainable Development Goal 4—however, without any mention of the UN CRPD (FME 2016, 11). With this translation, the Nigerian discourse updates the perennial struggle to universalize access to mass schooling for all children and youth. Overall, the goal of educational change has thus not changed fundamentally over the decades, nor have the challenges of implementing rules and policies already in place. What has changed is the framework in which this struggle is negotiated. In the 1950s, it were the UPE programs to foster self-determination by educational expansion, and in the 1960–1970s the NPE to foster national unity after independence. Since the 1990s, UBE has been the main vehicle promoting socioeconomic development, with inclusive education as the key strategy to realize EFA, a concern that will be continued in the context of SDG 4.

FOUR

Germany

Inclusive Education as a Source of Conflict
over School Structures to Preserve Special Education

The translation of Article 24 UN CRPD's human rights paradigm into educational change in Germany is confronted with an expansive, but at the same time highly segregated, school system. This system is characterized by the professional and structural divide between regular and special education and dates back to the establishment of special schools. Since the mid-nineteenth century, these schools have paved the way for physically and mentally impaired as well as socially disadvantaged children to enter the formal education system. Even though more disabled children have gained access to regular schools since the 2009 ratification of the UN CRPD, the placement of some two-thirds of children with special needs in special schools continues unabated (KMK 2020). What difference does the human rights paradigm of inclusive education now make in realizing equal access and participation? This is the central question of this case study. To answer it, I first delineate the historical development and current characteristics of Germany's school systems and then reconstruct the federal policy discourse on inclusive education.

Setting the Scene: The Formal School System—Policy Development and Current Realities

From the nineteenth century until today, structural stratification according to ability is the distinctive feature and cornerstone of the German school system. Despite decisive historical junctures—two world wars, the creation of two separate, politically opposed states, and their eventual reunification—this logic not only survived but thrived over the last decades, making Germany one of the few European states with no comprehensive education.

Critical Historical Junctures

The advent of Germany's formal, publicly funded school system dates back to the introduction of compulsory education in the 1760s by the Kingdom of Prussia, far earlier than in England or France (Stübig 2013, 45). Educational developments in the several Germanic states in the years following, though not uniform, displayed crucial similarities, including the strict separation between higher schools, serving a small group of children from the nobility, and lower elementary schools (Wittmütz 2007, 26), as well as the introduction of special schools for impaired children.[1]

Educational developments began to converge across the different Germanic states after the foundation of the unitary German Reich in 1870. In response to the socioeconomic developments in an industrializing world, the Prussian minister of education introduced General Provisions on Elementary Schools and Teacher Training (*Allgemeine Bestimmungen betreffend das Volksschul-, Präparanden- und Seminarwesen*) and a School Supervision Law (*Schulaufsichtsgesetz*) in 1872 (Wittmütz 2007, 29). These regulations solidified the hierarchical organization of formal education. The lower-school system provided basic education for working-class children in public elementary schools (*Elementarschulen*)—to which 100 percent of school-age children had access beginning in the 1880s (Lundgreen 1980, 93 in Stübig 2013, 35). In addition, these schools prepared middle-class children for skilled employment in commerce and for administration in technically oriented middle schools (*Mittelschulen*). Scientifically oriented higher secondary schools (*Gymnasium*) allowed the upper class to gain access to public service and universities (Geißler 2011, chap. 4.2; Konrad 2012, chap. 4). This system was supplemented by an evolving arrangement of support classes and schools for children with learning and behavioral problems.

Beginning in 1859, children who failed in public elementary schools were separated into special education classes and, ultimately, segregated into specialized support schools (*Hilfsschulen*) (Powell [2011] 2016, 151–53; Hänsel 2005, 102). Support schools are a German peculiarity, providing an organizational and pedagogical solution to serve the group of "weakly gifted" children (Pfahl 2011, 85–86; Hänsel 2006, 18). In the nineteenth century, these children were, on the whole, poverty-stricken, neglected, and disadvantaged, that is, hardest hit by the impact of the industrial revolution but not disabled because of an impairment (Pfahl 2011, 90, 116; Moser and Sasse 2008, 33–34).

After World War I and the end of the monarchical German Reich, the newly founded Weimar Republic reformed the school system to reflect its novel democratic orientation. The reform attempts were, however, accompanied by fierce parliamentary disagreements. These were eventually solved with the 1920 Weimar School Compromise (*Weimarer Schulkompromiss*) establishing a four-grade primary school compulsory for *all* children (*Grundschule*). After completion of this joint schooling period, students were sorted into the three prevailing types of basic, middle, and higher secondary schools (Geißler 2011, chap. 5.3.). Parallel to this, support schools developed into an independent type for underachieving poor students, as a particular special education strand of "therapeutic education" (*Heilpädagogik*) was thriving (Powell [2011] 2016, 153; Moser 2012, 264; Pfahl 2011, 90). The expansion of special schools for children hard of hearing or seeing, though, stagnated (Ellger-Rüttgardt 2016, 21). In sum, these special education arrangements "both supported and marginalized particular groups of people with disabilities," as Carol Poore acknowledges in her seminal book *Disability in Twentieth-Century German Culture* (2009, 48).

With the 1933 government takeover by the National Socialists, the school system was centralized to propagate their racist and anti-Semitic ideology through education (Giesecke 1999, 126–127; Bäumer-Schleinkofer 1995). Structurally, the four-grade primary school system and the three-tiered secondary school system remained intact. However, the selection of children for the different school types intensified, as beliefs about natural giftedness intersected with racial ideas about preserving the German nation (Nyssen 1979, 129–30; Ellger-Rüttgardt 1995, 78). For that reason, fewer children gained access to higher secondary schools, while the image of lower secondary schools was strengthened. In fact, combined elementary and lower secondary schools (*Volksschulen*) became compulsory for most children, and support schools—tasked with identifying "uneducable" children—strengthened their achievement orientation (Hänsel 2006, 145–148.; Giesecke 1999, 127; Powell [2011] 2016, 155).[2] The selection of children out of support schools prepared for their forced sterilizations and murder in line with the 1933 Law for the Prevention of Hereditarily Diseased Offspring (*Gesetz zur Verhütung erbkranken Nachwuchses*) (Poore 2009, 75–76; also Ley and Hinz-Wessels 2012). In this way, the status of support schools as an integral part of the special school system was strengthened (Hänsel 2014). After World War II, the restoration of the shattered school system took place in two ideologically opposed postwar German states—the Federal Republic of Germany in the West, and the German Democratic Republic in the East.

In the East, a socialist school system was introduced, reflected in the 1959 Law on the Socialist Development of Education (*Gesetz über die sozialistische Entwicklung des Schulwesens*), in 1965 replaced by the Law on the Unified Socialist Education System (*Gesetz über das einheitliche sozialistische Bildungssystem*). With these laws, the polytechnic school (*Polytechnische Oberschule*) was established, that is, a ten-year comprehensive general school that overcame the distinction between lower, middle, and higher secondary schools (Anweiler 1988, 86, 89). Children who were selected to continue education beyond the tenth grade learned for two more years in an extended secondary school (*Erweiterte Oberschule*), qualifying for access to universities (Anweiler 1988, 64, 101). Children who, however, did not succeed in this compulsory school were segregated into different special schools based on their perceived educability.[3] Special schools (*Sonderschulen*) served children with physical and sensory disabilities, while special education institutions (*Sonderschuleinrichtungen*) were meant for students with learning or mental disabilities. Children labeled uneducable and untrainable were sent to day care centers as well as asylums (*Tagesstätten oder Wochen/Heime for schulbildungsunfähige förderungsfähige Kinder*). (Poore 2009, 257; Sander 1969, 36, 45; Ministerium für Gesundheitswesen and Akademie für Ärztliche Fortbildung 1978, 25, 27) As any private initiative of parents or disability rights groups was suppressed, integrated education could neither be advocated for nor implemented in the German Democratic Republic (Poore 2009, 48).

In West Germany, the postwar restoration of the school system was also characterized by an institutional expansion and diversification of special education. Two documents, issued by the Standing Conference of the Ministers of Education and Cultural Affairs of the Federal States (*Kultusministerkonferenz* [KMK]), were decisive for the reaffirmation of segregation: the 1960 Recommendations on the Structure of the Special Education System (*Gutachten zur Ordnung des Sonderschulwesens*) as well as the 1972 Recommendation for the Organization of the Special School System (*Empfehlung zur Ordnung des Sonderschulwesens*). With these documents, ten different special school types were institutionalized. In this process, the *Hilfsschule* was differentiated into a special school for students with learning disabilities (*Schule für Lernbehinderte/Förderschule*) as well as a separate special school for children with intellectual disabilities (*Schule für geis-*

tig Behinderte) (Powell [2011] 2016, 82, 84; Möckel 2007, 236–37). The regular school system, in a similar way, reverted to prewar models. The education minister's 1964 Hamburg Agreement (*Hamburger Abkommen*) provided for a four-year primary school (*Grundschule*) and distinguished between a five-year lower secondary school (*Hauptschule*), a six-year middle school (*Realschule*), and a nine-year grammar school (*Gymnasium*) (Geißler 2011, 833). Since the late 1970s, these secondary schools have been supplemented by comprehensive secondary schools (*Gesamtschulen*) only in some states, as their introduction was politically highly controversial (Wiborg 2010). These debates also galvanized discussions about the segregation of disabled children (Powell [2011] 2016, 208–9). These debates culminated in the 1973 Recommendations on the Educational Support for Children and Youth with Disabilities (*Empfehlung zur pädagogischen Förderung behinderter und von Behinderung bedrohter Kinder und Jugendlicher*) issued by the German Education Council (*Deutscher Bildungsrat*) (Powell [2011] 2016, 163–64), a commission for the joint planning of education between the federal government and the federal states that existed between 1966 and 1975 (Leschinsky 2005, 818). These recommendations advocated for the integration of disabled children into regular schools (Weigt 1998). Given the fierce political opposition to comprehensive schools, integration could then only be realized in some model projects (Ellger-Rüttgardt 2016, 22; Hildeschmidt and Schnell 1998).

With reunification of Germany in 1990, the West German school system was in large parts taken over by the newly created Eastern federal states, sustaining the independence of a special school system. However, the system was reformed, a process to which two decisive developments contributed. In 1994, Germany's constitution, the Basic Law (*Grundgesetz*), was amended, prohibiting in Article 3 any discrimination based on disability (Heyer 2015, 102–3). The same year, the state education ministers jointly introduced Recommendations on Special Education in Schools (*Empfehlungen zur sonderpädagogischen Förderung in den Schulen der Bundesrepublik Deutschland*) (KMK 1994), which "would bring substantial reform in official education goals and principles" (Powell [2011] 2016, 166). Most importantly, these recommendations introduced a new classification system for special educational needs, which no longer certifies the need for special schooling (*Sonderschulbedürftigkeit*), as the one established in 1972 did. Instead, classifications from now on assert support needs in several areas, which I will detail soon (KMK 1994, 10–13). In addition, the document introduced joint learning as one form of special education delivery, with special schooling being the standard option (KMK 1994, 13–15).

Given the legislative and administrative prerogative of the sixteen federal states in education, special education diagnostic and placement practices vary considerably though (for an overview see Sälzer et al. 2015). In 2009, Germany ratified the UN CRPD (UN 2021). Subsequently, the federal government released a National Action Plan (NAP) for its implementation in 2011 (BMAS 2011a), which was updated in 2016 (BMAS 2016). The NAP states that every child is entitled to individual support and education, and that the choice of either a regular or special school depends on the parent's decision (BMAS 2011a, 14; for an evaluation of the NAP see Prognos 2014). Shortly after ratification of the UN CRPD, the education ministries of the sixteen states issued common resolutions: in 2010, for example, the position paper Pedagogical and Legal Aspects of the Implementation of the UN CRPD in School Education (*Pädagogische und rechtliche Aspekte der Umsetzung des Übereinkommens der Vereinten Nationen vom 13. Dezember 2006 über die Rechte von Menschen mit Behinderungen in der schulischen Bildung*) (KMK 2010) and in 2011 recommendations on the Inclusive Education of Children and Youth with Disabilities in Schools (*Inklusive Bildung von Kindern und Jugendlichen mit Behinderungen in Schulen*) (KMK 2011). These documents provide the national framework under which each federal state independently develops an inclusive school system.[4] Despite the existence of these national frameworks, significant differences therefore exist between the different states regarding the educational provisions for children with disabilities (Blanck, Edelstein, and Powell 2013; Blanck 2015). And even though most of the sixteen states have changed their school laws in recent years, most do not yet comprehensively meet the requirements of the UN CRPD (Mißling and Übert 2014).[5] For that reason, segregation is still prevailing in Germany, which the UN has repeatedly criticized in recent years, for example, in the 2015 concluding observations on the initial UN CRPD state party report (CRPD 2015a), but already in the 2007 report of the UN Special Rapporteur on the Right to Education (UNHRC 2007). Currently, inclusive education change is further promoted in the context of the Sustainable Development Goals (SDGs) (BuReg 2020).

Current Characteristics

Germany has one of the world's most segregated general school systems, comprising ability-stratified regular education as well as special education schools. The regular school system consists of a four- or six-year comprehensive primary school (*Grundschule*), which is followed by secondary

TABLE 7. Historical Development of the Formal School System in Germany

Year	Developments at the National Level	
Pre-1910s: Foundation of a formal, public system of compulsory schooling		
1763	Introduction of compulsory education in Prussia	
1850s-1890s	Foundation of asylums and special schools for children with impairments	
1871–1918	*German Empire*	
1872	Formation of a class-based school system	
Beginning 1860s	Foundation of support schools for the group of the so-called 'weakly gifted'	
1910s-1980s: Manifestation of a segregated school system		
1920	Weimar School Compromise establishing a four-grade primary school	
1933–1945	*National Socialism*	
1930s–1940s	Increased educational selection strengthening the role of support schools	
	Division of Germany into the	
	Federal Republic of Germany (West)	*German Democratic Republic (East)*
End 1940s to 1980s	Introduction of a three-tiered regular school system supplemented by a diversified special school system	Introduction of a comprehensive regular school system supplemented by a system of special schools
1990s–today: Reform of the segregated school system		
1990	*Reunification of Germany*	
	West German school system adopted in eastern federal states, sustaining the independence of a special school system	
1994	KMK Recommendations on Special Education in Schools and amendment of the Basic Law prohibiting discrimination on the base of disability	
2009	Ratification of the UN CRPD	
2010	KMK position paper on Pedagogical and Legal Aspects of the Implementation of the UN CRPD	
2011	KMK recommendations on Inclusive Education of Children and Youth with Disabilities in Schools and National Action Plan for the Implementation of the UN CRPD	
2013	First UN CRPD state party report	
2015	Concluding Observations of the Committee on the Rights of Persons with Disabilities on Germany's first state party report	

schools differentiated into achievement-based school forms: the lowest tier is made of lower secondary schools (*Hauptschulen*), followed by mid-level secondary schools (*Realschulen*), while higher secondary schools (*Gymnasium*) are at the top. Some states also provide comprehensive secondary schools (*Gesamtschulen*). Children who do not meet the achievement expectations linked to these distinct school forms are sorted into various special

TABLE 8. The General Education System in Germany

General school system			
Special education system	Regular education system		

Primary education level

Special schools (*Sonder– oder Förderschulen*)	Primary education school (*Grundschule*)		

Secondary education level

Special schools (*Sonder– oder Förderschulen*)	Lower secondary school (*Hauptschule*)	Mid-level secondary school (*Realschule*)	Comprehensive secondary school (*Gesamtschule*)	Higher secondary school (*Gymnasium*)

Source: Based on KMK 2017, 2.

schools according to their educational needs based on state-specific regulations (Blanck 2014). Special schools (*Sonderschulen/Förderschulen*) are part of an independent special education system, which is not only segregated from the regular school system but explicitly defines itself in contrast to it (Hänsel 2003, 593; 2006, 20). In an English publication, the Conference of Education Ministers defines a *Förderschule* as a "special school—school establishment for pupils whose development cannot be adequately assisted at mainstream schools on account of disability. Also known as *Förderzentrum*" (KMK 2019, 376; also KMK 2017, 5). For that reason, I also use the term "special school" to refer to the various special education institutions when they segregate students based on disability.

A finely calibrated system of classifications—which interconnects impairment, disadvantage, and difficulty—allows the selection of students for special schools (Powell and Pfahl 2012, 727–28; also Pfahl and Powell 2011; Kottmann 2006). Based on the premise that better educational results are achieved in homogenous learning groups, this selection aims to increase homogeneity within the different regular schools and classrooms (Powell and Pfahl 2012, 736; Blanck, Edelstein, and Powell 2014, 98–99). To guarantee that students achieve similar results, they are measured against school-form specific average abilities, attainment, and behavior (Powell and Pfahl 2012, 727). When a child cannot meet these expectations, a special education need is officially diagnosed in one of following support areas (*sonderpädagogische Förderschwerpunkte*): learning (*Lernen*), seeing (*Sehen*), hearing (*Hören*), speaking (*Sprache*), body and motor development (*körperliche und motorische Entwicklung*), intellectual development (*geistige Entwicklung*), emotional and social development (*emotionale und soziale Entwicklung*), long-term illness (*Krankheit*), and multiple / not classified (*mehrfach / nicht klassifiziert*) (KMK 1994, 10–13). It is worth noting that the German notion of "learning disability" refers to a negative deviation from achievement and behavior of average students, not intellectual-cognitive challenges (Pfahl and Powell 2011, 87; Opp 1992). Therefore, primarily socioeconomically disadvantaged students are served by this category and not those who are low achieving (Pfahl 2010; Schnell 2016). In this way, social inequalities are often reproduced in special schools, and social problems are reinterpreted within individual special-needs categories (Schnell 2016, 886; also Bruce and Venkatesh 2014; Minello and Blossfeld 2016).

In 2018, half a million students received special education support, that are about 7 percent of all pupils (KMK 2020, XVI).[6] One-third had a support need because of a "learning disability" and 17 percent in the areas of "intellectual development" and "emotional and social development" respectively (KMK 2020, XV; see also KMK 2018, XV; 2016, XV).[7] The smallest special-needs group consists of children with physical impairments such as hearing (about 4 percent) and seeing (less than 2 percent) (KMK 2020, XV; see also KMK 2018, XV; 2016, XV). Three groups are overrepresented among all children with special needs: boys, children from poorer socioeconomic backgrounds, and children with a non-German nationality (KMK 2020, XXIV; see also KMK 2018, XXII; 2016, XXII; Autorengruppe Bildungsberichterstattung 2014, 179).

Nationwide, about 60 percent of all children with a special education need learn in special schools (KMK 2020, XVII–XVIII; see also KMK 2018, XVI–XVII; 2016, XVI–XVII). By far the largest groups are learning-disabled children and students with support needs in "intellectual development" (about one-fourth), followed by students facing challenges in their "emotional and social development" (one-tenth) (KMK 2020, XVII; see also KMK 2018, XVI; 2016, XVI). The lowest share is accounted for by students with hearing impairments (3.2 percent) and visual impairments (1.4 percent) (KMK 2020, XVIII; see also KMK 2018, XV; 2016, XVII).[8]

In recent years, the number of children with special needs learning in regular schools has increased by 20 percent, rising from roughly 95,000 in 2009 to 235,000 in 2018; they are currently about 40 percent of all children receiving special education support (KMK 2020, XX). Most children with special needs who are integrated in regular schools learn in primary schools (about 40 percent), integrated comprehensive schools (about 25 percent), or lower secondary schools (about 10 percent) (KMK 2020, XIX; see also KMK 2018, XVIII; 2016, XVII). Most often, children with support needs in emotional and social development or language learn in regular schools, least often, children with a support need in mental development (KMK 2020, XXI; see also KMK 2018, XX; 2016, XIX). Here they achieve significantly better results than comparable pupils in special schools (Müller et al. 2017; Kocaj et al. 2014, 2015). Fifteen-year-old students in special schools lag in skills development by up to 2.5 school years in comparison to their peers in lower secondary schools (Autorengruppe Bildungsberichterstattung 2014, 180). Hence, three-fourths of pupils in special schools graduate without a basic school-leaving certificate (*Hauptschulabschluss*) (Autorengruppe Bildungsberichterstattung 2014, 181; also Gebhardt et al. 2015).

The increasing participation of children with special needs in regular schools is, however, not due to a reduction in special schooling but a growing number of children with special needs. Over the last decade, the portion of pupils in special schools only slightly decreased, from 4.8 percent in 2009 to 4.2 percent in 2018, while the total number of students identified as having a special educational need climbed from about 480,000 to 556,000 during the same time period (KMK 2020, XVII, 3). This pattern evidences the expansion of special-needs classifications and the stability of special schools as a viable and steadfast pillar of the segregated German school system. In addition, it points to the delicate relation between labeling and funding: special-needs categories secure resources that are only provided in an independent special school system (Füssel and Kretschmann 1993). These current characteristics of schooling in Germany underline the institutional reality of ability-based segregation challenged by the human rights paradigm of inclusive education.

Getting Started: Reconstructing the German Discourse on Inclusive Education

Against the background of educational segregation, how is Article 24 UN CRPD's "program of change" now translated into educational change in Germany? How does its reform mandate—to ensure an inclusive school system—and its agenda—to make all schools accessible and available for all—connect with contextual ideas about education already in place? And with what effect on the rules, norms, and beliefs that facilitate the institution of schooling? To answer these questions, I now turn to my empirical work: the reconstruction of the German discourse on inclusive education that took place on the federal level between 2009 and 2015. This period covers the UN CRPD ratification and first cycle of state party reporting. The analysis therefore represents a snapshot of ongoing policy debates. These were crucial to analyze, as they, in generating a logic of change, frame and thus set the national stage for the development of inclusive school systems. Portraying a moving target, though, these initial deliberations can neither depict actual implementation processes nor account for specific material changes in each school system. Despite the prerogative of the sixteen states on schooling, the focus is on the federal level, as policy actors here coordinate positions on inclusive education. In addition, federal policy actors are responsible for converting the international human rights treaty into domestic federal law, developing a national policy framework and, eventually, presenting and defending progress in front of the UN Committee on the Rights of Persons with Disabilities. In terms of translation, the key question is therefore how Article 24's "program of change" is negotiated in light of the differences between the states.

The German case study offers an individual case of Article 24's translations. To reconstruct this translation, I follow a sociology-of-knowledge approach to discourse (Keller 2011) and analyze the knowledge policy actors (re)produce about inclusive education when they "engage one another in a 'coordinative' discourse about policy construction" (Schmidt 2008, 310). This analysis is based on data I collected in the capital, Berlin, in 2014 and 2015. I contacted federal policy actors, including representatives from federal ministries, non-governmental organizations (NGOs) and disabled persons organizations (DPOs). In line with Article 33 UN CRPD, they are involved in the convention's implementation, the state actors given their legislative and administrative capacity, and the civil society actors as target groups. These policy actors are integral for the translation of global human rights ideas, because they are "involved in the creation, elaboration, and justification of policy and programmatic ideas" (Schmidt 2008, 31). In this process, they "convey ideas from one context to another, adapting and reframing them from the way they attach to a source context to one that resonates with the new location" (Levitt and Merry 2009, 448).

Nationally, the key responsibility for complying with the UN CRPD lies with the federal government (*Bundesregierung*) and its Federal Ministry of Labor and Social Affairs (*Bundesministerium für Arbeit und Soziales*). The latter serves as the national focal point, the governing body that controls and regulates the implementation process on the basis of a National Action

Plan (BMAS 2011a). In addition, the federal government has appointed a Federal Commissioner for Matters relating to Persons with Disabilities (*Beauftragte der Bundesregierung für die Belange von Menschen mit Behinderungen*) (2021), who serves as the coordinator linking civil society and state actors. The Federal German Parliament (*Bundestag*) and the Federal Council (*Bundesrat*) have delegated the role of independent monitoring mechanism to the German Institute for Human Rights (*Deutsches Institut für Menschenrechte*) (DIMR 2021). The implementation process is also monitored by different civil society actors, most importantly the German UN CRPD Alliance (*BRK-Allianz*). This network of more than seventy NGOs has joined forces to coordinate a shadow report supplementing the first state party report (BRK-Allianz 2013). As the prerogative power for school legislation and administration rests with the sixteen states the Conference of Education Ministers (*Kultusministerkonferenz*) is also involved in inclusive education policymaking (KMK 2010, 2011). Furthermore, professional associations developed positions on the obligations deriving from the UN CRPD, for example, the German Philologists' Association (*Deutscher Philologenverband*) (DPhV 2010, 2011). An overview of all corpus data is provided in the appendix.[9]

By making this selection, I do not assume that the selected policy actors can influence policymaking or debates to the same extent; indeed, state actors are more powerful than civil society actors. However, it is important to juxtapose their views because in confronting the problem of inclusive education, this wide range of policy actors negotiates Article 24's human rights paradigm in a coordinative policy discourse; they therefore form an organizational field that constitutes the discursive space of translations (Benzecry and Krause 2010, 419; Scott 1994, 71).

The data I gathered consist of policy documents produced by various actors, paired with expert interviews. Both data sources are characterized by a dynamic connection between words, meanings, and policy actions (Prior 2008, 479). While documents foreground codified knowledge, interviews allow us to gain a deeper insight into the negotiation of change by accessing tacit knowledge. Documents are written texts produced by organizations (Salheiser 2014, 813). For this study, I was particularly interested in official and publicly available publications, such as positions papers, action plans, mission statements, and leaflets. In containing organizational positions, these documents are artifacts of communicative practices carrying policy actors' approaches to inclusive education. Interviews, on the other hand, are, as transcribed, written texts that result from a communicative interaction and are produced by the researcher (Helfferich 2014, 559). I conducted interviews with representatives of organizations that are involved in policy debates. In total, I analyzed fifty-three documents and seven interviews in-depth, an overview of which is available in the appendix. These data allow me to reveal how policy actors coordinate positions on inclusive education at the federal level and thus reflect the complex realities of realizing Article 24—with the federal government responsible for the implementation of human rights treaties, but the federal states responsible for school systems. In topically dealing with inclusive education, Article 24, and disability-based exclusions in education, these data are discourse fragments that I analyzed through grounded-theory-based and content-driven qualitative analysis (Charmaz 2014; Keller 2011). In this process, I abstracted from the original data to reveal the overarching knowledge formation driving the German discourse on inclusive education. In presenting the results, I will, however, quote from some original data to illustrate the points made.

Negotiating Inclusive Education Change:
The German UN CRPD Implementation Discourse

In Germany, the topic of inclusive education emerges within a discourse about the UN CRPD implementation. Most documents analyzed were composed in reaction to Germany's ratification of the treaty, the subsequent development of a national action plan, and the first state party report, the three events also referred to in most interviews. In other words, there would not have been a federal policy debate on inclusive education if it were not for the ratification of the UN CRPD conveying legal and normative pressures to ensure inclusive schooling.

The ratification sparked a huge controversy, as the act transferring the convention into federal law entailed a translated convention text in which the German word for inclusion (*Inklusion*) was replaced by "integration" (*Integration*). Accordingly, Article 24's reform mandate was not to ensure an inclusive education system but an integrative one (Bundestag and Bundesrat 2008, Art. 24, para. 1). The substitution of terms was already criticized by the UN Special Rapporteur on the Right to Education, Vernor Muñoz, in his report on the 2007 mission in Germany. Here, he qualified the German notion of integration as "problematic" as it requires individuals to "adapt to a predetermined model" of schooling (UNHRC 2007, para. 76). Inclusion, in contrast, would necessitate responding "to the needs and rights of individuals and renders it incumbent on the State to ensure that all children receive education together in the same school environment" (para. 77). By carrying this confusion forward, the German translation of the convention's text fueled fierce debates about the distinctive implications of the two terms. During an interview, one state actor recollected that "this mistranslation . . . was more or less an own goal," as it has attracted "enormous attention" to the fact that integration and inclusion are "not one and the same" (G_2: 113–17).[10] Fearing that the political translation would weaken the human rights reform mandate entailed in Article 24, DPOs jointly produced a "shadow translation" (*Schattenübersetzung*) in which several linguistic mistakes were amended, including the one on education (Netzwerk Artikel 3 2010). In this way, civil society actors were able to revive the 1970s and 1980s efforts to integrate disabled children in mainstream schools, which were politically controversial at the time and could thus not be implemented on a nationwide scale. In this way, the apparent mistake in the verbatim translation, and even more so the efforts to correct it, ushered in the heated implementation discourse.

To reconstruct this discourse, I am going to combine the typified assumptions of federal policy actors about inclusive education into a specific form—a "process of change"—and identify its goal, scope, and dimensions (see Keller 2011, 58). The process of change, in sum, displays the typified assumptions of federal policy actors about the development of an inclusive school system for children with disabilities in Nigeria.

Goal of Change

All policy actors share the understanding that the development of an inclusive school system necessitates allowing more disabled students to learn with their nondisabled peers in regular schools. Whether this necessity applies to all disabled students or only some is, however, disputed, as will be detailed shortly. In its 2011 position paper, the Conference of Education Ministers, for example, states that "the basis of inclusive education is the joint learning and education of children and adolescents with and without disabilities" (KMK 2011, 7).[11] Striving for the same goal, one parent initiative, however, points out that the "growing up and learning together of young people with and without disabilities is still the exception" (Gemeinsam Leben Gemeinsam Lernen 2015, 3).[12] In making these statements, actors share the understanding that the transformation Article 24 aims for is that more disabled students can learn outside special schools.

In addition to this understanding, some policy actors introduce a broader context of inclusive education. One nonstate actor, for example, points out that the organization the individual is working for has "a much broader understanding" of inclusive education: "It's about human diversity and inclusion in the one society," and therefore "schools must be for everyone" (G_1: 465–68).[13] In other words, the interviewee regards disability as one dimension of human diversity to be catered for in schools. In contrast, a state actor rejects a broader approach as impracticable, explaining, "We want to concentrate on inclusion . . . as the learning of disabled and nondisabled people, because everything beyond that, that may all make sense and be right, but if we don't focus on that, then we get bogged down" (G_6: 159–62).[14] From this actor's point of view, the focus on other social factors than disability that contribute to discrimination, such as sexual orientation, would diminish the effectiveness of any reform process directed toward inclusive education.

In sum, these examples prove that all policy actors strive to make more regular schools accessible for children with disabilities. Based on this common denominator, the goal aimed for with the development of an inclusive school system is to increase the joint learning of students with and without disabilities.

Scope of Change

Policy actors, nonetheless, disagree on the scope of change necessary to realize the joint learning. Two groups argumentatively oppose each other. One such group consists of NGOs, especially DPOs. They advocate for a major transformation of organizational structures; their viewpoints are summarized in a transformative line of argumentation. The other group consists of political decision-makers and includes the federal government and state education ministers as well as teachers unions. They, in contrast, advocate for gradual changes summarized in a conservative line of argumentation.

Within the transformative line of argumentation, policy actors highlight the ratification of Article 24 as a historical turning point for school structure reform, remembered by one DPO-representative as follows:

> So especially with regard to education, I have the feeling that a plug has been pulled in our country. . . . And with the convention, this international debate, linked to this bad translation—"inclusion" and "integration"—factually spilled over into Germany. (G_3: 405–11)[15]

The interviewee celebrates the treaty's ratification as a vehicle for inclusive education to finally become relevant as a human rights norm on the national level. For this group of policy actors, Article 24 therefore provides the argumentative bedrock to identify interschool segregation as the main barrier to inclusion. Their argumentative focus is hence on the right to inclusive education concluded to require that all children with disabilities have unconditional access to regular schools.

Within the conservative line of argumentation, policy actors in contrast emphasize the peculiarities of Germany's school system with its elaborated special schools to fend off major reforms. The German Philologists' Association, an association of teachers at grammar and higher secondary schools, for example, welcomes the UN convention in a 2010 position paper and argues:

> The German school system already meets it to a high degree through its comprehensive offer with very differentiated, special support in special-needs schools for people with disabilities. (DPhV 2010, 3)[16]

In making this statement, the association highlights the essential function of special schools, which is to include disabled children in the general school system in the first place. In this way, the premise of functional selectivity the German school system is built upon is sustained. This fact lets the organization conclude that the requirements of Article 24 are already met in large part, so that the UN CRPD only stipulates minor reforms. One document sustains this line of reasoning, the federal government's 2008 memorandum on the UN CRPD (BuReg 2008). In parts it uses wording identical to the recommendations on special education issued by the Conference of Education Ministers in 1994, which provide for the possibility that disabled children will learn in regular schools *if* the necessary special education support is provided there (KMK 1994).

(KMK 1994, 4, 18)	(BuReg 2008, 58)[17]
Special education is intended to realize the right of children and adolescents with disabilities and those at risk of becoming disabled to a school education and upbringing in accordance with their personal possibilities.	Special education in integrative education is intended to realize the right of children and adolescents with disabilities and those at risk of becoming disabled to a school education and upbringing in accordance with their personal possibilities.
Special education takes place in a variety of fields and forms of action.	Special education as an indispensable part of integrative education takes place in diverse fields of activity and forms of action.

These two almost identical passages qualify a special education system with various placement options as necessary to realize the right to education for disabled children and youth. Regarding the implementation of Article 24, the focus in this line of argumentation is therefore on the overall right of persons with disabilities to education, which according to the actors, first and foremost demands not excluding these children from formal schooling.

These two opposing lines of argumentation characterize the federal discourse on inclusive education; they do not, however, constitute distinct discourse strands or subdiscourses. This is because both argumentations gear toward the same goal, "joint learning in regular schools," but disagree on the scope of change: transformists argue for the abolishment of special schooling to integrate all children in regular schools, while conservatists defend special education segregation. The common theme of the discourse is therefore the lack of consensus about legitimate places to offer special education for children with disabilities in the future—whether exclusively in regular schools or not.

Dimensions of Change

Given these opposing lines of argumentation, actors negotiate educational reforms in three dimensions: structural changes pertaining to the segregated organization of schooling, legal changes essential for complying with Article 24, and, eventually, professional changes necessary to enable teachers to realize joint education.

Structural Changes

The problem of school structure reform is paramount within the discourse and pertains to the segregation between regular and special schools. Within the conservative line of argumentation, interschool segregation is defended. This is because state actors and professional associations consider the school system to be inclusive *when* children with disabilities participate in compulsory education, that is, when outright exclusion is overcome. Special schools then make it possible to meet the special needs of children with disabilities. In its first state party report, the federal government accordingly asserts that "the special-needs school has a special function" in the German school system, as it is "specialized in specific special educational, counseling, and support services" (BMAS 2011b, 54).[18] Basically, the federal government is reaffirming that special schools segregating children on the basis of disability are a constitutive sine qua non element of the general school system. This line of reasoning eventually implies that special schools must be maintained; conservatists consider them to be in the disabled children's best interest, as an adequate education could otherwise not be guaranteed. To take a case in point, the teacher association DPhV argues in its 2011 position paper on inclusive education:

> Our society [must] offer different types of schools, education courses and school-leaving qualifications . . . in order to respond in a differentiated way to the broad spectrum of individual talents and the different demands of society, and not to decouple school and labor market. (DPhV 2011, 2)[19]

In other words, the association deems the provision of ability-specific segregated school types as necessary to reflect the diversity among children. In a similar way, a state actor defends special schools by affirming that they have "enriched" the "already very structured and divided" German school system (G_5: 122–23).[20] From this perspective, interschool segregation cannot be outrightly rejected, even when attempting to incrementally increase the number of disabled children in regular schools. On the contrary, the reasoning goes, special schools must be defended as the education system's historical beacon that allowed disabled children to be integrated into mass schooling in the first place. Hence, conservatists see the criticism of special schools as the actual problem for the implementation of Article 24.

In contrast, interschool segregation is criticized within the transformative line of argumentation. Here, special schools embody the exact opposite of an inclusive school system, as they create segregated learning spaces. Their maintenance is therefore seen as hampering any meaningful change that would make regular schools more accessible for disabled pupils. In a joint statement, DPOs thus criticize the 2010 Conference of Education Ministers' draft recommendations on inclusive education; there, education ministers would "declare special schools to be a constitutive part of inclusive education . . . and thus give the impression that the German special school system already meets the objectives of the CRPD" (DPOs 2011a, 2). For DPOs, "the opposite is true": the convention "requires profound changes in the German education system for the benefit of disabled children, which must go far beyond the previous integration" (DPOs 2011a, 2).[21] In other words, DPOs argue that the implementation of Article 24 requires a dismantling of the dual structures of special and regular schooling. Similarly, the German Human Rights Institute declares in its 2015 parallel report to Germany's first state report that the "adherence to a dual structure hinders the transformation process needed in the state party, which could shift existing special education resources and competencies to mainstream schools" (DIMR 2015, 27).[22] The maintenance of both—special schools alongside regular schools—is thus seen as tying up special education resources and specially trained teachers otherwise needed in regular schools. This vision of structural change is sustained by the argument that it is no longer the child who must adapt to regular schools, but regular schools who must accommodate disabled children, a vision that fundamentally contradicts the ability-selective school types and forms characteristic of Germany's school system. Along the same lines, the German Trade Union Confederation asserts in a 2015 position paper outlining criteria for inclusive schooling:

> A good inclusive school is the opposite of the traditional German selective school system. It does not separate, relegate, or segregate. If the German school system remains structurally stratified, there will be limits to the process of inclusion, one more reason to give the school structure debate a new dynamic through the inclusion mandate. (DGB 2015, 7)[23]

From this perspective, interschool segregation emerges as the main barrier to complying with the human right of inclusive education. Hence, policy actors advocate for fundamental structural reforms to establish a school system that recreates the diversity of students not within structures but regular schools and classrooms.

To summarize, the scope of structural changes is contested among policy actors: transformatists insist that special schools are the epitome of segregation and thus the main barrier to inclusion. At the same time, conservatists regard special schools as the epitome of inclusion and thus cherish them as the main vector by which to realize the disabled child's right to education. These opposing positions are carried forward by both argumentative coalitions with regard to legal changes.

Legal Changes

The legal action dominating the discourse is the right of parental choice (*Elternwahlrecht*). It is advanced by policy actors defending special schools to prevent the forced inclusion of all disabled children in regular schools but rejected by those advocating for their dissolution as sustaining the forced exclusion of children with disabilities from regular schools. These diverging positions are based on actors' opposing evaluations of legal obligations deriving from Article 24. Defenders of special schools conclude that the right to inclusive education requires that the state not exclude children from the general school system on the basis of disability. The federal government, in a text accompanying the 2014 National Education Report, accordingly emphasizes that "the guiding principle of Article 24 UN CRPD is equal access to education for people with and without disabilities" (BuReg 2014a, IV).[24] Based on this understanding, policy actors sustain the conservative attitude toward segregation in two ways. First, they declare that all disabled children and youth have their right to education already realized and, furthermore, the option to access all regular schools *if* they meet the type-specific ability expectations. Second, they highlight the fact that most state school laws already stipulate the option of joint education in regular schools. This reasoning, in turn, implies that the maintenance of special schools remains a political necessity. The Philologists' Association, therefore, deplores the tendency of "many advocates of inclusion" wishing to "de facto abolish parental choice," as "parents usually know in which type of school their child can be best supported" (DPhV 2010, 2).[25] In making this argument, the organization hints at the constitutional right of parents to care for their children—a duty incumbent upon them as guaranteed in Article 6 of the Basic Law. It too implies that special education resources could only be transferred from special into regular schools to the extent that parents opt for their children learning there. To put it another way, conservatists reject the devaluation of special schools as they, first and foremost, would secure the constitutional rights of parents to have their children taken care of as they wish. This is the argumentative backdrop that eventually allows the German state party to contend in a comment on the first draft of the General Comment on Article 24: "There can only be talk of 'segregation' in the context of 'educating students in separate environments,' if this is being done against the will of the parents; the definition of 'segregation' should be complemented by this addition" (Germany 2015, 2; original in English). Within the conservative argumentation, the right of parental choice thus provides the solution to comply with Article 24 without eliminating the segregated special school structures.

By contrast, actors following the transformative line of thought criticize the right of parental choice. They conclude that Article 24 obliges states not to exclude disabled children from regular schools. The CRPD Alliance—a collaboration of NGOs and DPOs founded in 2011 to monitor the UN CRPD implementation—therefore complains in its first civil society report that "students with disabilities are not legally guaranteed access to mainstream schools" (BRK-Allianz 2013, 54; original in English). Based on this understanding, policy actors sustain the transformative attitude toward segregation in two ways. They first deduce that Article 24 entails a "right to regular schools" (DPOs 2011b, 3) and, second, they argue that state school laws do not comply with human rights obligations as long as they don't grant this right. This reasoning implies that transformatists suspect that the right of parental choice is politically misused to downplay the need for structural reforms. One nonstate actor, for example, observed that "parents would actually choose joint education" if there were "a choice between . . . things that are equally good, equally equipped" (G_1: 263–67).[26] In making this argument, the interviewee points out that a genuine right to choose would require two equally resourced and staffed systems that offer disabled students equivalent support in special and regular schools. Ultimately, the interviewee regards the right of parental choice as a double-edged privilege, as parents would only opt for special schools because of the disadvantages their disabled children experience in underresourced regular schools. In other words, transformatists criticize the parental right to choose for allowing the state to retain the parallel structures of regular and special education. This reasoning becomes particularly clear in the 2013 shadow state party report by the CRPD Alliance, in which civil society actors object that "some Länder consider the parental right to choose to represent a de facto implementation of the CRPD" (BRK-Allianz 2013, 55; original in English). In addition, they "deplore the fact that politicians misuse the parental right to choose in order to question the fundamental right to an inclusive education in a mainstream school that is close to the student's place of residence" (BRK-Allianz 2013, 55; original in English). Within the transformative argumentation, the right of parental choice thus provides a major legal barrier to realizing the right to inclusive education.

Professional Changes

Notwithstanding the argumentative dissension on structural and legal reforms, both lines of argumentation present a more united front concerning necessary professional changes required to realize joint learning. They advocate for a transfer of special education resources and expertise into regular schools. Why? Because otherwise they deem it impossible to respond to the special needs of disabled students in regular schools and classrooms.

In a 2010 paper, the Conference of Education Ministers, a fierce defender of special schools, argues that "the provision of special needs education in an increasingly inclusive mainstream school is a complex and ongoing task" requiring to increase the "competencies of the regular school in dealing with the heterogeneity of students" (KMK 2010, 8).[27] Along a similar line, the German Human Rights Institute, a fierce critic of special schools, declares in its 2015 shadow report to the UN Committee on the Rights of Persons with Disabilities that "one can only speak of a change of course toward an 'inclusive system' when special-needs education is systematically and structurally anchored in the regular school" (DIMR 2015, 27).[28] Even though disagreeing on structural changes, both groups corroborate the idea that regular schools become inclusive when they offer special education.

To realize the transfer of special education, policy actors consistently advocate for the establishment of "multiprofessional teams" allowing for the cooperation of special educators with regular teachers as well as therapeutic and medical staff in regular schools.[29] These teams are going to "fulfil the complex professional duties when dealing with diversity," as the Conference of Education Ministers outlines in a joint resolution with the German Rectors' Conference (*Hochschulrektorenkonferenz*) (KMK and HRK 2015, 3; original in English). Envisioning the future of teacher training, both actors outline "essential elements of a career in teaching," which include a teacher's "professional attitude to the limits of their own competence, the knowledge of the potential offered by other professions and the readiness to work with colleagues" (KMK and HRK 2015, 3; original in English). In making these recommendations, distinctive competences of teachers are defined, thus upholding the professional boundaries between regular and special education. But also the CRPD Alliance criticizes the lack of a "nation-wide personnel scheme that defines the joint responsibilities of different professions with regard to inclusion," as well as the fact that "special needs teachers and social education workers are by no means part of the staff at all mainstream schools" (BRK-Allianz 2013, 58; original in English). With this reasoning, policy actors ultimately strengthen the role of special education expertise.

While regular teachers were not required hither to be trained in special education, they will increasingly need to acquire such expertise. Special teachers, however, remain the guarantors of effective special education. The Conferences of Education Ministers and Rectors thus demand from a conservative standpoint that "all teachers should be educated and continuously trained in a way that will allow them to acquire fundamental transferable competences in general teaching and in special needs education" (KMK and HRK 2015, 3; original in English). From a transformative standpoint, the German Trade Union Confederation similarly envisions that "modules on special education, heterogeneity, and inclusion, as well as on cooperation with the different professions," be "mandatory in all teacher training courses" (2015, 7).[30] Policy actors hence concur on the retention of special education professionalism as advantageous and thus inevitable for the quality education of disabled children in regular schools. What will become of the special schools then? Across both lines of argumentation, policy actors envision their transformation into centers of competence (*Kompetenzzentren*), partially, to aid regular schools in accommodating children with special educational needs as the education ministers maintain (KMK 2010, 6), or fully, to become schools without pupils, as DPOs argue (DPOs 2010, 10). In this way, special schools lose some of their legitimacy as the *only* learning space for children with special needs. However, the provision of special education outside of special schools gains legitimacy as the ultimate means to integrate disabled children into regular schools.

The envisaged development of an inclusive school system, for that reason, effectively contributes to the amalgamation of the two professional practices of regular and special education under the roof of regular schools. In other words, the special education system is extended into regular schools, and parallel to special schools, as their future role is not yet determined. The availability of special education in regular schools is therefore the factor determining whether disabled and disadvantaged pupils can access them. In mimicking the provision of special education in regular schools, inclusive education gains legitimacy so that a professionalized special education, however organized and structured, becomes the pivotal institutional resource with which to realize joint learning.

To summarize, the process of change negotiated in the UN CRPD implementation discourse centers on a conflict on special schools, impacting how policy actors envision changes to realize joint learning: considering most of Article 24's obligations already met in the current system, conservatists advocate for a parallel system of special and regular schools based on the right of parents to choose where their disabled children learn. Transformatists, on the other hand, advocate for the closure of special school to realize the right of disabled children in regular schools. Whereas the continued existence of special schools is disputed between discourse coalitions, special education as a professional practice is not. In both lines of argumentation, policy actors agree on the need to transfer special education resources and expertise into regular schools to expand joint learning. The argumentative conflict therefore does not center on the nature of the problem—policy actors acknowledge that the organization of special education is the main problem to be addressed with inclusive education change. Instead, the conflict centers on solutions, which elevate the discourse on inclusive education to a conflict about school structures.

Therefore, the discursively (re)produced knowledge primarily calls for new legislation to effectuate modifications of the segregated special education structures. These changes, however, do not threaten but, eventually, reinforce selection according to ability, and this no longer only between special and regular schools, but increasingly also in regular schools. Special schools, even though losing some leverage, therefore remain functional; even more, they are extended into regular schools. In this way, the institutional path of interschool segregation is complemented by intraschool segregation.

Speaker and Subject Positions

In envisioning the development of an inclusive school system, policy actors speak from the position of critics or defenders of special schools. Their opposing positions fuel mutual accusations regarding each other's supposedly incorrect understanding of the UN CRPD's Article 24.

The dissension between these discourse coalitions was born the moment the treaty was ratified, as the German translation of the convention text replaced the word "inclusion" with "integration." With this verbatim translation, the special school defenders were able to contend that the German special education system is a facilitator of the disabled child's right to education (and thus already meets the UN CRPD obligations). In qualifying special schooling as a barrier to inclusion, critics were in turn able to contest any such assumptions (which is why they call for transformative structural changes). These divergent assessments allowed federal policy actors to perceive themselves as parties to a conflict about school structures. In other words, their opposing positions on special schools made policy actors perceptible to each other as speakers in the UN CRPD implementation discourse. In this way, the ratification of the UN CRPD provided the stage on which argumentative routines, coined in debates, for example, about the introduction of comprehensive schools in the 1970s or integration in the 1980s, could be reworked and extended.

Critics see themselves as human rights advocates, who in arguing against special schools demonstrate an appropriate understanding of Article 24's reform challenge. Conversely, they consider defenders of special schools to be human rights deniers whose positions obstruct any meaningful change toward inclusive education. One nonstate actor, for example, explains that, in debates with state actors, "this human rights foundation is simply something completely new" (G_3: 60–62).[31] When critics suggest that defenders ignore the human rights component of inclusive education, they do not blame them for negating the UN CRPD as a legal document. However, they blame them for negating the human rights promise implied in Article 24, that is, to improve the educational situation of children with disabilities. In other words, critics do not question the serious will of defenders to implement the UN CRPD, but their willingness to include children with disabilities in regular schools. According to critics, the very act of believing in the legitimacy of special schools compromises the defenders' credibility.

Conversely, defenders of segregated school structures see themselves as realists, and therefore as the only ones advocating for practically feasible changes. One state actor, accordingly, reports having observed "very ideological discussions about this topic, where one does not try to think from the child's point of view"; instead, the opposing side would have "a goal in mind," arguing "that this is now a human right and that must now simply be implemented" (G_6: 178–85).[32] While defenders of special schools see the human rights-oriented view of critics as driven by ideology, they do not blame them for pursuing the development of an inclusive school system. Instead, they deplore the tendency to conclude that an abolition of special schools would improve the educational situation of children with disabilities. In other words, defenders do not challenge critics' commitment to inclusive education, but they suspect them of pursuing the ideologically driven goal of "one school for all," a goal that is linked to contentious political attempts to introduce comprehensive schools in the 1980s. Questioning the legitimacy of special schools thus fuels suspicions of ideology, which requires defenders to intervene as realists.

What qualifies critics of segregated structures to position themselves as human rights advocates is the reason for defenders to view them as ideologists: namely the demand for transformative change toward inclusive education by overcoming segregation in special schools. Consequently, the reason that defenders position themselves as realists is the very same reason that critics consider them to be human rights deniers: the demand for incremental change toward inclusive education that does not give up special schools as segregated learning spaces. Defenders' categorizing critics as "ideologists" and critics' labeling of defenders as "human rights deniers" allow both discourse coalitions to become parties in a conflict about school

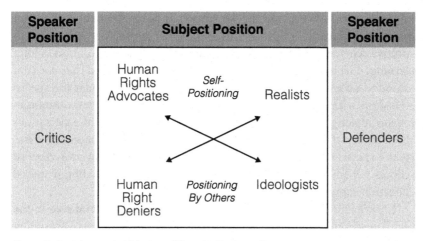

Speaker Position	Subject Position			Speaker Position
	Human Rights Advocates	*Self-Positioning*	Realists	
Critics				Defenders
	Human Right Deniers	*Positioning By Others*	Ideologists	

Figure 8. Speaker and subject positions in German discourse

structures, a disagreement that is maintained by the self-positioning of critics as human rights advocates and defenders as realists.

Interpretative Frame

As critics or defenders of special schools, policy actors share ideas about appropriate ways of making regular schools more accessible. These ideas are based on knowledge about disabled children's special needs and the school system's capacity to provide for their special education. Reproduced discursively, this knowledge frames the development of an inclusive school system as a process of retaining special education professionalism. This interpretative frame—defined as a "fundamental meaning and action-generating schemata" (Keller 2011, 57)—is what links the ideas entailed in the global rights package of Article 24 to preexisting ideas and institutions of disabled children's education (see Levitt and Merry 2009, 451–52).

Having developed historically, knowledge about the special educational needs of disabled children builds on the institutionalization of segregated special school structures and exclusive professional responsibilities (Pfahl and Powell 2011). The ability-based, structural, and professional distinction between regular and special education is based on the premise that homogenous learning groups provide a better learning environment. Within the discourse, these ideas are articulated when policy actors in both lines of argumentation advocate for a transfer of special educational expertise and resources into regular schools. The amalgamation of regular and special education professionalism in regular schools becomes the constitutive scheme to negotiate the realization of inclusive education as joint learning. The lack of consensus on the structural segregation thus does not extend to a conflict about the professional separation of regular and special education within regular schools. Exclusive professional responsibilities remain intact so that the discourse sustains institutionalized expectations about ability: if a child is not able to function in regular schools and classrooms, special education support needs to be provided. Conversely, special schools remain a legitimate learning space for disabled children if special education support cannot be provided in regular settings.

Knowledge about the large special education capacity available in the German school system builds on the institutionalization of mass schooling in an ability-stratified system. Historically, the provision of education for disabled and disadvantaged children in special schools allowed to surmount their overall educational exclusion. While both lines of argumentation acknowledge this past contribution of special schools, the current importance accorded to this school type is especially pronounced in discourse fragments following a conservative line of argumentation. There, the historical achievement of having overcome outright exclusion is used to point out the lack of educational provisions for disabled children in other world regions. A teacher's union for example asserts,

> To properly assess the claim and significance of the UN convention, it is important to know that 98 percent of people with disabilities worldwide still have no access to educational institutions. Against this background, the UN convention is a decisive step forward. It obliges the signatory states to enable people with disabilities to participate in society through participation in education. Germany has already implemented this with its multitiered school system. (DPhV 2010, 1)[33]

The essence of this statement is that Article 24's requirements are already fulfilled in the segregated German school system. Even more, the delivery of education in special schools confirms the major educational success the German system has achieved on a global scale by including children not able to function in regular education into the general school system. Pivotal in realizing mass schooling, the institutionalization of a special education system is therefore considered to provide a global advantage, for which special schools cannot be dismantled. Contesting special schools, transformatists nonetheless advocate the safeguarding of Germany's special education capacity. One nonstate actor, though regretting the poor organization of special education, highlights the "high level of professionalism [and] training of special educators for the diverse areas, which other countries don't have at all, and we definitely have something to offer here" (G_1: 560–64).[34] Such a showcasing of Germany's special education capacity sustains a belief in the advantages of ability-distinctive education for access and participation. This belief, eventually, allows both stances: to defend special education resources and expertise across both lines of argumentation while, simultaneously, maintaining diverging positions on the role of special schools.

Disabled children's inability to succeed in regular education and the German school system's capacity to provide for their special education are facts outside yet crucial for the discourse. Therefore, the development of an inclusive school system in Germany becomes a concern over retaining special education. The boundaries of the discourse are set accordingly: it is impossible for policy actors not to speak about special education and special schools when negotiating the development of an inclusive school system. Inclusive education change thus strengthens the relevance of special education professionalism. Accordingly, the historically institutional path is only slightly amended: special schools, even though losing leverage as the exclusive school form for disabled children and youth, remain functional and ready to be integrated into regular schools. The discourse therefore does not change the institutional path but confirms one thing essential for the segregated logic of Germany's school system: that special education is inevitable.

Wrapping Up: The German Story about Inclusive Education Change

Having reconstructed the interpretative repertoire of the UN CRPD implementation discourse, the empirical results are now summarized in a story about the development of an inclusive school system in Germany (see Keller 2011, 59). As an interim result, this story entails the distinct set of ideas with which Article 24's "program of change" is translated in the German discourse on inclusive education.

According to this story, the development of an inclusive school system is closely linked to the ratification of the UN CRPD, which gave the impetus to a federal policy debate between state and civil society policy actors. In these debates, policy actors agree that the goal of inclusive education change is the expansion of the joint learning of children with and without disabilities in regular schools, a process that necessitates the transfer of special education resources and expertise into regular schools. However, policy actors disagree if these changes must occur at the expense of the continued existence of special schools as segregated learning spaces. Defenders of segregated structures argue, based on parents' right to choose, for the preservation of special schools as the historical beacons of inclusion into education. Critics of segregated special education structures, on the other hand, qualify them as outdated, arguing that the UN CRPD postulates the child's right to access regular schools. In light of this dissension on the reorganization of special education, the development of an inclusive school system depends on the retention of special education professionalism outside of special schools.

With this story, the German discourse responds to global as well as institutionalized ideas about the education of children with disabilities. Global ideas pertain to Article 24's reform mandate to ensure an inclusive school system, accepted by all policy. The reform agenda of "all schools for all," on the other hand, remains controversial among policy actors and is modified on grounds of practical and contextual considerations. These considerations are based on institutionalized ideas and norms regarding children's inability to learn in regular education and the school system's extensive special education capacity, with the result that the development of an inclusive school systems turns into concern over retaining special education professionalism.

In sum, the German case study constitutes a direct translation of Article 24 UN CRPD; ideas and norms taken up are explicitly linked to the human rights treaty. As a document, the convention initiated a controversial debate

TABLE 9. The Story of Inclusive Education Change in Germany

Ideational dimensions	Content
Cause for change	UN CRPD ratification
Aim of change	Development of an inclusive school system
Value of change	Realization of the best possible (special) education for children with disabilities
Goal to be achieved	Expansion of joint learning in regular schools
Problem to be addressed	Reorganization of special education in segregated structures
Solutions to be applied	Structures: closure vs. maintenance of special schools; Legislation: parent's right to choose vs. right to regular schools; Professionalism: transfer of special education into regular schools
Norms to be applied	Special education professionalism
Roles taken	Critics and defenders of special schools

in which its "program of change" is appropriated through the norms and beliefs of the institutionalized special education system. All policy actors accept Article 24 as a legitimate legal and normative document demanding context-specific educational changes to ensure an inclusive school system. However, policy actors disagree on the scope of change required to meet this goal. Whereas the continued existence of special schools is disputed between discourse coalitions, special education as a professional practice is not. Inclusive education change is therefore about transferring special education resources into regular schools. In this way, the discourse confirms the inevitability of ability selection to realize the right to education for children and youth with disabilities.

FIVE

Comparing Translations

The "Special Educationalization of Inclusion"

The comparison of the Nigerian and German cases assesses the impact of the divergent local contexts of schooling on translations of the global human rights package entailed in Article 24 of the UN CRPD. In having selected Nigeria and Germany as case study contexts, I consider the institutional differences that exist between the school systems as relevant for the translation of human rights into educational change.

The Nigerian and German case studies reflect the global variance of noninclusive education as well as dissimilar institutional conditions for Article 24 to gain influence (see Berg-Schlosser and Meur 2009, 25; Przeworski and Teune 1970, 34–35). The case selection criterion—maximum country context variation for two contrasting school systems—therefore also entails the logic of comparison. Instructed by a neoinstitutional theoretical framework, the comparison is concerned with the question of how the different respective institutional environments of formal education impact human rights translations. This, in turn, determines the influence Article 24 can have on the development of inclusive school systems. Analytically, the focus is therefore on the link between Article 24 and the institutional change of school systems, which is negotiated in discourses. It is this discursive negotiation that both human rights translations have in common and that constitutes the *tertium comparationis* (see Waterkamp 2006, 194–96; Alheit 2012, 89). Given the contrasting institutional logics the German and Nigerian school systems follow—exclusion vs. segregation—,

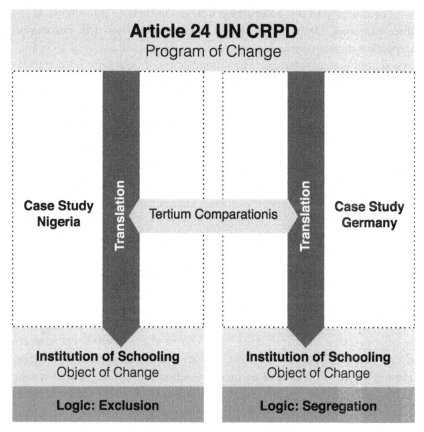

Article 24 UN CRPD
Program of Change

Case Study
Nigeria

Translation

Tertium Comparationis

Translation

Case Study
Germany

Institution of Schooling
Object of Change

Institution of Schooling
Object of Change

Logic: Exclusion

Logic: Segregation

Figure 9. Comparative case study design

these translational discourses are, however, formed in different institutional environments. Translations are thus similar yet separate enough to treat them—as Charles Ragin promotes—"comparable instances of the same social phenomenon" (1992, 1); that phenomenon is the influence of Article 24 on the development of inclusive school systems.

The influence of the UN CRPD on institutional change in two such different school systems depends on the meaning policy actors confer on Article 24 as a document and "program of change." This meaning is generated in discourses when global ideas about inclusive education blend with institutionalized ideas about schooling. To capture the analytically equivalent phenomena of Article 24's influence, the translational discourses are therefore the research object (see Locke and Thelen 1998, 9). This way I can compare human rights translations.

The first step of this comparison is to juxtapose both translations at the discourse level. Despite crucial differences, this analysis will uncover an important similarity, which is the "special educationalization of inclusion" as a shared logic of change. The second step is to compare both translations at the institutional level to explain this translational similarity.

Comparing Translation at the Discourse Level

The Nigerian and German translations of Article 24 are fascinating in both the scale of difference and the minutiae of similarities. In particular, the paradox of disability segregation being maintained despite rhetorical and legal support for inclusive education counters long-held views on the fundamental differences of reform processes in contrasting world regions.

Relation between Translations

Discerning the relation between translations allows to reveal how the Nigerian and German discourses react to Article 24 as an exogenous reform pressure. The principal questions of this analytical exercise are these: What difference does the UN CRPD make in and for discourses? How is the development of an inclusive school system negotiated among federal policy actors in each country? And what role do the different logics that both school systems follow play in these negotiations?

The Role of Article 24 UN CRPD

As a document, Article 24 is a nonevent in the Nigerian discourse, but a crucial event in the German discourse. This difference is due to the divergent contexts of discourse production: while the topic of inclusive education is debated in relation to the implementation of universal basic education (UBE) in Nigeria, it revolves around the implementation of the UN CRPD in Germany.

In Nigeria, the 2004 UBE Act is the symbolic carrier generating and framing a discourse about its implementation to meet the development objective of Education for All (EFA). In this discourse, the realization of inclusive schooling is understood to provide for the special education of largely excluded groups, negotiated in several subdiscourses; the one on children with disabilities was reconstructed for this analysis in detail. Within this subdiscourse, the right of children with disabilities to basic education is the argumentative base and common reference point for federal policy actors. The prominence of UBE affects the role of Article 24 in two ways: first, the human rights treaty is of no importance in the discourse—a discursive non-event—, as all relevant information pertaining to making schooling inclusive is already conveyed with the UBE Act; a fact further reinforced by the nondomestication of the UN CRPD. Second, the development of an inclusive school system becomes relevant for policy actors as a key strategy to implement UBE in a developmental framework of educational expansion. In this way, the Nigerian discourse reverts to international education policy discussions of the 1990s, which coined inclusive education as a concept and strategy to realize the right to education for marginalized and excluded children in the pursuit of EFA (e.g., the Salamanca Statement [World Conference on Special Needs Education 1994]). In this way, Article 24's "program of change" is central for the discourse yet is not tied to Article 24 as a document; the development of an inclusive school system is concerned with realizing the right to basic education, not the right to inclusive education.

In Germany, on the other hand, Article 24 is the symbolic carrier that generates and frames a discourse about its implementation. The crucial discourse event is UN CRPD's ratification as it—based on an erroneous translation by the German government, replacing the original term "inclusion" with the term "integration"—sparked a controversy among policy actors. This controversy centered around the question of whether a segregated special education systems, where most children with disabilities and special needs learn, is still legitimate or constitutes a barrier to realizing inclusive education as joint learning. With this question, historic conflicts about Germany's segregated school structures were rekindled, resulting in the formation of two opposing discourse coalitions: defenders and critics of special schools. The controversy between these discourse coalitions characterizes public consultations pertaining to the National Action Plan (BMAS 2011a), the first State Party Report (BMAS 2011b) as well as Recommendations on Inclusive Education by the education ministers of the federal states (KMK 2011). In all these debates, Article 24 is the argumentative base and common reference point for federal policy actors, either to advocate for transformative change to overcome segregated school structures or, conversely, for their conservation as a historical achievement.

In this sense, the German discourse can be characterized as a direct translation of Article 24, in which the UN CRPD is the main discourse event explicitly negotiated by policy actors. The Nigerian discourse, in contrast, can be characterized as an indirect translation, given that ideas pertaining to inclusive education as a global human rights paradigm are conveyed with the EFA development frame of UBE and not the UN CRPD.

Processes of Change

Confronted with the reality of exclusion, Nigerian policy actors aim at the inclusion of all children in the formal school system. For them, the main barrier to accessing schools is evident in the lack of any support structure that would allow educators to address and respond to disabled children's special educational needs—the very reason they are excluded in the first place. Therefore, policy actors advocate for the provision of special-needs education in special schools and classes, as well as assistive devices. The goal pursued with the development of an inclusive school system is thus educational expansion by special-needs education. This goal represents the first, crucial step of educational progress by which, at a later stage, inclusive education as joint learning can be established. Within the Nigerian discourse, an inclusive school system is therefore understood to be a formal school system that can provide for the special education of excluded groups, to realize their individual right to education and to meet the developmental objective of EFA.

In Germany, in contrast, policy actors intend, with the development of an inclusive school system, to expand the joint learning of children with and without disabilities in regular schools. However, it remains controversial if pursuing this goal also implies the closure of special schools: while critics of special schools see them as the main barrier to realizing inclusive education, understood as the right to attend regular schools, defenders see them as the guarantors of the disabled child's right to education and their parents' right to choose the school. Despite these differences, policy actors agree that to realize joint learning, special educational expertise and resources need to be transferred out of special and into regular schools. Within the German discourse, an inclusive school system is therefore understood to be a system that provides special education no longer exclusively in special schools, but increasingly in regular schools.

Both discourses are thus concerned with the development of an inclusive school system. Only in Germany does this, however, currently mean pursuing the goal of expanding the possibilities for joint learning. In Nigeria, this goal is relegated to a later stage of educational progression after educational expansion by special education is achieved. Albeit pursuing different goals, the discursive rationale for doing so is identical in the two countries and based on the understanding that inclusive education—as an organizational principle and classroom practice to realize the joint learning of students with and without disabilities—depends on one condition: that special education is provided in regular schools for disabled children. Based on the reality of exclusion, this understanding implies in the Nigerian discourse that a special education support system needs to be institutionalized first. In Germany, on the other hand, it implies that the already available special education support system can be progressively extended into regular schools.

Based on this understanding, the argument that inclusion demands the closure of special schools, as advanced in the German discourse, could not be made in Nigeria, as their establishment is perceived as the very condition needed to overcome the outright exclusion of disabled children and youth. By contrast, the argument that inclusion means the realization of disabled children's right to education, as advanced in the Nigerian discourse, can be made in Germany. Indeed, it is put forward by conservatives to maintain that the German school system is already inclusive as disabled children have access to formal education. Both discourses—though pointing to different aspects of the right specified in Article 24—therefore corroborate each other in the idea of different evolutionary stages of educational progress: exclusion must be overcome with a segregated and separated special education system before it can be transferred into regular schools to realize joint learning at the final stage. This idea is captured in the metaphor of "moving up the inclusive education ladder."

The two discourses thus address different problems with the development of an inclusive school system: access to formal education in Nigeria and placement in schools in Germany. In Nigeria, speaking about inclusive education indicates compliance with the already established UBE framework, whereas in Germany it indicates a conflict about school structures. In addressing these different problems, both discourses acknowledge that the institutional logics their school systems follow are challenged by the global human rights paradigm of inclusive education—exclusion in Nigeria and segregation in Germany.

In addressing different problems, both discourses proffer different solutions to inclusive education change, which, however, similarly depend on the provision of special-needs education. Special-needs education is regarded as an institutional resource to be provided in special schools and classes in Nigeria, and in Germany to also be increasingly offered in regular schools. In this way, a special education fix is proposed in both discourses. In Nigeria, it serves to realize the right to education for disabled children, while it serves to realize their access to regular schools in Germany. This call for special education is based on claims about gaps in support for disabled children and youth—in Nigeria with regard the school system itself, and in Germany regarding regular schools. This claim substitutes the inevitability of special education as the way to realize their right to education—be it in regular or special schools. Why is a special education system the crucial institutional resource necessary to pursue inclusive education change in both countries? Answering this question requires a comparison of the role that the two countries' relative contexts play in and for discourses.

Role of Context

The contextual particularity policy actors see as important in speaking about inclusive education change is, in Germany, the highly professionalized special education system, and, in Nigeria, its absence. From now on, I will use the terms "special education" and "special-needs education" synonymously to refer to educational settings envisioned by federal policy actors in both countries for children with a disability.

The expansive special education capacity available in Germany and other countries of the global North confirms for policy actors in *both* discourses the educational progress achieved by means of a segregated special education system. On the other hand, it is the limited special education capacity in Nigeria and other countries of the global South, emblematic of a world region struggling to achieve EFA, that confirms for policy actors in *both* discourses the developmental need to first include all children with disabilities in education instead of pursuing their joint instruction with nondisabled peers.

In both discourses, the capacity for special education is thus taken as a global indicator to measure how far countries have progressed in realizing EFA by "moving up the inclusive ladder." Therefore, the provision of special education can in either discourse not be separated from the accomplishment of including all children into formal education, nor from realizing joint learning. Instead, inclusion in education and inclusive education equally depend on the provision of special-needs education and differ only with respect to where it is provided—in special schools alone or also in regular schools and classrooms. In this way, both discourses create not only boundaries but hierarchies between school systems based on their special education capacity. This makes it seem as if Germany is less challenged by the mandate to ensure an inclusive education system than Nigeria.

Maintaining the division of regular and special education, be it between

TABLE 10. Contextual Sources of Change I

		Nigeria	Germany
		Low level of special education capacity	High level of special education capacity
Nigeria & Germany	Ability to succeed in regular education	"Expansion of special education"	"Retention of special education"
	Inability to succeed in regular education		

Source: Author's representation inspired by Mahoney and Thelen 2010, 19.
Note: Underlining indicates discursive spaces of translations.

or within schools, both discourses sustain numerous beliefs: that learning groups cannot be too heterogeneous, that children with disabilities require a more or less sheltered environment (*Schonraum*), and that only special educators are sufficiently qualified to teach students with special needs appropriately (see Pfahl 2011, 248). Deploying the image of disabled children with special educational needs allows to define the boundaries to heterogeneity that can exist in regular schools and classrooms. Discursively, children with disabilities are the proxy for the ability expectations upon which a special education system can be institutionalized.

For both discourses, the contextually appropriate way to align the image of disabled children with special educational needs with the image of school systems (in)capable of providing for their special education is to understand the development of an inclusive school system as a process of "moving up the inclusive education ladder." In Nigeria, that requires the expansion of special education and, in Germany, its retention.

In both discourses, the focus on special education is based on the conviction that whatever equal opportunities and nondiscriminatory learning environments are for children with disabilities, they must be realized with and through a special education system. In both discourses this focus is equally legitimized with the contextual particularities of the respective school systems. In Germany, this is the long tradition of special education, which has produced a highly elaborated and professionalized, segregated school system. In Nigeria, it is the absence of such a system in light of the perennial struggle to expand access to education.

To summarize, both discourses contextually appropriate global human rights ideas about inclusive education—be it as a strategy to realize EFA as UBE in Nigeria, or as a process to implement Article 24 in Germany. In negotiating the development of an inclusive school system, both discourses equally challenge the institutional logics their respective school systems follow—exclusion in Nigeria and segregation in Germany. Likewise, they also doubt that the goal of "all schools for all" can be attained because of the contextual particularities linked to these logics—a low level of special education capacity in Nigeria, and a high level in Germany. Sustained by a belief in the inability of disabled children to succeed in regular education, the provision of special education emerges as the contextually most appropriate means. Therefore, the development of an inclusive school system is in Nigeria concerned with the "expansion of a special education system." Conversely, in Germany, it is about the "retention of special education" outside of special schools.

With this knowledge, the relation between translations is characterized by an obvious difference and a concealed similarity. The difference relates to the role of Article 24 in and for both discourses. As a document, the convention is overshadowed by the UBE framework in Nigeria and has therefore no direct influence on the discourse. In Germany, it is, however, the central point of reference, generating and framing a discourse. Consequently, the discourses differ most with regard to the level of directness with which Article 24's ideas and norms are translated. The institutional contexts of schooling—even though they vary considerably—are nonetheless equally used to make the development of an inclusive school system dependent on the provision of special education, be it in special or regular schools. For that reason, both translations are similar in their focus on contextual particularities to justify the reliance on institutionalized special education in developing an inclusive school system.

Relation between Translations and Article 24 UN CRPD

Discerning the relation between translations and Article 24 of the UN CRPD allows to reveal the positions both translations take toward global human rights ideas. The principal question is, to what extent do the Nigerian and German discourses comply with Article 24's "program of change"?

The Nigerian discourse recognizes Article 24's reform mandate to ensure an inclusive education system. This recognition is, however, implicit, as the process of change envisioned is not negotiated in relation to the UN CRPD, but to the UBE Act and its implementation. Against this background, the development of an inclusive school system is acknowledged by federal policy actors as a tool to realize the right to basic education for children with disabilities, and to thus meet the developmental objective of

TABLE 11. Points of Comparison between Translations

	Nigeria	Germany
	Context of discourse production	
Role of Article 24 UN CRPD	UBE implementation	UN CRPD ratification
	Institutional carriers	
	Art 24 UN CRPD noncarrier	Art 24 UN CRPD symbolic carrier
	Goal of change	
	Educational expansion by special-needs education	Joint learning
	Problem	
Processes of change	Access to education due to a lack of support for children with disabilities	Placement in schools due to the organization of special education in segregated structures
	Scope of change	
	Realizing the right to education for children with disabilities	Transformation of school structures vs. minor reforms
	Solution	
	Provision of special-needs education and assistive devices	Transfer of special education into regular schools, conflict about special schools
Role of context	*Interpretative schemes*	
	"Expansion of special education" given the restricted special education capacity	"Retention of special education professionalism" given the large special education capacity

EFA. For that reason, recognizing the reform mandate is rather a socioeconomic necessity than a legal obligation under international human rights law, especially as the UN CRPD was not domesticated into Nigerian law at the time of data collection. In pursuing inclusive education change as a process of educational expansion by special education, the Nigerian discourse does not reject but indirectly answers to the reform mandate.

The reform agenda, on the other hand, is explicitly negotiated within the discourse. Policy actors reflect on the goal of "all schools for all children," coined on the international level, against the exclusionary reality of schooling on the national level. Given the lack of any support system that would allow for the inclusion of disabled children in basic education, they conclude that this goal is currently not attainable and therefore restrict it for practical and contextual reasons. In pushing inclusive education as a key strategy for EFA, the UBE implementation discourse thus indirectly answers Article 24's reform mandate with a progress-based reform agenda that advances the link between educational expansion and the provision of special-needs education.

Generated and framed by the UN CRPD, the German discourse fully recognizes the reform mandate to develop an inclusive school system; Article 24's reform mandate is the legitimate reason for and main concern of federal policy debates on the topic. However, Article 24's reform agenda remains controversial given the argumentative dissension between policy actors trying to reform interschool segregation and their opponents trying to preserve special schools. Negotiating the organization of special education, the German discourse thus answers Article 24's reform mandate with a reform agenda that responds to the norms and beliefs of Germany's segregated special education system.[1] The goal of "all schools for all children" is therefore neither utterly rejected nor truly met, but restricted for practical and contextual reasons.

As a result, the Nigerian and German discourses partially comply with Article 24's "program of change." This relation is illustrated in Figure 10, positioning both discourses within the translational space along a continuum of recognition to rejection with regard to Article 24's reform mandate on the horizontal x-axis and its reform agenda on the y-axis (see Clarke 2012, 233–37).

As both discourses recognize the global reform mandate to ensure an inclusive education system but reject the global reform agenda of "all schools for all," they are positioned in the map's bottom right quadrant II. For practical and contextual reasons, Nigerian actors pursue with inclusive education the institutionalization of a special education system that segregates or separates children based on disability. German actors, on the other hand, pursue the extension of such a system from special schools into regular schools. In doing this, both discourses decouple the aim of Article 24 from its goal and ultimately create a paradox for the time being: to realize inclusive education by adhering to ability selection in schooling instead of challenging such a system based on the global human rights norm.

To summarize, the crucial difference between the African and European discourses and Article 24 is not that the basic concern and objective of the human rights paradigm of inclusive education is misunderstood. Instead,

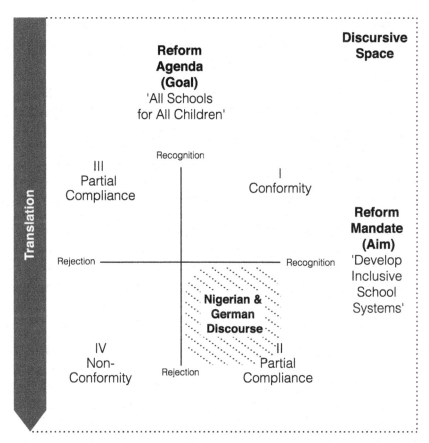

Figure 10. Position map of discourses. Author's representation based on Clarke 2012, 233.

it is the paradoxical relation between inclusion and segregation advanced in either discourse. While Nigerian and German policy actors discursively claim they are complementary considering each system's particularities, the General Comment on Article 24 clearly states that the provision of education in separated environments is incompatible with the systematic reform process of overcoming barriers that impede equal access and participation (CRPD 2016, para. 11).

Result: The "Special Educationalization of Inclusion"

The comparison of Nigerian and German discourses on inclusive education has revealed considerable differences and similarities. In sum, they produce a result as unexpected as it is impressive: in adhering to the reform mandate to develop inclusive school systems, both translations similarly reject the reform goal of "all schools for all" based on their school systems' contrasting special education capacities. In Germany, this is because of the long tradition of special education, which, it is argued, has allowed the inclusion of all disabled children in education in the first place. In Nigeria, it is because of a lack of this tradition, which is perceived as preventing educational progress. To demonstrate contextual appropriateness, both discourses similarly advance the "special educationalization of inclusion."

With this terminology, I build on discussions about the "education-alization of social problems," which are concerned with the "perceived intersection between distinct social practices, one of which is education" (Tröhler 2016, 1; see also Proske 2001, 2002; Depaepe and Smeyers 2008). In this way, the term "special educationalization of inclusion" points out the intersection between the professional practice of special education and the human rights paradigm of inclusive education. Advanced in both dis-courses, this intersection is based on the perceived and institutionalized differences between the distinct educational practices of special and regu-lar education; these are expected to move closer together in light of Article 24's "program of change." Considering the country-specific capacities to provide special education, policy actors understand the development of an inclusive school system in two ways accordingly: they either regard it as a problem of expanding special education to include all children with dis-abilities in formal mass schooling, or as one of retaining special education outside of special schools to enable the joint learning of children with and without disabilities in regular schools. In either case, the main responsibil-ity for the education of children with disabilities is handed over to spe-cial education professionals, who are assigned to cope with problems that occur when they access the school system in Nigeria or regular schools in Germany. Discursively, policy actors therefore react to the challenge of developing an inclusive school system with the provision of more and better special education; this is understood to be the engine for both, inclu-sion in education and joint learning (see Tröhler 2016, 7).

In both translations, the trust in special education follows the idea that it has an infinite advantage in creating school systems that select children based on disability out of regular education settings. The implicit hope is that this selection is more beneficial for the education of children with *and* without disabilities than the restrictions it brings by segregating or separat-ing them. This hope allowed the realization of a system of mass schooling in Germany in the nineteenth century, and it is this same hope that currently drives the quest for educational expansion in Nigeria. In acknowledging the needs of disabled children, a special education system is therefore the cage neither discourse can escape. The focus on special education systems allows speakers in the discourses to demonstrate the contextual appropriateness of the modified reform agendas to realize inclusive schooling. Otherwise, they would violate global hierarchies between school systems that have struggled to realize EFA or continue to do so. Therefore, educational change is negotiated in both discourses as a question of resources for the provision for special education. In Germany, this materializes as a conflict about school structures, while it takes shape as a developmental project of educational progress to realize EFA in Nigeria. In addressing the problem of exclusion in Nigeria and segregation in Germany, the "special educationalization of inclusion" is fundamentally connected to the development of an inclusive school system in both countries. It provides the foundation upon which the modification of Article 24's reform agenda of "all schools for all" could take place in the first place (see Proske 2001, 21).

In modifying the reform agenda, the "special educationalization of inclusion" eventually indicates the direction of change. At the ideational level of discourses, this direction instructs the material aspects of educational change to realize inclusive education—in Nigeria the expansion of special education, and in Germany its retention. With these characteristics, the "special educationalization of inclusion" is an institutional logic of change (see Thornton, Ocasio, and Lounsbury 2012, 2; Thornton and Ocasio 1999, 804; 2008, 100–1; Friedland and Alford 1991, 243). The logic of change is defined as the discursively (re)produced knowledge about the (in)ability of children and youth with disabilities to participate in regular education and the (in)capacity of school systems to accommodate special education. These ability-capacity expectations motivate policy actors to organize the development of an inclusive school system as a contextually appropriate process of expanding or retaining special education to realize the human right to inclusive education.

The argument is not that the two human rights translations are the same or identical. Rather, their inner connection—their isomorphy—is that both discourses make a special education system their point of reference to express practical problems and contextual particularities relevant for inclusive education change. In this way, the appropriation of global ideas is successful, but in neither case does it aid the implementation of Article 24's human rights reform agenda.

To theoretically explain how and why the institutional logics of change converge across translations, the institutional processes leading to the "special educationalization of inclusion" are analyzed in the next step. This

TABLE 12. Contextual Sources of Change II

		Nigeria	Germany
		Low level of special education capacity	High level of special education capacity
Nigeria & Germany	Ability to succeed in regular education	"Expansion of special education"	"Retention of special education"
	Inability to succeed in regular education		

Institutional logic of change: "special educationalization of inclusion"

Source: Author's representation inspired by Mahoney and Thelen 2010, 19.
Note: Underlining indicates discursive spaces of translations.

analysis will show that this logic of change is not an arbitrary result of discourses, but a finely calibrated translational outcome, produced with much effort.

Comparing Translations at the Institutional Level

Why must it be claimed by policy actors in both discourses that special education is inevitable in the development of inclusive school systems—not despite, but because of, their contrasting realities of schooling? To answer this question, the institutional processes that have led to isomorphic translations—institutional logics of change becoming similar across discourses—are traced (see George and Bennett 2005). With process tracing, the focus is on the institutional environments in which discourses take place. Setting discourses in relation to their outside, this theoretical analysis works backward from the "special educationalization of inclusion" to the discursive-institutional processes that facilitate this logic of change to emerge (see Traue, Pfahl, and Schürmann 2014, 505; Reilly 2010, 734).

The Institutional Mechanism of Paradoxical Solution

The first step in tracing the institutional processes that can explain the "special educationalization of inclusion" is to focus on the institutional mechanism through which this translational outcome could have been produced in both discourses.

In general, institutional mechanisms denote the procedures "through which institutional isomorphic change occurs" (DiMaggio and Powell

1983, 150). They are distinguished as coercive, normative, or mimetic mechanisms of diffusion of institutional pressures (DiMaggio and Powell 1983, 150; Scott 2008, 51). The coercive mechanism emphasizes the influence of regulative rules for isomorphism; the normative mechanism the effect of binding expectations of, for instance, professional norms and values; and the mimetic mechanism the role of constitutive schemes found in common beliefs and shared understandings (Scott 2003, 881). None of these mechanisms, however, can on their own comprehensively explain why both discourses produce the "special educationalization of inclusion" in contextually appropriating the global human rights paradigm of inclusive education. Why? Because neither the rules and obligations of Article 24, nor the expectations and beliefs related to the differently institutionalized special education systems alone, pressure each discourse into generating this paradox. Only the German discourse directly negotiates Article 24 as a legal and normative framework of change, as in Nigeria it is linked to the EFA framework and the question of educational expansion. Challenged by the rules and expectations of making schooling inclusive, the German discourse is characterized by a conflict over the organization of its highly professionalized special education system. Conversely, the Nigerian discourse identifies the absence of such a system as the main barrier to realizing EFA. For these reasons, I argue that it must be a combination of both— the global human rights paradigm of inclusive education *and* the differently institutionalized special education systems—that is effective in spreading the "special educationalization of inclusion" as the logic of change across both cases. The institutional mechanism that explains the creation of isomorphic translations might thus rather be one of paradoxical solution.

In the following, I conceptualize the mechanism of paradoxical solution based on the works of Smith and Lewis (2011) and Jay (2013). Smith and Lewis define a paradox as "contradictory yet interrelated elements that exist simultaneously and persist over time" (2011, 382). In addition, they identify "paradoxical resolution" as a management strategy to deal with organizational tensions (389). Transferring these ideas from the organizational to the ideational level of translations, I adjust the term slightly and do not speak of paradoxical *resolution* but paradoxical *solution*. The reason is that both translations, by using the "special educationalization of inclusion," indeed solve the tension "between global intentions and national persistence" in educational change (Richardson and Powell 2011, 258). However, they do not *re*solve the tension between the professional practice and organizational principle of special education segregation and the human rights paradigm of inclusive education; while the former is based on the premise of ability selection, the latter calls for their overcoming (CRPD 2016). On the contrary, this intricate tension is strengthened as discourses modify the global reform agenda and therewith juxtapose the development of an inclusive school system with the expansion or retention of special education. To conceptualize the mechanism of paradoxical solution, I furthermore take up Jay's (2013) argument that the navigation of paradoxes can be a mechanism of change amid institutional complexity, and again transfer it from the organizational to the ideational level of translations. On this conceptual basis, I now probe the mode of action through which the mechanism of paradoxical solution produces the "special educationalization of inclusion" in the Nigerian and German discourses.

The mechanism of paradoxical solution in translations evolves in two steps inferred from the two components that constitute a paradox: first, an "underlying tension" between "elements that seem logical individually but inconsistent and even absurd when juxtaposed" and, second, "responses that embrace [this] tension simultaneously" (Smith and Lewis 2011, 382). Based on this definition, I begin by showing which underlying tension is confronted in both discourses and then how it is embraced discursively.

Paradoxical solution drives the blend of global and context-specific ideas about the education of disabled children in the Nigerian and German discourses. Both take up the global paradigm of inclusive education to negotiate changes to their school systems for this group. For change to happen, policy actors feed global ideas, which are not yet institutionalized knowledge, into coordinative policy discourses to challenge exclusion in Nigeria and segregation in Germany. In other words, the mechanism of paradoxical solution could not take effect if policy actors would not support their stance on educational change with the human rights paradigm of inclusive education. In Nigeria, it is derived from the EFA framework as a key strategy to expand access to formal education, while it is based on Article 24 as an obligation under international law in Germany. In negotiating educational change, the Nigerian and German discourses confront a tension arising between the paradigm's inherent "program of change" and the contextual particularities of their school systems.

In envisioning context-appropriate reforms, this tension is embraced in both cases. The result is a similar paradox: the development of an inclusive school system by segregating and separating children within and between schools on the basis of disability. Yet this practice is a discriminatory understanding of Article 24 and contradicts the objective of realizing the human right to education for persons with disabilities on an equal basis with others. In its General Comment on Article 24, the

Committee on the Rights of Persons with Disabilities clearly states that "the right to non-discrimination includes the right not to be segregated" (CRPD 2016, para. 13).

The translational paradox is hence produced in discourses that construct a "process of change" that adheres to the reform mandate to develop an inclusive school system but rejects the reform agenda of "all schools for all." In Nigeria, this is because of the absence of a segregated special education system, while in Germany it is because of its availability. Even more, in openly negotiating this institutional tension, translations accentuate this paradoxical solution: the more policy actors negotiate the human rights paradigm of inclusive education, the more they highlight disabled children's need for special education. And the more they advocate for the development of an inclusive school system, the more they are compelled to expand or retain ability-selective schooling. Therefore, both cases of translations are characterized by a weak link between the discursively produced "process of change" and the global reform agenda of "all schools for all." Yet—and this is of utmost importance—there remains a strong link between the discursively produced "process of change" and the reform mandate to develop inclusive school systems.

If the paradoxical solution occurs in a discourse that indirectly translates Article 24, policy actors negotiate the development of an inclusive school system in relation to the global development framework of EFA. In Nigeria, this negotiation draws attention to the fundamental flaws of a failing system of mass schooling, which excludes the largest number of children of any country worldwide. Agreeing that the lack of special education provision contributes to the exclusion of disabled children, policy actors support, through the development of an inclusive school system, the institutionalization of a special education system. If the paradoxical solution occurs, on the other hand, in a discourse that directly translates Article 24, policy actors negotiate the scope of change implied in the human rights "program of change." In Germany, this negotiation is a conflict-laden process unfolding between two discourse coalitions taking opposing positions on the future of special schools while agreeing on the inevitability of special education. Both forms of paradoxical solution allow for the creation of the "special educationalization of inclusion."

With paradoxical solution, the important point is that translations do not exist despite, but because of, the human rights paradigm of inclusive education. It is the reform mandate to develop inclusive school systems that initiates discourses about institutional change. Yet in these discourses the reform agenda is modified, reflecting the two school systems' divergent special education capacities. In these translations, Article 24 and the institutions of schooling engage with each other, albeit—at this stage—in a paradoxical way.

The Discursive Strategy of Decoupling to Comply

Which translational strategy allows to achieve the paradoxical fusion of global and local ideas about the education of disabled children? To answer this question, I adapt the concept of decoupling, as it allows me to detail the deliberate disconnection of the global reform mandate from its agenda in the Nigerian and German discourses.

Originally, decoupling describes a strategy by which organizations disconnect their formal structure from activities to signal correspondence with competing demands from outside and within (Meyer and Rowan 1977; Boxenbaum and Jonsson 2008, 90). In ceremonially adapting to these environmental expectations without following them through, organizations maintain their legitimacy.[2]

Transferring the concept of decoupling from the organizational to the ideational level of translations, I extend it to *decoupling to comply*. This is because decoupling would imply that discourses, in envisioning educational change, ceremonially adapt the global reform mandate *and* agenda for reasons of legitimacy, without pursuing them for practical and contextual reasons. However, the reform agenda "all schools for all" is explicitly rejected in both discourses to signal compliance with the reform mandate of ensuring inclusive education systems, either by pursuing "special schools for disabled children" in Nigeria, or "some regular schools for some disabled children" in Germany. Ceremonial compliance would not have required the extensive elaboration of practical requirements and contextual particularities necessitating the modification of aims pursued with inclusive education change.

Decoupling to comply is therefore defined as a discursive strategy to disconnect the goal of developing inclusive school systems deliberately and explicitly from the aim of making "all schools for all" to demonstrate the contextual appropriateness of human rights translations. It allows speakers in the discourses to solve the tension between Article 24's "program of change" and the contextual particularities of their school systems in a paradoxical way. The mechanism of paradoxical solution hence relies on the discursive strategy of decoupling to comply in order to generate the "special educationalization of inclusion" as a context-appropriate logic of change. For the theory of neoinstitutionalism, this implies that decoupling can not only be understood as a deliberate organizational strategy to negotiate competing institutional demands. Rather, it can also describe a discursive strategy in human rights translations to juxtapose competing global and local demands in a paradoxical way. Yet, why are discourses pressured to decouple the global reform mandate from its agenda? To answer this question, we need to widen the focus of analysis and examine the role of institutional environments in supporting the "special educationalization of inclusion" as a necessity for inclusive education change.

The Institutional Environment as Ability-Capacity Expectations

To theoretically engage with institutional environments requires a focus on the discursively (re)produced knowledge about children's (in)ability to participate in regular education, and school system's (in)capacity to provide for their special education accordingly. Constructed as facts outside of discourses, these distinctions provide the basis upon which the "special educationalization of inclusion" can be similarly asserted as the logic of change in both cases. For that reason, I conceptualize the expectations entailed in both distinctions as the institutional environments in which the Nigerian and German translations of Article 24 become isomorphic.

Focusing on the special needs of disabled children, both discourses reproduce knowledge about children who deviate from a compulsory norm of ableness (Hutcheon and Wolbring 2012, 1; Powell [2011] 2016, 66–69). In Nigeria, these are children with "visual, hearing, physical, speech or cognitive impairments" or "emotional and behavioral disorders" (FRN 2004b). As one among different special groups, disabled children are excessively excluded from education, which policy actors relate to the fact that no special education support system is available. In Germany, children with special needs are those who require special support in the areas of learning, language, emotional-social development, mental disabilities, physical impairment, hearing, seeing, and because of a disease (KMK 1994). These children are excessively selected for special schools corresponding to the special support required. In both discourses, speaking about disabled children with special educational needs points to a group that is not expected to function in regular education settings, where certain abilities are valued and promoted over others (see Wolbring 2008, 253; Weisser 2007). The appraisal of disability-based special educational needs hence depends on the assessment that something that is expected to be possible is not possible, thus causing a sorting of students into segregated schools and separated classrooms (Weisser 2005, 18–19). To put it another way, disability is understood as entailing "a source of tension that must be avoided" in regular education rather than "an important site worthy of examination" in all schools and classrooms (Dei et al. 2006, 208). Consequently, ability expectations form the basis of ability-selective school systems in which children with average abilities and needs become the norm, while children who do not meet this norm become those with special needs (see Rioux 2007, 114; Slee 1998, 102; Florian 2007, 13). Special needs, conversely, justify the provision of special education in segregated or separated learning spaces. In other words, if school systems view children with disabilities as having special needs, they will utilize special education systems as the primary mode to respond to difference; even more so as they are validated on a global level as being the most appropriate way to deal with ability-related differences in mass schooling (see Weisser 2005, 76).

Disabled children with special needs, who face exclusion in Nigeria and segregation in Germany, in turn, validate contextual particularities designated in both discourses as relevant for the development of inclusive school systems. In Nigeria, this is the absence of a special education system, while, in Germany, it is its highly professionalized character. Focusing on this (in)capacity, both discourses (re)produce knowledge about school systems that still struggle to achieve EFA and those that have already achieved this aim (Richardson and Powell 2011, 128–29; also Chataika et al. 2012; Dei et al. 2006; D'Alessio, Donnelly, and Watkins 2010; Miles and Singal 2010; Peters 2007; Werning et al. 2016). In both discourses, the developmental norm of EFA serves to position school systems hierarchically at different stages of the "inclusive education ladder." An extensive special education capacity accordingly indicates lower reform pressures, as disabled children have already gained access to formal education, even though in mostly segregated settings. In contrast, a limited special education capacity increases reform pressures, as it proves that disabled children receive no support whatsoever. These capacity expectations reflect that having a special education system is valued in both discourses as an expression of educational progress; it is therefore promoted over not having one, eventually justifying the "special educationalization of inclusion" in both, the global North and the global South context.

Together, the distinction between children (un)able to participate in regular education and school systems (in)capable of providing for their special education facilitates expectations about how to develop an inclusive school system: in Nigeria, this is through the expansion of a special education system and, in Germany, through the retention of special education professionalism (the question of whether this is exclusively inside or outside of special schools remains controversial). Therefore, what cannot be

TABLE 13. Institutional Sources of Change I

			Environmental expectation	
			Nigeria	Germany
			Low level of special education capacity	High level of special education capacity
Environmental expectation	**Nigeria & Germany**	Ability to succeed in regular education	"Expansion of special education"	"Retention of special education"
		Inability to succeed in regular education		

Institutional logic of change: "special educationalization of inclusion"

Source: Author's representation inspired by Mahoney and Thelen 2010, 19.
Note: Underlining indicates discursive spaces of translations. Italics indicate the institutional environment framing these spaces.

said about the development of an inclusive school system in each discourse is that it is practically feasible and contextually appropriate to make all schools available and accessible for all children.[3]

Constructed as facts outside of both discourses, these ability-capacity expectations constitute the institutional environments that pressure both discourses into decoupling the human rights goal and aim of inclusive education change (see Meyer and Rowan 1977, 341; Boxenbaum and Jonsson 2008, 80–81; Becker-Ritterspach and Becker-Ritterspach 2006, 107). In other words, the factors leading to the isomorphy of translations—the logics of change becoming similar across discourses because of their contrasting contexts—are the expectations about children's (in)abilities and school systems' (in)capacities. For the theory of neoinstitutionalism, this argumentation implies that institutional environments are not just "out there." Instead, institutional environments first need to be actively constructed by actors in order to subsequently exert their homogenizing pressures. This construction occurs in and through discourses, where knowledge is (re)produced for the negotiation of institutional changes. One question remains, though: why do these ability-capacity expectations become relevant in translations of Article 24?

The Institutional Myth of the Inevitability of Ability Selection

Widening the focus of analysis further, the emphasis is now on the institutional source through which ability-capacity expectations gain power to modify the reform agenda in relation to the development of inclusive school systems. To this end, I take up the concept of institutional myth, which is used in neoinstitutional organization theory to refer to widely held social understandings about rational ways of organizing. Organizations that align their structure and form with these understandings become similar to each other. In this way, they generate environmental expectations about how organizations should look and function, and upon which their legitimacy depends (Meyer and Rowan 1977; Greenwood et al. 2008, 3; Koch 2009, 113–14; Boxenbaum and Jonsson 2008, 78).[4]

Transferred from the organizational to the ideational level of translations, the concept of institutional myth allows us to capture the prime understanding that prevails in the Nigerian and the German discourses: that good schooling for disabled children requires a special education system. This understanding is based on knowledge about children's (in)ability to participate in regular education and school systems' (in)capacity to provide special education. Both discourses (re)produce this knowledge as environmental expectations imposed on them as outside facts. Reinforcing each other, these ability-capacity expectations build up to an institutional myth about the inevitability of ability selection in schooling. In other words, the institutionalized expectations that discourses incorporate as outside facts function as an institutional myth (see Tacke 2006, 95).

Institutionally, the mythological point of the inevitability of ability selection is that special educational needs are understood as an essential characteristic of children with disabilities, which school systems cannot control but only provide for. Therefore, the capacity of school systems to provide special education becomes the crucial contextual particularity, which must be respected while translating the human rights paradigm of inclusive education. Believing in the special needs of children with disabilities, policy actors in both discourses can hence only argue differently about the organization and structures of a special education system, but not question its fundamental necessity (see Rottenburg 2002, 142). Consequently, the development of an inclusive school system can, in Nigeria, require nothing else than the expansion of special-needs education, while, in Germany, it requires its retention in- and outside of special schools.

In organizing ideas about the development of inclusive school systems, the myth enhances the legitimacy of translational outcomes, that is, in each case the "special educationalization of inclusion." This legitimacy is gained as both discourses not only maintain but eventually sustain ability-capacity expectations; they are the respective tokens of contextual appropriateness (see Suchman 1995, 382; Scott 2008, 61). In other words, discourses that conform with, *and* thus confirm, ability-capacity expectations demonstrate

TABLE 14. Institutional Sources of Change II

			Environmental expectation	
			Nigeria	Germany
Institutional myth of the inevitability of ability selection in schooling			Low level of special education capacity	High level of special education capacity
Environmental expectation	**Nigeria & Germany**	Ability to succeed in regular education	"Expansion of special education"	"Retention of special education"
		Inability to succeed in regular education		

Institutional logic of change: "special educationalization of inclusion"

Source: Author's representation inspired by Mahoney and Thelen 2010, 19.
Note: Underlining indicates discursive spaces of translations. Italics indicate the institutional environment framing these spaces.

that the development of inclusive school systems depends on a special education system. This happens in both discourses not despite, but because of, their contrasting school systems (see Meyer and Scott 1983, 201).

The point is not that the Nigerian and German discourses share an institutional environment, but that these institutional environments similarly perpetuate ability-capacity expectations that make inclusive schooling a concern of special education systems. In other words, the isomorphic pressures that make the institutional logic of change in the Nigerian discourse similar to the one in the German discourse are grounded in expectations about children's (in)abilities and school systems' (in)capacities. The translational legitimacy of a "special educationalization of inclusion" thus depends on two components: first, the discursive recognition of the reform mandate to develop inclusive school systems, and, second, the discursive compliance with environmental ability-capacity expectations.

With this analysis, I do not allege that a causal relation exists between special education systems and the development of inclusive school systems in Nigeria and Germany. Instead, the argument is that this relation is constructed in and through discourses. That means the "special educationalization of inclusion" does not derive from an institutional myth. Rather, it is the myth of the inevitability of ability selection that can be inferred from the "special educationalization of inclusion." In other words, the myth does not cause but enables this logic of change; it is the phenomenon to which both discourses refer, and which is constructed as standing outside of them (*Diskursgegenstand*) (see Traue, Pfahl, and Schürmann 2014, 498).

Therefore, the relation between institutional myth and the isomorphy of translational outcomes must be understood as a discursive one. This conclusion has implications for neoinstitutional theory as well as the development of inclusive school systems. Theoretically, the role of actors must be strengthened; myths can only become powerful when the expectation they institutionalize—be it about rational ways of organizing or good schooling for disabled children—are actively (re)produced by actors in and for institutional change. That means that institutional myths need to be discursively constructed as such; that is, they must become the subject matter of discourses (*Diskursgegenstände*). This was achieved in the Nigerian and German discourses on inclusive education, in which the myth of the inevitability of ability selection necessitated and legitimized the "special educationalization of inclusion." For the development of inclusive school systems, this implies that the ability-selectivity of school systems could not be challenged but was further strengthened. Even more, the belief in the disabled child with special needs as a challenge for regular education settings, and in special education systems as an advantage in the global development of mass schooling, became "objectively available and subjectively plausible" facts in and through discourses (Berger and Luckmann [1966] 1984, 110). It is here that the global power of both discourses becomes apparent. They essentialize the abilities of individuals and capacities of school systems. In this way, they initiate institutional changes in Africa and Europe that are similarly governed by ableist expectations about the inevitability of special education. Accordingly, inclusion emerges as an evolutionary and linear process of educational expansion that depends on institutionalized special education, not as a right of persons with disabilities to be realized in local schools and on equal basis with others. The crucial factor undermining the realization of Article 24 is therefore the discursive-institutional power of special education to corroborate each nation's progress, or lack of progress, in providing education for all—both nationally and internationally.

Summary: Institutionalized Translations

In both cases of translation, the "special educationalization of inclusion" could be similarly produced with the institutional mechanism of paradoxical solution. With this mechanism at work, the tension between Article 24's "program of change" and the contextual particularities of the exclusionary Nigerian and the segregated German school systems—with their differing capacity to provide special education—could be embraced in each

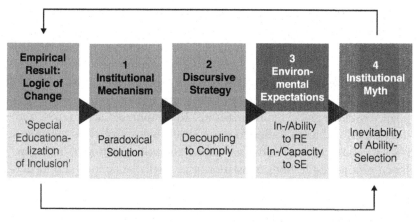

Figure 11. Elements of institutionalized translations. Adapted from Meyer 1994, 33. Note. RE means regular education, SE special education.

discourse through the generation of a paradox: the reliance on a special education system to realize the right to education for disabled children in an inclusive school system.

For this paradox to emerge, Article 24's reform mandate needed to be decoupled from its reform agenda. Indeed, the development of inclusive school systems is the main concern of policy actors in both discourses. But in considering their school systems' divergent capacities to provide special education, they modified the goal of "all schools for all," in Nigeria to become "special schools for disabled children" and in Germany to "some regular schools for some disabled children."

These modifications are attributable to the social beliefs in children's (in)ability to participate in regular education and school systems (in)capacities to provide special education accordingly. Constructed as facts outside of both discourses, these distinctions entail expectations that provided for the institutional environments that framed both translations. Reinforcing each other, these ability-capacity expectations eventually built up to an institutional myth about the inevitability of ability-selective schooling, specifying what good education for disabled children looks like. Effective in both discourses, this myth not only necessitated but eventually legitimized the "special educationalization of inclusion." The relation between both—the logic of change and the institutional myth—is therefore a circular one: the myth could not become powerful without its discursive (re) production as the logic of change, and translations could not legitimately result in the "special educationalization of inclusion" for contextual reasons without falling back on this myth.

In both translations, the circular relation between the logic of change and the institutional myth evidences the institutional embeddedness of human rights translations: their discourses not only are framed by institutional environments, but construct these environments. The results are institutionalized translations in which the "special educationalization of inclusion" is both a confirmation of the myth and a confirmation of compliance with the global reform mandate. To paraphrase Latour (1986, 276): the institutional myth is therefore not what holds translations together, it is what is held together with the "special educationalization of inclusion." Based on this result, both translations can finally be defined as a form of discursive institutional work that, in contextually appropriating global ideas, are involved in the maintenance of ability-selective school systems and thus hamper the realization of the human right to inclusive education for persons with disabilities.

SIX

Conclusion

The Global-Local Nexus in Human Rights Translations

This book answers the question of how Article 24 UN CRPD influenced the development of inclusive school systems in Nigeria and Germany. The focus is on the context-specific understandings of Article 24 that, generated in discourses, translate the human rights paradigm of inclusive education into institutional change on the ground.

This translational model of institutional change assumes that the vernacularization of human rights depends on the knowledge policy actors (re)produce in and through communicative actions that make up discourses. These regulated practices of knowledge (re)production mediate between the human right to inclusive education and its realization. To reconstruct such translations, theoretical insights from discourse and institutional analysis were combined (Keller 2011; Scott 2008; Meyer and Rowan 1977). The empirical research, in a comparative case study design, emphasized the dissimilarity of two school systems of UN CRPD state parties. Maximizing variance in institutionalized education, Nigeria and Germany were selected given the different institutional logics of their school systems—exclusion versus segregation. For the collection and analysis of empirical data, a sociology-of-knowledge approach to discourse (Keller 2011) was combined with grounded theory (Charmaz 2014). For the within- and cross-case analysis, the method of process tracing was chosen to engage with and uncover the relationship between translations and the institutional environments in which they are embedded (George and Bennett 2005).

The Nigerian case study revealed that the topic of inclusive education is a concern for federal policy actors committed to implementing universal basic education (UBE) in order to achieve the developmental goal of Education for All (EFA). To include children with disabilities in the basic education system, policy actors advocate for educational expansion by special-needs education. Pursuing this goal is regarded as the prerequisite to overcome the widespread outright exclusion of disabled children from formal education. It is also the precondition that would allow, at a later stage of educational progression, for their education alongside nondisabled peers. In this way, the Nigerian discourse on inclusive education is working to shift the institutional logic of schooling from exclusion to segregation and separation. At this point, it is important to remind ourselves that the policy debates about the inclusion of disabled children and youth in UBE occurred in a separate subdiscourse. Other subdiscourses targeted the inclusion of nomads, almajirais, or illiterate adults and youth via special education programs.

In Germany, on the other hand, the topic of inclusive education has been negotiated in relation to the implementation of Article 24. The discourse is characterized by two lines of argumentation. Policy actors who follow a conservative line defend special schools as a legitimate learning space, while those who follow a transformative line reject this position and propose the closure of special schools. Though disagreeing on the future of special schools, policy actors have agreed on the need to retain special education resources and expertise outside of special schools to realize joint learning for some disabled children in regular schools. In this way, the discourse supports interschool segregation that is supplemented with intraschool separation, more in some regions than others.

Comparing these contrasting cases of translation shows that policy actors in Nigeria as well as Germany engage in what Heyer (2015, 206) calls "mobilizing global norms": to contest current educational provisions for disabled children, they align and legitimate their own argumentations with the global *reform mandate* to ensure inclusive school systems. In Germany, policy actors derive this mandate directly from Article 24. In Nigeria they do so from the EFA development goal anchored in historical precursors to the UN CRPD, such as the 1994 Salamanca Statement, which first internationally introduced inclusive education as a strategy to achieve EFA. If this principle obtained the status of a human right via the UN CRPD, it has since been confirmed in the Sustainable Development Goals.

In both countries, however, the global *reform agenda* associated with the development of inclusive school systems, that is, to create schools that are available and accessible for all, is modified as it is translated. For practical and contextual reasons, the aim of inclusive education reform in Nigeria is to provide special schools and classes for disabled children. In Germany, the goal is to make some regular schools accessible for some disabled children. In this way, discourses in both countries—and policy actors—react to the challenge of inclusive schooling with more and better special education provisions, either to include disabled children in mass schooling or regular schools. The comparative analysis thus reveals an important, and paradoxical, similarity, despite the vastly different educational conditions that characterize the most populous countries of Africa and Europe, respectively: the segregation of pupils based on disability is extended or maintained in the name of rhetorical and legal support for *inclusive* education. The analytical task is to explain this paradox, the institutional processes that led to the "special educationalization of inclusion" in both countries, despite their very different school systems.

To this end, I introduced the institutional mechanism of "paradoxical solution" to denote the procedure through which global and local institutional pressures diffused into the discursive spaces of these multilevel translations. These pressures equally emanated from human rights ideas entailed in Article 24's values package as well as domestic ideas institutionalized in the rules, norms, and beliefs of an exclusionary and segregated school system. Opposites, these ideas generated a tension that was embraced in both discourses through the generation of this paradox: to pursue the development of *inclusive* school systems by expanding or retaining *segregated* special education systems, with the consequences that "all schools for all" cannot be realized. To conceptually account for th deliberate disconnection of reform mandate and agenda of inclusive education change as promoted with Article 24, I developed the concept of "decoupling to comply," the discursive strategy that paradoxically solves the tension between human rights requirements and contextual demands in translations. This is because the global "program of change" was not only ceremonially adopted in discourses, but explicitly modified to demonstrate the appropriateness of reform processes: in Nigeria due to the lack of any support system for children with disabilities, but in Germany because of the high level of special education resources and professionalization available mainly special schools for this group.

The need to alter the goals associated with inclusive education was in both discourses grounded in expectations about children's (in)ability to succeed in regular education, and school systems' (in)capacity to provide special education. These ability-capacity expectations reinforced each other and, eventually, built an institutional myth about the inevitability of ability selection in education in order to realize disabled children's inclusion into education. Indicative of a country's progress toward realizing a formal system of mass schooling, this myth was equally maintained in both national discourses as a rationale to demand or defend a special education system (however organized). For that reason, both translations have a similar outcome, which is the "special educationalization of inclusion."

Countering long-held views on the fundamental differences among reform processes in contrasting world regions, this result reveals that the translations of Article 24's human rights paradigm into educational change were similarly mediated by the "special educationalization of inclusion" in Nigeria and Germany. When talking about inclusive education, policy actors in both countries first and foremost considered the resources available to aid the special education of disabled children. This yielded change processes that framed the development of inclusive education system either as a process of expanding special education (Nigeria) or retaining special education within, and partly also outside of, special schools (Germany).

Global Expectations—Local Translations

Both discourses are influenced by global expectations about the development of formal systems of mass schooling. At their core is the idea that the realization of EFA locally follows a universal path globally. This path is best captured in the image of "moving up the inclusive education ladder," which was introduced by a Nigerian interviewee. In order to realize mass schooling, its implicit global narrative goes, states are required to overcome the exclusion of disabled children, first by providing for their special education in special schools, later in special classes, and eventually, regular classrooms. Ultimately, this framing implies that historical developments in the institutionalization of special education systems in Western countries serve as a template to be replicated in the rest of the world in the pursuit of inclusion. Indeed, this is what we witness in the Nigerian and German discourses.

Given the reality of exclusion, Nigeria is positioned on the lowest step of the inclusion ladder, striving to institutionalize a special education system. As such a system is already available in Germany, its school system is positioned on the second highest step, and reforms pertain only the organization of special education. In other words, knowledge production on inclusive education in the global North discourse is dominated by the historical achievement of realizing mass schooling by special education, a practice fundamentally characterized by ableism (Tomlinson 2017). The global South discourse, in turn, reinforces this historical development to eventually become a universal model of educational progression driving both, the inclusion of persons with disabilities in formal education as well as their continued exclusion from regular schools and classrooms. The translation of human rights in education is therefore tied to global educational hierarchies. These hierarchies—embedded in the distinction between early and late adopters of a standard model of mass schooling— structure power in discourses on inclusive education.

The Global Standard Model of Mass Schooling

Historically, the evolution of state-funded systems of mass schooling was closely linked to the industrial revolution of the eighteenth and nineteenth centuries in Europe. The dramatic surge in demand by public and private employers for elementary literacy and technical skills during this period prompted the expansion of mass schooling systems and marked the beginning of legislation for compulsory primary education (Weymann 2010, 67; Richardson and Powell 2011, 64–65). Countries that were particularly rapidly industrializing took the lead in this trend. This is illustrated by the introduction of a state-led public education system in Germany, widely regarded as a model for less industrialized nations to follow (Ramirez and Boli 1987, 4–5). Other major economies in the western hemisphere, notably Britain and France, developed their own education systems with similar characteristics (Ramirez and Boli 1987, 8–9). Due to the economic and military power of these countries and the fact that most of them possessed colonial empires, these mass education systems provided the blueprint to be adopted by the rest of the world (Richardson and Powell 2011, 97; Power 2015, 251). The education systems established by colonial agents and missionaries—not for all but a minority of children and youth—were clearly reproducing the key features of the "Western model of schooling" (Meyer et al. 1997; Adick 2003, 179; Koch and Schemmann 2009, 9), a trend that rapidly accelerated in the postcolonial era, when the newly independent nations adopted the compulsory and state-sponsored mass schooling system across the board from the late 1950s onward (Richardson and Powell 2011, 165; Baker and LeTendre 2005, 6). The latest manifestation of the prevalence of the "Western model" of schooling can be found in the EFA agenda introduced by several UN institutions and the World Bank in 1990 to accelerate the realization of mass schooling globally (Brock-Utne

2000). What, then, are the defining characteristics of this standard model of mass schooling?

In a structural sense, it is characterized by separating the provision of education into primary, secondary, and tertiary cycles regardless of social, political, and economic differences of the respective national contexts (Meyer and Ramirez 2000, 121; Baker and LeTendre 2005, 6). In an organizational sense, the model is characterized by the provision of education in schools and classrooms by professionalized teachers (Meyer and Ramirez 2000, 125–26; Baker and LeTendre 2005, 104–5). Moreover, from the outset onward, Western education systems segregated children with disabilities into special systems, initially based on a charitable approach that eventually morphed into a support-based approach (Tomlinson 2017, 20–21). In their comparative study of special education systems globally, Richardson and Powell even show that "special education predated compulsory schooling" in Europe and America and eventually "led to the expansion of general education" (2011, 125). Indeed, they argue that "special education is seen as a criterion of mature nationhood" (2011, 128). The exclusion of disabled children from regular education settings is thus being replicated by countries in the quest to close the educational gaps in mass schooling resulting, according to Tomlinson, in "an expanded and expensive 'SEN' industry" underpinning "mass education systems in developed and developing countries" (2012, 267).

The historical divide between school system in realizing a global standard model of mass schooling reemerges in translations of Article 24. It is entailed in metaphor of the "inclusive ladder," which advances the narrative that formal school systems with a large special education capacity have a global advantage in including disabled children in mass schooling. In this way, a specific historical development in one world region is transformed into a universal model of educational progress toward EFA impacting human rights translations.

The Global Narrative Vernacularized

Resonating equally in Nigeria and Germany, the global narrative of moving up the inclusive ladder considers the capacity of school systems to provide special education within and outside of special schools as an essential prerequisite for including disabled children in mass schooling. In view of the respective positioning of school systems on the inclusive education ladder, this narrative allowed policy actors in both countries to foreground the realities of their respective school systems as crucial for the translations of disability rights in education. In this way, policy actors were not only able to acknowledge the contextual predicaments they face in light of the global reform challenge but could eventually escape them. After all, Nigerian and German policy actors are well aware of two things: first, that the human rights goal associated with the development of inclusive school systems is to make "all schools available and accessible for all"; and, second, that their school systems are directly and essentially challenged by this vision—because they either exclude or segregate children on the basis of disability. Actors can, however, discursively escape this tension by fore-grounding contextual particularities given their position on the inclusive education ladder impeding the realization of this goal, even when the UN CRPD has been ratified. In Nigeria, with the worldwide highest number of out-of-school children, this is the lack of any support system for disabled children, and in Germany, having already achieved mass schooling at the end of last century, the availability of a well-resourced, highly diversified special education system.

In light of these national particularities, the human rights aim of ensuring inclusive school systems was deliberately and explicitly decoupled from its ultimate goal of making all schools available and accessible to all children and youth. For neoinstitutional theory, this finding implies that decoupling not only allows actors to juxtapose competing institutional demands, but to eventually dissolve them in a paradoxical way. Even more, similar institutional demands can be perpetuated in dissimilar contexts through powerful global narratives—as found in the image of the inclusive ladder—that, additionally, supersede the human rights paradigm.

The act of diverging from the principles embodied in Article 24 of the UN CRPD for contextual reasons—as contrasting as these are—is based on the steadfast and shared belief that school systems that place students in special education have an essential advantage in realizing the right to education for persons with disabilities. This belief is backed by a cycle of ableist assumptions that buttress and reinforce each other in negotiations of inclusive education reform: first, that persons with disabilities have "special educational needs" that prevent them from participating in regular education and, second, that school systems must provide special education in order to include this group in the first place (even as inclusive education globally shows this is not the case). Because of these ability-capacity expectations, special education structures and practices co-opt the inclusive education agenda in human rights translations, in Nigeria trying to achieve EFA, and in Germany defending this achievement.

Summarized in the inclusive education ladder, inclusion accordingly emerges not as the radical transformation realizing the right to education for persons with disabilities on an equal basis with others many advocates hoped for, but rather as an evolutionary and linear process of educational expansion that depends on institutionalized special education. The hierarchical positioning of early (Germany) and late adopters (Nigeria) of a standard global model of formal mass schooling, which the newer inclusive education ladder perpetuates, hence equally interferes with the enforcement of disabled children's human rights in contrasting world regions.

This insight not only counters long-held views on the fundamental differences among reform processes in Africa and Europe. It also expands Chua's observation that "human rights generate some potent effects, but they are not a dominant power" (2018, 131). Even though human rights ideas became highly relevant for discourses on inclusive education in Nigeria and Germany, they were trumped by a global narrative that perpetuates a universal path of educational advancement. Consider that when talking about inclusive education, policy actors in both countries first and foremost examined the resources available to aid the special education of disabled children in formal schooling. This insight, in addition, expands Merry and Levitt's argument that human rights translations need to draw on local narratives, images, and conceptions in order to gain traction on the ground (Levitt and Merry 2009; Merry and Levitt 2017). It reveals that images through which human rights are presented locally also rely on global narratives. Even more, the use of global narratives can allow translators to foreground contextual particularities in the first place. Here it was the image of the inclusive education ladder that enabled policy actors to accentuate different levels of educational progress in discourses on inclusive education. To be precise, in Nigeria and Germany, the same global narrative of educational progression was deployed to generate contextually appropriate—and thus less transformative—translations of Article 24's human rights package. Remarkably, these translations, though vernacularized, also generated a similar logic of change. According to the "special educationalization of inclusion," the development of an inclusive school system was either framed as a process of expanding special education (Nigeria) or retaining special education in special schools, but also offering special education support in regular schools (Germany). Thus, I show that human rights translations may set in motion a type of institutional change labeled "change without attainment": the transformation of school systems to comply with the mandate of developing inclusive school systems, yet through change processes that reinforce disability-based segregation and separation supposed to be overcome with Article 24. Local translations of global human rights ideas thus simultaneously drive the inclusion of persons with disability in formal education as well as their continued exclusion from regular schools, and this equally in contexts of the global South and the global North. A crucial factor contributing to the *nonimplementation* of Article 24 is hence the discursive-institutional power of special education systems to define and corroborate educational progress—or the lack of it—globally and locally.

A Human Rights Models of Disability in Education

Seeing special educational needs as given, indeed inexorable, and requiring ability selection in schooling shifts the ways in which the human right to inclusive education is understood. It undermines notions of equal access and participation of all children in local schools, no matter their impairment or ability level. In addition, this traditional view of catering for the needs of disabled students reinforces global hierarchies. These overstate the diverse special education capacities of contrasting school systems as a crucial contextual factor to be considered while translating human rights into educational change. Seeing the structures and practices of special education, by contrast, as a major cause of disablement emphasizes the ability-capacity expectations that undergird the idea of a universal, evolutionary path toward inclusion, as illustrated in the inclusive education ladder. In the name of educational advancement, ability-capacity expectations encourage segregation and separation in school systems at different ends of the spectrum of achieved mass schooling globally. Further, these expectations of the necessity of special education, even in inclusive education reforms, discourage the contestation of discursive-institutional processes that, above all, facilitate the "act of disabling a person" through special-needs classifications and education in segregated, stigmatizing facilities (Powell [2011] 2016, 40).

To counter mistranslations of the UN CRPD's Article 24—discourses that not only legitimate but ultimately foster ability selection in the name of the human right to inclusive education—the human rights model of disability offers crucial insights. This model, according to Degener—a long-term member of Committee on the Rights of Persons with Disability who has been instrumental in shaping disability in a human rights context—offers "a tool to implement the CRPD" (2017, 41). Why? Because it declares that "impairment does not hinder human rights capacity" (43). In other words, persons with disabilities are rights holders to the same extent as persons without disabilities. Degener, in a joint paper with Begg, therefore unequivocally states: "To deny or restrict rights on the basis of impairment is a form of disability-based discrimination" (2019, 54).

Accordingly, a human rights model in education endorses the legal fact that inclusive education, as a human right anchored in international law, is a legally enforceable duty, not solely a policy commitment. It focuses on the commonality of all children and youth to learn on an equal basis with others in nondiscriminatory ways. Without the focus on the human rights principles of equal opportunity and nondiscrimination, the idea of inclusive education can easily slip into a rhetoric of special education that champions the special needs of disabled children and focuses on the provision and availability of special education capacities. These vary considerably across the world (Richardson and Powell 2011), evolving gradually, expanding, and thus increasingly "manufacturing inability" (Tomlinson 2017).

Even though the special education argument has won (and stills wins) supporters for the inclusion of marginalized and excluded groups in education in the first place, the maintenance of special education systems is not sufficient to realize—or indeed counteracts—the right to inclusive education. While special education systems have historically been instrumental in overcoming the outright exclusion of disabled children from mass schooling, these gains have rarely translated into better educational outcomes. Organizing schooling on the basis of antiquated, deficit-oriented models of disability, special education systems increase the likelihood of segregation, separation, and stigmatization. In this way, ability selection in schooling is strengthened, which in turn contributes to exclusion from local schools and reduces the potential of inclusive schooling. Children with disabilities, and indeed other excluded children, would not need to be segregated from their peers were it not for the problems that ability-selective school systems construct on the premise that there is a limit to accepting heterogeneity in regular schools and classrooms. From a human rights perspective, I argue that such institutionalized myths are the root cause of disability-based inequity in education. However, to dismantle barriers that impede equal access and participation, the solution cannot be to deny differences in abilities or the real needs of children in the hope of ending their exclusion and segregation. On the contrary, the focus on different abilities and needs must be strengthened to underline the duty of each schools to accommodate all children living in their community. This is because, as Degener (2017, 47) points out, "The human rights model values impairment as part of human diversity." The scarcest resource for the development of inclusive school systems thus is not necessarily a lack of special education provisions, but of a critical examination and understanding of Article 24's human rights paradigm.

Consequently, a human rights model of disability in education needs to confront universalizing assumptions about the realization of inclusion as a space in which discrimination unfortunately continues to be sustained. These assumptions are entailed in the ability-selective and progression-based rationalities that drive the "special educationalization of inclusion." Because if there is anything equally challenging for contrasting school systems like the exclusionary Nigerian and the segregated German one, it is to comprehend that special education is far more complicated than just allowing access and participation. This does not mean that the current differences between school systems do not matter for the development of inclusive school systems and their analysis. Nor does it mean that children with disabilities face the same problems in all education systems; certainly, securing educational opportunities for children in exclusionary, underresourced systems is more precarious. This point, however, could be made without a sole focus on the availability of special education and its organization, because this obscures two crucial realities: first, that all school systems worldwide are challenged by the human rights paradigm of inclusive education, and, second, that alternative ways exist to realize the right to inclusive education for all by recognizing and valorizing diversity. The ultimate question is therefore actually this: do school systems need to be ability selective because children with disabilities have special needs? Or, do ability-selective school systems tend to disallow children with disabilities—and indeed many other excluded children—to learn together with their peers because more emphasis and value is placed on special education capacities to demonstrate educational "progress"?[1]

In conclusion, the human rights model of disability in education enables the use of Article 24 UN CRPD as "a roadmap for change" (Degener 2017, 54). It offers a way to engage critically with the ableist assumptions that foster the global politics of mass schooling that maintain segregated schools and separate classrooms and affect the translation of human rights into educational change. Stakeholders in academia, policy, and education are therefore called upon not only to focus on contextual particularities when engaging with the development of inclusive school systems, but also to reflect on, and counteract, a global narrative of "moving up the inclusive education ladder," often used to (mis)translate human rights in education. This is because on 13 December 2006, the day the UN General Assembly adopted the UN CRPD by Resolution 61/106, inclusive education became a human right (UNGA 2006). And children cannot be deprived of this right, even if they do not meet the ability expectations associated with different school tracks, types, and forms, and notwithstanding the respective school system's capacity to provide special education.

Appendix

Policy Documents Used in the Analysis

This appendix lists all policy documents I used to reconstruct the federal policy discourses on inclusive education in Nigeria and Germany. Topically dealing with inclusive education, Article 24 UN CRPD, or disability-based exclusions in education, these sources entail the discourse fragments that allowed to reconstruct how the global reform challenge is negotiated against the background of national policy frameworks and local realities of schooling.

Corpus Nigeria

Abatemi-Usman, Nurudeen. 2013. *Making a Case for Nigerians Living with Disabilities. Excerpt of a Paper Delivered by Senator Nurudeen Abatemi-Usman at a Programme Organised by Women with Disabilities in Abuja, 06 Feb. 2013.* Hardcopy.

Al-makura, Umaru Tanko. 2015. *Being Text of a Keynote Address Delivered by His Excellency, Umaru Tanko Al-makura, Governor of Nasarawa State, on the Occasion of International Conference on Disabilities, Lagos: Monday, 22nd June, 2015.* Hardcopy.

Basharu, Danlami. 2015. *Disability, the Media and Legal and Policy Framework for Making Nigeria Disability Friendly. Paper Presented at the Media Training Session for the International Conference on Disabilities, Lagos, 25th June, 2015.* Hardcopy.

CCD (Centre for Citizens with Disabilities). 2012. *Memorandum of the Centre for Citizens with Disabilities Presented to: The Chairman, Joint Committee on the Review of the Constitution (JCRC).* Softcopy.

CSACEFA (Civil Society Action Coalition on Education for All). 2010. *Millennium Development Goals: Nigeria Struggles to Meet Target to Educate over 10m Out of School Children.* Hardcopy.

ERT (The Equal Rights Trust). 2011. *ERT's Submission to President Goodluck Jonathan Regarding the Nigeria Disability Bill.* Online, http://www.equalrightstrust .org/ertdocumentbank//GOODLUCK%20JONATHAN%20SUBMISSION .pdf (Last accessed October 27, 2021).

ESSPIN (Education Sector Support Programme in Nigeria). 2009. *Access and Equity Position Paper Doc. No.: ESSPIN 028.* Online, http://www.esspin.org/re ports/download/58-file-1259916849-access_equity.pdf (Last accessed October 27, 2021).

ESSPIN (Education Sector Support Programme in Nigeria). 2012. *Access and Equity Strategy 2011–2014, Report Number: ESSPIN 056.* Online, http://www .esspin.org/reports/download/337-file-ESSPIN-058-Access-and-Equity-Strat egy-2011-2014.pdf (Last accessed October 27, 2021).

ESSPIN (Education Sector Support Programme in Nigeria). 2013. *Inclusive Education Approach Paper Doc No.: ESSPIN 064.* http://www.esspin.org/reports/do wnload/352-file-ESSPIN-064-%20Inclusive-Education-Approach-Paper.pdf (Last accessed October 27, 2021).

FME (Federal Ministry of Education). 2005. *Nigeria Education Sector Diagnosis—a Condensed Version. A Framework for Re-engineering the Education Sector.* Online, https://planipolis.iiep.unesco.org/sites/default/files/ressources/nigeria_educati on_sector_diagnosis.pdf (Last accessed October 27, 2021).

FME (Federal Ministry of Education). 2007. *Federal Ministry of Education 10 Year Strategic Plan, Draft 8 05 March 2007.* Online , http://planipolis.iiep.unesco.org /sites/planipolis/files/ressources/nigeria_10_year_federal_education_plan_dra ft.pdf (Last accessed October 27, 2021).

FME (Federal Ministry of Education). 2008. *The Development of Education: National Report by the Federal Ministry of Education for the Forty-Eighth Session of the International Conference on Education (ICE), Theme: Inclusive Education: The Way of the Future, Geneva, Switzerland 25–28 November, 2008.* Online, http://www.ibe.un esco.org/fileadmin/user_upload/archive/National_Reports/ICE_2008/nigeria _NR08.pdf (Last accessed October 27, 2021).

FME (Federal Ministry of Education). 2009. *Tips on Inclusive Education (Leaflet).* Hardcopy.

FME (Federal Ministry of Education). 2010. *Training Manual on Adaptation and Implementation of Inclusive Education in Nigeria.* Hardcopy.

FME (Federal Ministry of Education). 2012a. *4-Year Strategic Plan for the Development of the Education Sector.* Hardcopy.

FME (Federal Ministry of Education). 2012b. *2012 Implementation Report of the 4-Year Strategic Development Plan for the Education Sector.* Hardcopy.

FME (Federal Ministry of Education). 2015. *Education for All—a Collective Responsibility. Nigeria EFA Review Report 2000–2014. Strides and Milestones.* Online, http://unesdoc.unesco.org/images/0023/002310/231081e.pdf (Last accessed October 27, 2021).

FME (Federal Ministry of Education). 2016. *National Policy on Inclusive Education in Nigeria (Draft)*. Softcopy.

FME (Federal Ministry of Education). n.d.. *Implementation Plan for Special Needs Education Strategy*. Hardcopy.

FMWA (Federal Ministry of Women Affairs and Social Development). 2011. *Report of the National Baseline Survey in Persons with Disabilities (PWDs) in Nigeria, Funded by the Millennium Development Goals (MDGs) Office, with Statistical Support from the National Bureau of Statistics (NBS)*. Softcopy.

FRN (Federal Republic of Nigeria). 2004a. *Compulsory, Free Universal Basic Education Act*. Online, http://www.unesco.org/education/edurights/media/docs/7b dbc8b2a9a9188909f3ed44baf5392c3b68f844.pdf (Last accessed October 27, 2021).

FRN (Federal Republic of Nigeria). 2004b. *National Policy on Education, 4th Edition*. Hardcopy.

FRN (Federal Republic of Nigeria). 2009. *National Report Submitted in Accordance with Paragraph 15 (A) of the Annex to Human Rights Council Resolution 5/1. Nigeria*. UN Document A/HRC/WG.6/4/NGA/1.

FRN (Federal Republic of Nigeria). 2013a. *National Policy on Education, 6th Edition*. Softcopy.

FRN (Federal Republic of Nigeria). 2013b. *National Report Submitted in Accordance with Paragraph 5 of the Annex to Human Rights Council Resolution 16/21. Nigeria*. UN Document A/HRC/WG.6/17/NGA/1.

FRN (Federal Republic of Nigeria). 2015. *Nigeria 2015 Millennium Development Goals End-Point Report*. Online, https://planipolis.iiep.unesco.org/sites/default/files/ressources/nigeria_mdgs_report_2015_abridged_version.pdf (Last accessed October 27, 2021).

FRN (Federal Republic of Nigeria). 2018. *Discrimination against Persons with Disabilities (Prohibition) Act, 2018*. Softcopy and online, https://www.hrw.org/news/2019/01/25/nigeria-passes-disability-rights-law (Last accessed October 27, 2021).

FRN (Federal Republic of Nigeria). n.d. *National Action Plan (NAP) for Implementation of the UBE Programme to Achieve Education for All (EFA) and the Millennium Development Goals by 2015*. Hardcopy.

GPE (Global Partnership for Education Nigeria). 2013. *Federal Republic of Nigeria: Appraisal of Education Sector Plans of Five States of the North West Region*. Online, http://www.globalpartnership.org/content/appraisal-education-sector-plans-5-states-nigeria (Last accessed October 27, 2021).

Guar, N. & Ivom, D. (2010). *Ability in DisABILITY: A Handbook on Understanding Disability*. Abuja: Yaliam Press Limited.

House of Representatives, Federal Republic of Nigeria. 2008. *A Bill for an Act to Ensure Full Integration of Nigerians with Disability into the Society and to Establish a National Commission for Persons with Disability and Vest it with the Responsibilities* for *Their Education, Health Care and the Protection of Their Social, Economic, Civil and Political Rights*. Sponsors: Hon. Abike Dabiri and *17* other Hon. Softcopy.

ICD (International Conference on Disability). 2015. *Communique from the International Conference on Disability, Held on: 22nd–25th June, 2015 @ The Civic Centre Ozumba Mbadiwe Road Victoria Island, Lagos*. Softcopy and online, http://www .iabc-nigeria.com/wp-content/uploads/2015/09/ICD-Communique.pdf (Last accessed August 29, 2016).

JONAPWD (Joint National Association of Persons with Disabilities). 2012. *Memorandum Submitted to the National Assembly on Review of the 1999 Constitution of the Federal Republic of Nigeria*. Softcopy.

Minister of Education. 2008. *Nigeria. Inclusive Education: Public Policies*. Message to the International Conference on Education, 48th session, 25–28 November 2008 "Inclusive Education: The Way of the Future." Online, http://www.ibe .unesco.org/fileadmin/user_upload/Policy_Dialogue/48th_ICE/Messages/nig eria_MIN08.pdf (Last accessed October 27, 2021).

National Technical Working Group on Education. 2009. *Report of the Vision 2020 National Technical Working Group on Education*. Softcopy and online, https://de .scribd.com/document/245069453/Report-of-the-Vision-2020-National-Tec hnical-Working-Group-on-Education-Sector-in-Nigeria (Last accessed October 27, 2021).

NHRC (National Human Rights Commission). n.d.. *Response of the National Human Rights Commission of Nigeria to the Implementation of Article 33 of the Convention on the Rights of Persons with Disabilities*. Online, http://www2.ohchr.org/engli sh/issues/disability/docs/NigeriaHumanRightsCommission.doc (Last accessed October 27, 2021).

Permanent Mission of Nigeria to the United Nations. 2013. *Statement by Ambassador Usman Sarki at the Sixth Session of Conference of States Parties to the Convention on the Rights of Person's with Disabilities (COSP 6) on Agenda Item 5A: General Debate*. Softcopy.

Permanent Mission of Nigeria to the United Nations. 2014. *Statement by Dr. Habiba M. Lawal, Permanent Secretary Federal Ministry of Women Affairs and Social Development at the Seventh Session of Conference of States Parties to the Convention on the Rights of Persons with Disabilities on General Debate New York, 10–12 June 2014*. Softcopy.

The Senate, Federal Republic of Nigeria (2013). *A Bill for an Act to Ensure Full Integration of Persons with Disabilities into the Society and to Establish a National Commission for Persons with Disabilities and Vest it with the Responsibilities for Their Education, Health Care and the Protection of their Social, Economic, Civil Rights. Sponsored by Senator Nurudeen Abatemi-Usman*. Softcopy.

Special Interest Group for Persons with Disability. 2009. *Report of the Vision 2020 Special Interest Group for Persons with Disability*. Hardcopy.

UBEC (Universal Basic Education Commission). n.d. *Universal Basic Education Commission Standard Action Plan*. Online, http://planipolis.iiep.unesco.org/uplo

ad/Nigeria/Nigeria_ube_standard_action_plan.pdf (Last accessed October 27, 2021).

UNESCO (United Nations Educational, Scientific and Cultural Organization). 2008. *UNESCO National Education Support Strategy (UNESS) for Nigeria 2006–2015*. Online, https://unesdoc.unesco.org/ark:/48223/pf0000183136 (Last accessed October 27, 2021).

UNICEF (United Nations Children's Fund), and FME (Federal Ministry of Education). 2012. *All Children in School by 2015, Global Initiative on Out-of-School Children, Nigeria Country Study*. Online, https://unesdoc.unesco.org/ark:/48223/pf0000225788 (Last accessed October 27, 2021).

Corpus Germany

ASD (Allgemeiner Schulleitungsverband Deutschlands). 2011. *Stellungnahme des ASD Allgemeiner Schulleitungsverband Deutschlands e.V. zum Entwurf der KMK zu "Inklusive Bildung von Kindern und Jugendlichen mit Behinderungen in Schulen."* Online, https://www.schulleitungsverbaende.de/stellungnahmen/23-stellungn ahme-des-asd-allgemeiner-schulleitungsverband-deutschlands-e-v-zum-entw urf-der-kmk-zu-inklusive-bildung-von-kindern-und-jugendlichen-mit-behind erungen-in-schulen (Last accessed October 27, 2021).

Behindertenbeauftragte (Beauftragte für die Belange von Menschen mit Behinderungen von Bund und Ländern). 2014. *Stuttgarter Erklärung der Beauftragten für die Belange von Menschen mit Behinderungen von Bund und Ländern zum Recht auf inklusive schulische Bildung vom 14. November 2014*. Online, https://innen.hessen .de/sites/default/files/media/stuttgarter_erklaerung_vom_14.11.2014.pdf (Last accessed April 3, 2021).

BMAS (Bundesministerium für Arbeit und Soziales). 2011a. *Unser Weg in eine inklusive Gesellschaft: Der Nationale Aktionsplan der Bundesregierung zur Umsetzung der UN-Behindertenrechtskonvention*. Online, https://www.bmas.de/DE/Service/Pu blikationen/a740-aktionsplan-bundesregierung.html (Last accessed October 27, 2021).

BMAS (Bundesministerium für Arbeit und Soziales). 2011b. *Übereinkommen der Vereinten Nationen über Rechte von Menschen mit Behinderungen: Erster Staatenbericht der Bundesrepublik Deutschland. Vom Bundeskabinett beschlossen am 3. August 2011*. Online, https://www.bmas.de/SharedDocs/Downloads/DE/staatenberi cht-2011.pdf?__blob=publicationFile&v=1 (Last accessed October 27, 2021).

BMAS (Bundesministerium für Arbeit und Soziales). 2014. *Beantwortung der Fragen aus der "List of Issues" im Zusammenhang mit der ersten deutschen Staatenprüfung*. Online, http://www.gemeinsam-einfach-machen.de/SharedDocs/Downl oads/DE/AS/UN_BRK/LOI.pdf?__blob=publicationFile&v=3 (Last accessed October 27, 2021).

BRK-Allianz (Alliance of German Non-Governmental Organizations Regarding the UN Convention on the Rights of Persons with Disabilities). 2013. *For Independent Living, Equal Rights, Accessibility and Inclusion! First Civil Society Report on* the *Implementation of the UN Convention on the Rights of Persons with Disabilities in Germany.* Online, http://www.brk-allianz.de/attachments/article/93/Altern ative_Report_German_CRPD_Alliance_final.pdf (Last accessed October 27, 2021).

BRK-Allianz (Alliance of German Non-Governmental Organizations Regarding the UN Convention on the Rights of Persons with Disabilities). 2015. *Response from the German CRPD Alliance (BRK-Allianz) to List of Issues (CRPD/C/ DEU/Q/1) in Relation to the Initial Report of Germany.* Online, http://www.brk -allianz.de/attachments/article/104/EN-Response%20from%20the%20Germ an%20CRPD%20Alliance%20to%20LoI_FINAL.doc (Last accessed October 27, 2021).

Bundestag, and Bundesrat. 2008. *Gesetz zu dem Übereinkommen der Vereinten Nationen vom 13. Dezember 2006 über die Rechte von Menschen mit Behinderungen sowie zu dem Fakultativprotokoll vom 13. Dezember 2006 zum Übereinkommen der Vereinten Nationen über die Rechte von Menschen mit Behinderungen vom 21. Dezember 2008.* Online, http://www.bgbl.de/xaver/bgbl/start.xav?startbk=Bu ndesanzeiger_BGBl&jumpTo=bgbl208s1419.pdf (Last accessed October 27, 2021).

Bundesvereinigung Lebenshilfe. 2011. *Gemeinsames Leben braucht Gemeinsames Lernen in der Schule: Positionspapier.* Online, https://www.lebenshilfe.de/wData /downloads/themen-recht/empfehlung/Gemeinsames-Leben-braucht-gemein sames-Lernen-neu.pdf (Last accessed November 6, 2016).

Bundesvereinigung Lebenshilfe. 2012. *Stellungnahme der Bundesvereinigung Lebenshilfe für Menschen mit geistiger Behinderung e. V. zu den Empfehlungen "Inklusive Bildung von Kindern und Jugendlichen mit Behinderungen in Schulen" der Kultusministerkonferenz vom 20.10.2011.* Online, https://www.lebenshilfe.de/de/them en-recht/artikel/StellungnahmenBVLH.php?listLink=1NaN&pageId3bcc26 7f=5 (Last accessed November 6, 2016).

BuReg (Bundesregierung). 2008. *Denkschrift zum Übereinkommen der VN über die Rechte von Menschen mit Behinderungen.* Bundestags-Drucksache 16/10808. Online, http://dip21.bundestag.de/dip21/btd/16/108/1610808.pdf (Last accessed October 27, 2021).

BuReg (Bundesregierung). 2014a. *Unterrichtung durch die Bundesregierung: Nationaler Bildungsbericht—Bildung in Deutschland 2014 und Stellungnahme der Bundesregierung. Bundestags-Drucksache 18/2990.* Online, http://dipbt.bundestag.de /doc/btd/18/029/1802990.pdf (Last accessed October 27, 2021).

BuReg (Bundesregierung). 2014b. *Antwort der Bundesregierung auf die Kleine Anfrage der Abgeordneten Özcan Mutlu, Kai Gehring, Corinna Rüffer, weiterer Abgeordneter und der Fraktion BÜNDNIS 90/DIE GRÜNEN—Drucksache 18/2886—Stand und Perspektive schulischer Inklusion.* Bundestags-Drucksache 18/3101. Online, http://dipbt.bundestag.de/doc/btd/18/031/1803101.pdf (Last accessed October 27, 2021).

DBR (Deutscher Behindertenrat). 2011. *Schriftliche Stellungnahme zur öffentli-*

chen Anhörung von Sachverständigen in Berlin am 17. Oktober 2011: Nationaler Aktionsplan zur Umsetzung der UN-Behindertenrechtskonvention. Bundestags-Ausschussdrucksache 17(11)664. Online, http://webarchiv.bundestag.de/cgi/sh ow.php?fileToLoad=2962&id=1223 (Last accessed June 1, 2017).

DBR (Deutscher Behindertenrat). 2015. *6. Sitzung des Hochrangigen Beteiligungs-verfahrens BTHG—Positionen der DBR-Verbände zum Thema Inklusive Bildung (einschließlich Hochschulen)*. Online, https://www.vdk.de/deutscher-behinderten rat/mime/00087508D1425637604.pdf (Last accessed October 27, 2021).

Deutscher Caritasverband. 2011. *Schriftliche Stellungnahme zur öffentlichen Anhörung von Sachverständigen in Berlin am 17. Oktober 2011: Nationaler Aktionsplan zur Umsetzung der UN-Behindertenrechtskonvention. Bundestags-Ausschussdrucksache 17(11)652*. Online, http://webarchiv.bundestag.de/cgi/show.php?fileToLoad= 2962&id=1223 (Last accessed June 1, 2017).

DGB (Deutscher Gewerkschaftsbund). 2011. *Stellungnahme des Deutschen Gewerk-schaftsbundes (DGB): Nationaler Aktionsplan der Bundesregierung zur Umsetzung des UN-Übereinkommens über die Rechte von Menschen mit Behinderung*. Online, https://www.dgb.de/themen/++co++ab31dc08-8081-11e0-4f40-00188b4dc422 (Last accessed October 27, 2021).

DGB (Deutscher Gewerkschaftsbund). 2015. *Gemeinsam statt getrennt— gewerkschaftliche Kriterien für die Entwicklung inklusiver Schulen*. Online, https:// schule.dgb.de/++co++1e6920ce-adf5-11e4-99de-52540023ef1a (Last accessed October 27, 2021).

DIMR (Deutsches Institut für Menschenrechte). 2011a. *Stellungnahme der Monitoring-Stelle: Eckpunkte zur Verwirklichung eines inklusiven Bildungssystems (Primarstufe und Sekundarstufen I und II). Empfehlungen an die Länder, die Kultus-ministerkonferenz (KMK) und den Bund*. Online, https://www.institut-fuer-men schenrechte.de/fileadmin/_migrated/tx_commerce/stellungnahme_der_moni toring_stelle_eckpunkte_z_verwirklichung_eines_inklusiven_bildungssystems _31_03_2011.pdf (Last accessed October 27, 2021).

DIMR (Deutsches Institut für Menschenrechte). 2011b. *Stellungnahme zum Natio-nalen Aktionsplan der Bundesregierung anlässlich der Anhörung im Deutschen Bund-estag am 17. Oktober 2011*. Online, https://www.institut-fuer-menschenrech te.de/fileadmin/user_upload/Publikationen/Stellungnahmen/stellungnahme _zum_nationalen_aktionsplan_der_bundesregierung_17_10_2011.pdf (Last accessed October 27, 2021).

DIMR (Deutsches Institut für Menschenrechte). 2014. *Submission of the National CRPD Monitoring Body of Germany to the CRPD Committee on the Rights of Persons with Disabilities on the Occasion of the Preparation of a List of Issues by the Committee in the Review of Germany's Initial Report in 2014*. Online, http://tbinternet.ohchr .org/Treaties/CRPD/Shared%20Documents/DEU/INT_CRPD_IFL_DEU _16940_E.doc (Last accessed October 27, 2021).

DIMR (Deutsches Institut für Menschenrechte). 2015. *Parallelbericht an den UN-Fachausschuss für die Rechte von Menschen mit Behinderungen anlässlich der Prüfung des ersten Staatenberichts Deutschlands gemäß Artikel 35 der UN-Behindertenrechtskonvention.* Online, https://www.institut-fuer-menschenrech te.de/fileadmin/Redaktion/Publikationen/Parallelbericht/Parallelbericht_an _den_UN-Fachausschuss_fuer_Rechte_Menschen_mit_Behinderungen_Pruef ung_1_Staatenbericht.pdf (Last accessed October 27, 2021).

DL (Deutscher Lehrerverband). 2012. *Bildung in Deutschland—Diagnosen und Perspektiven des Deutschen Lehrerverbandes.* Online, https://www.lehrerverband.de /bildung-in-deutschland/ (Last accessed October 27, 2021).

DL (Deutscher Lehrerverband). 2013. *Positionspapier "Inklusion".* Online, http:// www.lehrerverband.de/Inklusion%20DL%202013.pdf (Last accessed November 6, 2016).

DPhV (Deutscher Philologenverband). 2010a. *Position des Deutschen Philologenverbands zum Thema "Inklusion".* Online, https://www.dphv.de/wp-content/uploa ds/2020/08/2010-Positionspapier_Inklusion_Bildungspoltische-Forderungen .pdf (Last accessed October 27, 2021).

DPhV (Deutscher Philologenverband). 2010b. *DPhV-Positionspapier zur Schulstrukturfrage.* Online, https://www.dphv.de/wp-content/uploads/2020/08/20 10-PositionspapierSchulstruktur.pdf (Last accessed October 27, 2021).

DPhV (Deutscher Philologenverband). 2011. *8 Thesen des DPhV zur Struktur und Qualität von Schulen und Abschlüssen.* Online, https://www.dphv.de/wp-content /uploads/2020/08/2011-Schule-und-Schulstruktur.pdf (Last accessed October 27, 2021).

DPhV (Deutscher Philologenverband). 2012. *Berufspolitische Forderungen des DPhV zur Durchführung der Inklusion in den Gymnasien.* Online, https://www.dphv.de /wp-content/uploads/2020/08/2012-Positionspapier_Inklusion_Berufspolitisc he-Forderungen.pdf (Last accessed October 27, 2021).

DPOs (Disabled Persons Organizations). 2010a. *Positionierung der Verbände zum Entwurf der KMK- Empfehlungen "Kinder und Jugendliche mit Behinderungen in Schulen" (Stand 6. August 2010).* Online, https://www.vdk.de/deutscher-behind ertenrat/mime/00064313D1308307730.pdf (Last accessed October 27, 2021).

DPOs (Disabled Persons Organizations) 2010b. *Beurteilung des KMK-Positionspapiers zu pädagogischen und rechtlichen Aspekten inklusiver Bildung nach Art. 24 BRK im Bereich schulischer Bildung aus Sicht behinderter Menschen und ihrer Verbände.* Online, https://www.vdk.de/deutscher-behindertenrat/mime /00060664D1276175808.pdf (Last accessed October 27, 2021).

DPOs (Disabled Persons Organizations). 2011a. *Stellungnahme der Verbände zu den KMK-Empfehlungen "Inklusive Bildung von Kindern und Jugendlichen mit Behinderungen in Schulen" vom 3.12.2010.* Online, https://www.vdk.de/deutscher-be hindertenrat/mime/00064313D1308307730.pdf (Last accessed October 27, 2021).

DPOs (Disabled Persons Organizations). 2011b. *Verbändeübergreifende Positionierung anlässlich der KMK-Amtschefkonferenz am 15. September 2011 zu den KMK-Empfehlungen "Inklusive Bildung von Kindern und Jugendlichen mit Behinderungen in Schulen" (Stand 17. Juni 2011).* Online, http://www.sovd.de/fileadmin/dow

nloads/pdf/stellungnahmen/TTTTStN_Verbaende_zur_Amtschefkonferenz
_mit_Logos_2011-8-31.pdf (Last accessed April 6, 2021).
DUK (Deutsche UNESCO Kommission). 2011. *Inklusive Bildung in Deutsch-land stärken, Resolution der 71. Hauptversammlung der Deutschen UNESCO-Kommission, Berlin, 24. Juni 2011.* Online, https://www.unesco.de/bildung/in
klusive-bildung/inklusive-bildung-deutschland/inklusive-bildung-deutschland
-staerken (Last accessed October 27, 2021).
DUK (Deutsche UNESCO Kommission). 2014. *Bonner Erklärung zur inklusiven Bildung.* Online, https://www.unesco.de/sites/default/files/2018-08/DUK_Bo
nner%20Erkl%C3%A4rung_2014.pdf (Last accessed October 27, 2021).
DVfR (Deutsche Vereinigung für Rehabilitation). 2011. *Schriftliche Stellungnahme zur öffentlichen Anhörung von Sachverständigen in Berlin am 17. Oktober 2011: Nationaler Aktionsplan zur Umsetzung der UN-Behindertenrechtskonvention. Bundestags-Ausschussdrucksache 17(11)658.* Online, http://webarchiv.bundestag
.de/cgi/show.php?fileToLoad=2962&id=1223 (Last accessed June 1, 2017).
FRG (Federal Republic of Germany). 2013. *Initial Report of Germany Submitted according to Article 35 of the CRPD.* UN Document CRPD/C/DEU/1.
Gemeinsam Leben Gemeinsam Lernen. 2015. *Eingabe an den UN Fachausschuss Bildung.* Online, http://www.gemeinsamleben-gemeinsamlernen.de/sites/all
/themes/skeletontheme/css//UN%20Fachausschuss%20M%C3%A4rz%2020
15.pdf (Last accessed November 6, 2016).
Germany. 2015. *German Statement concerning the Draft General Comment on Article 24 CRPD.* Online, http://www.ohchr.org/Documents/HRBodies/CRPD/GC
/RighttoEducation/Germany.pdf (Last accessed October 27, 2021).
GEW (Gewerkschaft Erziehung und Bildung). 2011. *GEW—Stellungnahme im Rahmen der schriftlichen Anhörung zum KMK-Entwurf zur Überarbeitung der "Empfehlungen zur sonderpädagogischen Förderung in den Schulen in der Bundesrepublik Deutschland".* Online, https://www.gew.de/index.php?eID=dumpFile&t
=f&f=24142&token=08a6689ee6a93f095fd56be885e2069c14d64253&sdownl
oad=&n=GEW_Stellungnahme_Empfehlungen_sopaed_KmK_HV_Beschlus
s1.pdf (Last accessed October 27, 2021).
KMK (Kultusministerkonferenz). 2010. *Pädagogische und rechtliche Aspekte der Umsetzung des Übereinkommens der Vereinten Nationen vom 13. Dezember 2006 über die Rechte von Menschen mit Behinderungen in der schulischen Bildung: Beschluss der Kultusministerkonferenz vom 18.11.2010.* Online, http://www.kmk.org/filea
dmin/Dateien/veroeffentlichungen_beschluesse/2010/2010_11_18-Behindert
enrechtkonvention.pdf (Last accessed October 27, 2021).
KMK (Kultusministerkonferenz). 2011. *Inklusive Bildung von Kindern und Jugendli-chen mit Behinderungen in Schulen: Beschluss der Kultusministerkonferenz vom 20.10.2011.* Online, http://www.kmk.org/fileadmin/Dateien/veroeffentlichu
ngen_beschluesse/2011/2011_10_20-Inklusive-Bildung.pdf (Last accessed on October 27, 2021).
KMK (Kultusministerkonferenz). 2014. *Standards für die Lehrerbildung: Bildung-swissenschaften (Beschluss der Kultusministerkonferenz vom 16.12.2004 i. d. F. vom*

12.06.2014). Online, http://www.akkreditierungsrat.de/fileadmin/Seiteninhal
te/KMK/Vorgaben/KMK_Lehrerbildung_Standards_Bildungswissenschaften
_aktuell.pdf (Last accessed November 6, 2020).

KMK (Kultusministerkonferenz), and HRK (Hochschulrektorenkonferenz). 2015.
*Lehrerbildung für eine Schule der Vielfalt / Englisch Version: Educating Teachers to
Embrace Diversity. Joint Recommendations by the German Rectors' Conference and
the Standing Conference of the Ministers of Education and Cultural Affairs of the
States in the Federal Republic of Germany (Resolution Passed by the Standing Conference of the Ministers of Education and Cultural Affairs of the States in the Federal
Republic of Germany.* Online, http://www.kmk.org/fileadmin/Dateien/veroeffen
tlichungen_beschluesse/2015/2015_03_12-KMK-HRK-Empfehlung-Vielfalt
-englisch.pdf (Last accessed October 27, 2021).

Minister of Education. 2008. *International Conference on Education, 48th session, 25–
28 November 2008 "Inclusive Education: The Way of the Future" Germany Ute
Erdsiek-Rave Minister for Education and Women's Affairs of the Land of Schleswig-
Holstein.* Online, http://www.ibe.unesco.org/fileadmin/user_upload/Policy_Di
alogue/48th_ICE/Messages/germany_MIN08.pdf (Last accessed October 27,
2021).

Netzwerk Artikel 3. 2010. *Schattenübersetzung des NETZWERK ARTIKEL 3 e.V.
Korrigierte Fassung der zwischen Deutschland, Liechtenstein, Österreich und der Schweiz abgestimmten Übersetzung, Übereinkommen über die Rechte von Menschen mit
Behinderungen.* Online, http://www.netzwerk-artikel-3.de/dokum/schattenueb
ersetzung-endgs.pdf (Last accessed October 27, 2021).

SoVD (Sozialverband Deutschland. 2011a. *Stellungnahme zum Nationalen
Aktionsplan der Bundesregierung—"einfach machen" unser Weg in eine inklusive Gesellschaft—zur Umsetzung des Übereinkommens der Vereinten Nationen
über die Rechte von Menschen mit Behinderungen. Bundestags-Ausschussdrucksache
17(11)553.* Online, https://www.sovd.de/fileadmin/downloads/pdf/stellungna
hmen/999-SoVD_Stellungnahme_NAP_Bundestag_9-2011.pdf (Last accessed
April 6, 2021).

SoVD (Sozialverband Deutschland) 2011b. *Stellungnahme des SoVD zum Ersten
Staatenbericht Deutschland zur Umsetzung der UN-Behindertenrechtskonvention.*
Online, https://www.sovd.de/fileadmin/downloads/pdf/stellungnahmen/XXX
-Stellungnahme_Staatenbericht_06-2011.pdf (Last accessed on April 6, 2021).

SoVD (Sozialverband Deutschland). 2015. *CRPD-General Comment on Article 24
(Right to Inclusive Education): Written Statement.* Online, https://www.sovd.de/fi
leadmin//downloads/pdf/stellungnahmen/2015-2-19-Stellungnahme_Art__24
_CRPD_General_Comment_2015doc.pdf (Last accessed April 6, 2021).

VBE (Verband Bildung und Erziehung). 2009. *Diskussionspapier zur Umsetzung der
UN-Konvention, Art. 24 (Inklusion).* Online, http://www.vbe.de/meinung/positi
onen/inklusion.html (Last accessed May 11, 2017).

VDS (Verband Sonderpädagogik). 2011. *Schulische Bildung von Kindern und
Jugendlichen mit schwersten Behinderungen: Positionen.* Online, http://www.verba

nd-sonderpaedagogik.de/upload/pdf/Positionen/Schwerstbehinderte_Neuaufl
age_2012.pdf (Last accessed October 27, 2021).

VDS (Verband Sonderpädagogik). 2012. *Leitlinien.* Online, http://www.verband
-sonderpaedagogik.de/upload/pdf/Positionen/Leitlinien_September_2012.pdf
(Last accessed October 27, 2021).

VDS (Verband Sonderpädagogik). 2013. *Inklusion braucht Professionalität—Teilhabe
gemeinsam gestalten.* Online, http://www.verband-sonderpaedagogik.de/uplo
ad/pdf/Positionen/Inklusion_braucht_Professionalitt-politisches_Papier.pdf
(Last accessed October 27, 2021).

VDS (Verband Sonderpädagogik. 2014. *Berufsbild Sonderpädagoginnen und Sonderpädagogen in inklusiven Systemen.* Online, http://www.verband-sonderpaedago
gik.de/upload/pdf/Positionen/3-2014-_Positionspapier-Kurzform-_Berufsb
ild_Sonderpdagoginnen_verabschiedet.pdf (Last accessed October 27, 2021).

Notes

Chapter 2

1. In addition to being available and accessible, education must be acceptable—relevant, culturally appropriate, and of high quality—as well as adaptable—adjusting to social conditions and values as well as individual needs (CRPD 2016, paras. 25, 26). These four core elements of the right to education—availability, accessibility, acceptability, and adaptability—were first enshrined in the 1999 General Comment No. 13 to the International Covenant on Economic, Social and Cultural Rights (CESCR 1999). This framework provides indicators upon which the realization of the human right to education can be monitored.

2. Mainstream schools—synonymous with "general education," "regular schools," and "ordinary schools"—are defined as schools that "receive students with or without impairments" and are thus opposed to "'special schools' that only receive students with impairments" (OHCHR 2013, para. 4).

3. It is important to note that countries use different methods and terminology to collect and compile data on special and inclusive education, which limits their comparability (D`Alessio and Watkins 2009; D'Alessio and Cowan 2013). Nonetheless, these data indicate the relation that exists between diagnoses of special education needs and segregated or separated learning environments and are therefore important to report.

4. For this conceptualization, I conjoin insights from Scandinavian institutionalism and discursive institutionalism. Scandinavian institutionalism has brought the notion of translation into institutional analysis (Wæraas and Nielsen 2016, 237; Czarniawska and Sevón 1996). Research in this tradition focuses on the circulation and adaptation of (management) ideas in organizations, and their transformation into actions and objects (Sahlin and Wedlin 2008, 225; Czarniawska and Joerges 1996, 39–40). From this work, I take the assumption that "to set something in a new place is to construct it anew" (Czarniawska and Sevón 2005b, 8; also Czarniawska 2012, 27). On this ground, it is imperative for this analysis to highlight the "com-

plex process of negotiation during which meanings, claims and interests" about the education of disabled children "change and gain ground," especially in considering the global "program for change" (Wæraas and Nielsen 2016, 237). To explore these negotiations, I turn to discursive institutionalism (Schmidt 2008; 2011). Why? Because for ideas about inclusive education to be translated into actions, they must be first "communicated via discourse" (Schmidt 2010, 4). In discourses, actors "generate, deliberate and/or legitimize" ideas about (political) actions (Schmidt 2011, 47; see also Deborah Stone 2012, 12). In other words, discourses not only represent ideas, but are also the "interactive processes" by and through which ideas are "generated" and "conveyed" in the "policy sphere" (Schmidt 2015, 171; 2008, 309).

5. In the tradition of sociology of knowledge, the translational model of institutional change assumes that reality is socially constructed by actors who (re)produce knowledge about the social world, which is provided by and objectified in institutions (Berger and Luckmann [1966] 1984; Keller 2011; Keller et al. 2005). Social actors—individuals or groups of persons who mobilize resources to achieve goals (Angermuller 2014, 25–26)—construct social reality in and through social interactions that give meaning to the world. Transmitted through language, this meaning is stored in knowledge about why, where, and how to interact in the social world (Knoblauch 2001, 208).

6. To theoretically frame this translational model, I combine neoinstitutional theory with discourse analysis; specifically, insights from organizational institutionalism (Meyer and Rowan 1977) and a sociology-of-knowledge approach to discourse (Keller 2011, 2013b). Neoinstitutional theory is characterized by a variety of analytical approaches given its historical evolution and application in different analytical and empirical fields (see Scott 2008, chaps. 1 and 2; Senge 2011, chap. 2). Common to all approaches is the assumption that institutions form and shape the actions of social actors and that social actors, in turn, generate, maintain, and change these institutions (Koch and Schemmann 2009, 7). In social sciences, discourse analysis is characterized by a wide variety of approaches (Traue, Pfahl, and Schürmann 2014). Despite different foci, all approaches share an interest in the ways in which social realities or phenomena are constructed through communicative processes (Angermuller 2015, 510). The combination of institutional and discourse theory allows me to depict the discursive nature of translations and to elucidate their institutional sources and effects on the change of schooling.

I want to briefly discuss why I do not use Scandinavian or discursive institutionalism to develop this theoretical framework, even though I referenced these theories to conceptualize the travel of Article 24 UN CRPD as a discursive process of translation. Scandinavian institutionalism focuses on the translation of ideas into actions (Czarniawska and Sevón 2005a; also Sahlin and Wedlin 2008), and discursive institutionalism on the role of policy ideas in discourses (Schmidt 2008). To explain institutional change from a translational perspective, however, requires focusing on the institutional sources and effects of knowledge that policy actors discursively (re)produce. For that reason, the relation between discourses and the institutional environments they are embedded in needs to come to the fore. This relation can be analyzed by resorting to organizational institutionalism. This theory is criticized, though, as it "devote[s] too much effort to analyzing the trajectories of macro-diffusion patterns" and therefore "underestimat[es] the meaning the spreading practices have . . . and the modifications—translations—they undergo in the course of their 'travels'" (R. E. Meyer 2008, 521). To address this criticism, I have recourse to a sociology-of-knowledge approach to discourses (Keller 2011).

7. The empirical analyses require methods that are open and flexible enough to capture context specifics yet ensure the commensurability of case studies. The collection and analysis of data is therefore based on a combination of a sociology-of-knowledge approach to discourse and grounded theory (Keller 2013a, 2011; Charmaz 2014, 2013; Corbin and Strauss 2008; also Truschkat 2013).

A sociology-of-knowledge approach to discourse provides the conceptual frame for the discourse analyses given its focus on "processes and practices of the production and circulation of knowledge" (Keller 2013a, 63; 2011, 57). Grounded theory, on the other hand, provides "a method of qualitative inquiry" that gains its strength from instructing a "fluid, interactive, and open-ended" research process (Charmaz 2013, 293; 2014, 320). In this circular process, the constant comparison of data within and between cases is central and supported by different techniques such as coding, memo writing, and theoretical sampling. Coding refers to the segmentation of data, which are abstracted into categories through memo writing and further specified through theoretical sampling, i.e., the deliberate choice of data to be collected and/or analyzed. Then a theory is developed that is grounded in data. Combined, both approaches allow collecting and analyzing data in context-sensitive yet equivalent ways to reconstruct knowledge configurations that link the human right to inclusive education and its realization.

8. As institutional carriers, symbolic and relational systems can release coercive, normative, or mimetic pressures on discourses. Coercive pressures emanate if carriers act in the regulative pillar so that policy actors may feel it expedient to follow Article 24's reform mandate in talking about inclusive education. If carriers, on the other hand, act in the normative pillar, discourses are confronted with normative pressures. Policy actors may then feel obligated to comply with expectations generated by the organizational and professional standards of school systems. If carriers, however, act in the cultural-cognitive pillar, discourses are confronted with mimetic pressures; meaning policy actors may comply with taken-for-granted understandings of "good" schooling. If actors perceive their own school system as appropriate, they may therefore try to preserve as many features as possible. However, if they are not convinced of the qualities of their school system, policy actors may want to learn from other countries.

9. If discourses advance changes in the regulative pillar, the focus is on "rule-setting, monitoring or sanctioning activities" (Scott 2008, 52), e.g., new legislation or policies. In the normative pillar of schooling, on the other hand, changes aim at the values and norms that impose binding expectations about appropriate ways to school children and would thus affect the organizational and professional standards (Scott 2008, 54). If discourses target changes in the cultural-cognitive pillar of schooling, though, policy actors would modify common frameworks of understanding that constitute what is to be taken for granted in school systems (Scott 2008, 57), e.g., what it means in educational terms to be disabled—to be segregated from peers or to learn on an equal basis with others.

10. These pressures can stem from regulative rules, binding expectations, and/

or constitutive schemes (Suchman 1995, 574; Meyer and Rowan 1977, 349; Scott 2008, 51, 61). Based on these pressures, three mechanisms of isomorphic change are distinguished: a coercive mechanism based on political influence and legal sanctions, a normative mechanism emanating from social obligations, and a mimetic mechanism facilitated by shared understandings (DiMaggio and Powell 1983, 150; Scott 2008, 51).

Chapter 3

1. One of the first schools were the Methodist mission's Nursery of the Infant Child, founded in 1843 in Badagry (Fafunwa [1974] 2018, 79), and the Roman Catholic Grammar School, founded in 1844 in Lagos (Niven 1967, 283). One of the first special schools was the Topo Industrial School for Delinquent Children, founded in 1876 by the Roman Catholic mission, and a school for children with visual impairments, founded in 1915 by the Sudan United Mission (Andzayi 2003, 24; Obiakor and Offor 2011, 15; Fafunwa [1974] 2018, 92).

2. The restricted expansion of Western education to Northern Nigeria was further solidified by the British policy of indirect rule preserving sociopolitical structures in place (Falola 1999, 70–71).

3. In 1912–13, a total of fifty-nine government primary schools and ninety-one mission schools were established in the south. In contrast, only twelve government and twenty-seven mission schools were available in the north, but 19,073 Koranic schools (Fafunwa [1974] 2018, 97, 109–110).

4. For attendance numbers in colonial and missionary schools in the 1920s see Okonkwo and Ezeh 2008, 192–195.

5. I focus on the fourth edition of the NPE released in 2004 alongside the UBE Act, but include references to the 2013 sixth edition where appropriate. While collecting data in Nigeria, I only came across the fourth edition; no one I met mentioned or had copies of the two later editions. The only reference I found to the fifth edition was in reports or research papers (e.g., FME 2015). In addition, papers or studies published after the fifth and sixth editions were released often refer only to the fourth edition (Ajuwon 2012; IOM 2014; Asiwe and Omiegbe 2014).

6. In recent years, data on the number of out-of-school children have been inconsistent, though. For 2010, the number of 10.5 million children circulated widely (see, for example, Omoeva et al. 2013), but was eventually revised to 8.7 by the UNESCO Institute of Statistics in 2014 based on new population estimates (Ajikobi 2017; Motunrayo 2019).

7. The data for boys are Nigeria-specific, while the data for girls are the average for sub-Saharan Africa (UNESCO 2014).

8. This trend is further alleviated by international donors, resulting in a growing business of education across Africa (Mundy and Menashy 2014; Caerus Capital 2017).

9. The administrative responsibility for basic education in schools is shared between the three tiers of government. The federal government is involved in the implementation of UBE through its Federal Ministry of Education (FME) and the Universal Basic Education Commission (UBEC). A parastatal established in 2004 under the FME, the UBEC coordinates the implementation of UBE across Nigerian states by managing the UBE fund into which 2 percent of the federal govern-

ment's Consolidated Revenue Fund is channeled (Amoo 2019; also Constitution of the Federal Republic of Nigeria 1999, Chapter V [80]). This fund depends heavily on oil revenues, so that slumps in oil prices have a direct effect on the UBE fund (World Bank 2015, 45). Yet despite the deterioration of public schools across the nation, these grants remain largely unassessed, as they must be matched by chronically cash-strapped states (UBEC 2019). Two percent of the UBE fund is held in a so-called Special Education Intervention Fund (Amoo 2019).

The operational authority over basic education lies with the state and local governments. State ministries of education develop and implement policies, while the maintenance of public schools lies in the hand of their state universal basic education boards. They are responsible for the administration and management of basic education in schools, including fund allocation and teacher deployment (FME 2015, 44; World Bank 2015, 43). Local government education authorities, on the other hand, assess the need for teachers, manage school facilities and learners, and distribute funds (FME 2015, 44; World Bank 2015, 23; Nnamani 2015). The shared, and often overlapping responsibilities, come with several challenges, including inflated bureaucracies, rivalry between actors across levels, and difficulties in estimating the total amount of expenditures (World Bank 2015, 22, 37).

10. Two of these documents were included after the initial analysis due to their importance for the discourse on inclusive education: the 2016 Draft Policy on Inclusive Education (FME 2016) and the 2018 Discrimination against Persons with Disabilities (Prohibition) Act (FRN 2018).

11. Given the realities of exclusion from education in public schools, this comprehensive structure is, however, practically stratified in two dimensions: first, based on children's (in)ability to access formal basic education in schools and, second, based on families' socioeconomic capacity to circumvent the state school system. For that reason, I see the need to also account for the distinction between regular and special schools as well as public and private schools.

12. The Federal Ministry of Education reports that the number of nomadic primary schools rose from 1,981 to 2,354 between 2004 and 2006 (FME 2008, ii). Another paper states that 1,680 nomadic schools were available in 2002 (Muhammad and Mohammed 2005, 26). In 2013, the number of Koranic/Islamic schools reported is 3,938, half of which follow an Islamic education curriculum and 45 percent the National Basic Education Curriculum (World Bank 2015, 22, 133).

13. Even though gifted and talented children are also mentioned as a special group to receive special-needs education, documents and interviewees hardly refer to them. For that reason, no subdiscourse could be identified for this group, so they are not included in the further analysis.

14. Similarly, the 2013 NPE stipulates the provision of various assistive devices, however without using the term "inclusive education" any longer (FRN 2013a, para. 122).

15. According the Disability Act, special facilities mean "any provision whether movable or immovable that enhances easy access and enjoyment in public buildings by persons with disabilities [i.e., a person who has] significantly decreased endurance so that he cannot perform his everyday routine, living and working without significantly increased hardship and vulnerability to everyday obstacles and hardships" (FRN 2018, para. 57; similarly The Senate 2013, para. 61).

16. As of 2020, several bills were before the National Assembly concerned with the establishment of teacher-training facilities, including Federal Colleges of Education (Special) in Birnin Kudu (Jigawa State) (HB. 169), Afon (Kwara State) (SB. 226), and Onueke Ezza South (Ebonyi State) (SB. 352) as well as a Federal University (Special) Oyo Town (SB. 363) (PLAC n.d.b).

17. Domestication, in accordance with Section 12 of the 1999 constitution, requires additional legislation. The National Assembly has to adopt a bill in order to make an international treaty effective in Nigeria (Egede 2007; Olutoyin 2014).

18. The latter include, for example, the power to "purchase or acquire any assets, business or property considered necessary for the proper conduct of its functions" (FRN 2018, para. 39(1), lit. b) and the power to "accept gift of land, money or other property on such terms and conditions, if any, as may be specified by the person or organisation making the gift, provided such terms and conditions are not inconsistent with any prevailing law" (FRN 2018, para. 46(1)). The commission is led by a governing council, whose members are "a part time chairman," "one person with disability from each geopolitical zone," and representatives from several federal ministries, including "Education, Health, Sports, Woman Affairs, Housing, Transport, Environment, Labour and Productivity, Justice and Finance" and, eventually, representatives from the National Human Rights Commission and National Planning Commission (FRN 2018, para. 32).

Chapter 4

1. The first state-funded school in the world for children who are hard of hearing was founded in 1778 in Leipzig (Sächsische Landesschule 2021), the first school for blind pupils in 1806 in Berlin (Zeune Schule 2021).

2. In addition, so-called selection schools (*Ausleseschulen*) were established to educate an elite in the National Socialist sense (Gelhaus and Hülter 2003); e.g., Adolf Hitler Schools (*Adolf-Hitler-Schulen*) (Feller and Feller 2001) and National Political Institutes of Education (*Nationalpolitische Erziehungsanstalten*) (C. Schneider, Stillke, and Leinweber 1996).

3. In addition, a system of specialized schools (*Spezialschulen*) was available to provide education for highly gifted children to hone their skills in music, sport, the Russian language, and the natural sciences (Anweiler 1988, 90–91).

4. Germany's Basic Law (*Grundgesetz*) guarantees the cultural sovereignty of each of the sixteen federal states (*Länder*), so that they may have the legislative and administrative prerogative in matters of education. Therefore, there is not one federal school law, but sixteen different state school laws, effectively resulting in sixteen different school systems. To maintain the unity of the school system, the ministers of education and cultural affairs of the states have formed a standing conference (*Kultusministerkonferenz* [KMK]) to set out common policy frameworks (KMK 2021). The transformation of these frameworks into state laws depends on the political priorities and legislative processes in each of the states. Accordingly, the state ministries of education have the highest legal authority over their respective school systems, which are supervised by school administrations in each state and managed by the local authorities (*Kommunen*). With regard to the UN CRPD implementation, this fact implies that each federal state has to develop an inclusive school system individually and without federal financial support.

5. Regarding the regular school system, reforms were triggered by the poor performance of German students in international comparative studies, which was below average in the 2000 Program for International Student Assessment (PISA). The so-called PISA shock exposed the close correlation between socioeconomic background and unequal educational performance in the German school system (Roeder 2003; Klemm and Roitsch 2015). In reaction, several federal states closed lower secondary schools (*Hauptschulen*) and transferred them into mid-level secondary schools (*Realschulen*); higher secondary schools (*Gymnasium*), however, were not affected by any changes (Helbig and Nikolai 2015, 99–103). In addition, common educational standards (IQB n.d.) were introduced as well as a biennial national education report (DIPF 2020).

6. However, regional variances exist. In 2014, the highest quota of children with special needs is reported for the state of Mecklenburg-Vorpommern (10.6 percent), the lowest for Rheinland Pfalz (5.6 percent) (Autorengruppe Bildungsberichterstattung 2016, 81).

7. Over the last decade, the number of children diagnosed as having a special need in the support area of "emotional and social development" has risen dramatically; their share among all special-needs children increased from 9.5 percent in 2005 to 16.1. percent in 2014, and 17.2 percent in 2018 (KMK 2016, XIV; 2020, XV).

8. The number of children with learning disabilities in special schools decreased over the last years. Again, huge regional disparities exist, with one of the highest rates of children in special schools in Baden Württemberg (71 percent), and one of the lowest in Bremen (23 percent) (Autorengruppe Bildungsberichterstattung 2016, 81).

9. Apart from the policy fields of education and disability, inclusive education and the UN CRPD implementation are also debated by policy actors with regard to international development cooperation. For example, the Federal Ministry for Economic Cooperation and Development (*Bundesministerium für wirtschaftliche Zusammenarbeit und Entwicklung*) issued an Action Plan for the Inclusion of Persons with Disabilities in 2013 (*Aktionsplan zur Inklusion von Menschen mit Behinderungen*) (BMZ 2013), which was replaced by a new strategy paper in 2019 (BMZ 2019). This process was likewise critically accompanied by civil society actors such as the Global Education Campaign (*Globale Bildungskampagne*, 2013) and VENRO (*Verband Entwicklungspolitik und Humanitäre Hilfe*, 2010), the umbrella organization of developmental and humanitarian nongovernmental organizations in Germany. Therefore, debates about inclusive education occur in two different federal policy arenas: one being education and disability, concerned with the UN CRPD's national implementation process, and one being development cooperation, concerned with its implementation in other countries. This parallelism of policy debates is evidenced in the federal government's 2014 overview of funded projects to realize inclusive education, which lists national and international initiatives that are largely unrelated (BuReg 2014b). Given the case study's focus on the influence of Article 24 on the change of Germany's school system, I did not collect data in the policy field of development cooperation. In Nigeria, in contrast, I did so, as development organizations are an integral part of domestic education policymaking.

10. "Diese Fehlübersetzung . . . , das war quasi ein Eigentor. . . . weil dadurch

der Diskurs angeheizt wurde, was ist eigentlich der Unterschied zwischen Integration und Inklusion. Und das hat echt das Bewusstsein stark befördert, dass es nicht ein und dasselbe ist" (G_2: 113–17).

11. "Grundlage inklusiver Bildung sind das gemeinsame Lernen und die gemeinsame Erziehung von Kindern und Jugendlichen mit und ohne Behinderungen" (KMK 2011, 7).

12. "Gemeinsames Aufwachsen und Lernen von jungen Menschen mit und ohne Behinderung in weiterhin die Ausnahme" (Gemeinsam Leben Gemeinsam Lernen 2015, 3).

13. "Wir haben ein sehr viel breiteres Verständnis, es geht um menschliche Vielfalt und Inklusion in die eine Gesellschaft, die Schulen müssen für Alle sein," (G_1: 465–68).

14. "Wir wollen uns konzentrieren, oder wir müssen uns konzentrieren auf Inklusion als . . . bei uns, in unserem Bereich, als Lernen von behinderten und nichtbehinderten Menschen, so. Weil, alles was man darüber hinaus noch, und das ist, mag alles sinnvoll und richtig sein, nur wenn wir nicht das fokusieren, dann verzettelt man sich" (G_6:159–62).

15. "Also speziell zu Bildung habe ich das Gefühl, dass bei uns so n Stopfen gezogen wurde. . . . Und mit der Konvention schwappte diese internationale Debatte, verknüpft an diese schlechte Übersetzung—Inklusion und Integration— faktisch nach Deutschland. Und es war für mich wie so ein Staudamm, der sozusagen jetzt sich ein Ventil verschafft hat abfließen zu können" (G_3: 405–11).

16. "Der Deutsche Philologenverband begrüßt die UN-Konvention und weist darauf hin, dass das deutsche Schulsystem dieser bereits jetzt in hohem Maße gerecht wird durch sein flächendeckendes Angebot mit einer sehr differenzierten, speziellen Förderung in Sonder- und Förderschulen für Menschen mit Behinderungen" (DPhV 2010, 3).

17. "Sonderpädagogische Förderung *in der integrativen Bildung* soll das Recht der behinderten und von Behinderung bedrohten Kinder und Jugendlichen auf eine ihren persönlichen Möglichkeiten entsprechende schulische Bildung und Erziehung verwirklichen" (BuReg 2008, 58).

18. "Im deutschen Schulwesen kommt der Förderschule eine besondere Funktion zu. Die Förderschulen sind auf spezifische sonderpädagogische Bildungs-, Beratungs- und Unterstützungsangebote spezialisiert" (BMAS 2011b, 54).

19. "Unsere Gesellschaft [muss] verschiedene Schularten, schulische Bildungsgänge und schulische Abschlüsse anbieten . . . , um auf das weite Spektrum der individuellen Begabungen und der unterschiedlichen gesellschaftlichen Anforderungen differenziert zu reagieren und Schule und Arbeitsmarkt nicht zu entkoppeln" (DPhV 2011, 2).

20. "Dieses sowieso schon sehr strukturierte und gegliederte Schulwesen wurde sozusagen, ich sag jetzt mal, bereichert durch das Sonderschulwesen" (G_5: 122–23).

21. "Die Verbände sehen einen klaren Widerspruch zu Art. 24 BRK, wenn die Empfehlungen nunmehr die Sonderschulen zu einem konstitutiven Teil inklusiver Bildungsangebote erklären und so den Eindruck erwecken, das deutsche Sonderschulsystem entspreche bereits den Zielsetzungen der BRK. Das Gegenteil ist richtig: Die UN-Behindertenrechtskonvention erfordert tiefgreifende Veränderungen

im deutschen Bildungssystem zugunsten behinderter Kinder, die weit über die bisherige Integration hinausgehen müssen" (DPOs 2011b, 2).

22. "Das Festhalten an einer Doppelstruktur behindert den im Vertragsstaat erforderlichen Transformationsprozess, in dessen Zuge die vorhandenen Ressourcen und Kompetenzen der sonderpädagogischen Förderung in die allgemeine Schule verlagert werden könnten" (DIMR 2015, 27).

23. "Eine gute inklusive Schule ist das Gegenteil vom traditionellen deutschen selektiven Schulsystem. Sie separiert nicht, schult nicht ab und sortiert nicht aus. Solange das deutsche Schulwesen in seiner Mehrgliedrigkeit bestehen bleibt, sind dem Inklusionsprozess Grenzen gesetzt. Ein Grund mehr, der Schulstrukturdebatte durch den Inklusionsauftrag eine neue Dynamik zu geben" (DGB 2015, 7).

24. "Leitbild des Artikels 24 UN-BRK ist der gleichberechtigte Zugang zu Bildung für Menschen mit und ohne Behinderungen" (BuReg 2014a, IV).

25. "Ein Aspekt von besonderem Gewicht ist in den aktuellen Kontroversen, dass viele Inklusionsbefürworter das Elternwahlrecht de facto abschaffen möchten, indem die Möglichkeit der Schulwahl, konkret der Sonder- und Förderschule, ausgeschlossen wird. Für das Elternwahlrecht gibt es gute Gründe, denn in der Regel wissen die Eltern, in welcher Schulart ihr Kind am besten gefördert werden kann" (DPhV 2010, 2).

26. "Da können Sie alle Eltern . . . fragen, wenn sie die Wahl haben aber die Bedingungen, also die Wahl kann eigentlich nur sein ne Wahl zwischen . . . Dingen die gleich gut sind, gleich ausgestattet sind und so weiter. Und dann würden eigentlich alle Eltern gemeinsame Erziehung wählen" (G_1: 263–67).

27. "Die Kompetenzen der allgemeinen Schule im Umgang mit der Heterogenität der Schülerschaft sind ebenso wie ihre Einstellungen zur Akzeptanz von Verschiedenheit zu stärken. Die Erweiterung des Angebots sonderpädagogischer Förderung in einer zunehmend inklusiven allgemeinen Schule ist eine komplexe und kontinuierliche Aufgabe" (KMK 2010, 8).

28. "Von einer Weichenstellung hin zu einem »inklusiven System« kann erst dann gesprochen werden, wenn die sonderpädagogische Förderung systematisch und strukturell in die allgemeine Schule verankert wird und gleichzeitig trennende Strukturen im Bereich der schulischen Bildung überwunden werden" (DIMR 2015, 27).

29. For an overview of the different arrangements of cooperation in regular schools to ensure the integration of children with special needs see Blanck 2014, 2015.

30. "In allen Lehramtsstudiengängen sind Module zur Sonderpädagogik, zu Heterogenität und Inklusion sowie zur Zusammenarbeit mit den unterschiedlichen Professionen verpflichtend vorzuhalten" (DGB 2015, 7).

31. "Und sozusagen diese menschenrechtliche Fundierung einfach für die ein komplett Neues, eine komplett neue Sichtweise ist" (G_3: 60–63).

32. "Es gibt häufiger sehr ideologisch behaftete Diskussionen um dieses Thema, wo man also nicht versucht gemeinsam vom Kind aus zu denken . . . , so was nutzt jetzt dem Kind tatsächlich im Lernen, in der Bildung . . . sondern man hat jetzt. . . . nen Ziel vor Augen und das wird jetzt verfolgt, so. . . . zum Teil dann eben argumentiert wird, da, dass ist jetzt ein Menschenrecht und das müssen wir jetzt, das muss jetzt einfach umgesetzt werden, Punkt" (G_6: 178–85).

33. "Um den Anspruch und die Bedeutung der UN-Konvention richtig einzuschätzen, muss man wissen, dass weltweit 98 Prozent der Menschen mit Behinderungen bis heute keinen Zugang zu Bildungseinrichtungen haben. Die UN-Konvention ist vor diesem Hintergrund ein entscheidender Schritt nach vorn. Sie nimmt die unterzeichnenden Staaten in die Pflicht, Menschen mit Behinderung über Teilhabe an der Bildung eine Teilhabe an der Gesellschaft zu ermöglichen. Deutschland hat dies mit seinem vielgliedrigen Schulsystem bereits umgesetzt" (DPhV 2010, 1).

34. "Unsere hohe Fachlichkeit, die wir haben, das ist also ne Rückmeldung, wir haben ein ausgeprägtes Sonderschulsystem aber deswegen haben wir dann auch nen ausgeprägtes . . . Ausbildung von Sonderpädagogen für die verschiedensten Bereiche, das haben die anderen Länder gar nicht so, und da haben wir durchaus was zu bieten" (G_1: 560–64).

Chapter 5

1. This is the case even though some critics of special schools claim to pursue the goal of "one school for all," which builds on the 1980s' heated policy discussions about integration and comprehensive schools (*Gesamtschulen*), and dissolves into statements that pursue the transfer of special education into regular schools. The crucial difference between the global goal of "all schools for all" and the contextual goal of "one school for all" is that the former is concerned with the human right to inclusive education, while the latter is concerned with school structures.

2. Although overlapping, the concept of decoupling differs from the more general concept of loose coupling, which refers to the weak links "between changing organizational practices and organizational decision making" (Boxenbaum and Jonsson 2008, 90). In other words, with the concept of loose coupling the disconnection of organizations' policy talks and policy actions amid competing demands come to the fore, while, with the concept of decoupling, their purposeful disentanglement for reasons of legitimacy comes into focus (see Meyer and Rowan 1977, 358–59; Steiner-Khamsi 2012, 467).

3. That it is highly contentious to even step a little beyond these boundaries that have traditionally circumscribed the parameters of special education becomes obvious in the German discourse when critics of special schools are accused of ideology.

4. Focusing on its contribution to isomorphy, the institutional concept of myth thus differs from its usage in a cultural, anthropological, or psychological sense (e.g., Assmann 1992; Beauvoir [1968] 2000; Boa 1994; Horkheimer and Adorno [1944] 1969).

Chapter 6

1. Phrasing inspired by Alderman 2017, 334.

References

Abang, Theresa B. 1992. "Special Education in Nigeria." *International Journal of Disability, Development and Education* 39 (1): 13–18.

Abdurrahman, Alhaji M., and Peter Canham. 1978. *The Ink of the Scholar.* Lagos: Macmillan Nigeria.

Achebe, Chinua. (1993) 2010. "The Education of a British-Protected Child." In *The Education of a British-Protected Child*, edited by Chinua Achebe, 3–24. London: Penguin Classics.

Adelani, Alli Ibrahim. 2014. "Management System of Islamic Private Schools in Nigeria, Madrasah Da'wah al-Islamiyyat, Case Study." *International Journal of Scientific and Research Publications* 4 (1): 1–6.

Adesina, Segun. 1988. *The Development of Modern Education in Nigeria.* Ibadan: Heinemann Educational Books Nigeria.

Adick, Christel. 2003. "Globale Trends weltweiter Schulentwicklung: Empirische Befunde und theoretische Erklärungen." *Zeitschrift für Erziehungswissenschaft* 6 (2): 173–87.

Agunloye, Olajide O. 2012. *Inclusive Education: Principles and Concepts.* Jos: Saniez.

Ajikobi, David. 2017. "Does Nigeria Have the World's Most Girls Out-of-School, as Malala Claimed?" Africa Check, August 10. https://africacheck.org/reports/nigeria-girls-school-worldwide-activist-malala-claimed/

Ajuwon, Paul M. 2012. "A Study of Nigerian Families Who Have a Family Member with Down Syndrome." *Journal on Developmental Disabilities* 18 (2): 36–49.

Akogun, Oladele, Sani Njobdi, and Adebayo Adebukola. 2018. "A Study of the Management and Implementation of the Policy on Special Needs and Disability for Improving Access of Persons with Disabilities to Nigeria's Basic Education." EDOREN (Education in Data, Research and Evaluation in Nigeria) Thematic Research Study #6. http://www.nigeria-education.org/edoren/wp-content/uploads/2018/08/EDOREN-SEND-Final-report.pdf

Alderman, Naomi. 2017. *The Power*. London: Penguin.

Alheit, Peter. 2012. "Zwischen den Kulturen." *Zeitschrift für Qualitative Forschung* 13 (1–2): 77–92.

Amoo, Abdulssalam. 2019. "How UBE Intervention Funds are Shared." EduCeleb. May 9. https://educeleb.com/ube-intervention-funds-sharing/

Andzayi, Charity A. 2003. *Introduction to Programmes and Services for Children with Special Needs in Nigeria*. Jos: Department of Special Education, University of Jos.

Angermuller, Johannes. 2014. "AkteurIn." In *DiskursNetz: Wörterbuch der interdisziplinären Diskursforschung*, edited by Daniel Wrana, Alexander Ziem, Martin Reisigl, Martin Nonhoff, and Johannes Angermuller, 25–26. Berlin: Suhrkamp.

Angermuller, Johannes. 2015. "Discourse Studies." In *International Encyclopedia of the Social & Behavioral Sciences*, edited by James D. Wright, 2nd ed., 510–15. Amsterdam: Elsevier.

Anweiler, Oskar. 1988. *Schulpolitik und Schulsystem in der DDR*. Opladen: Leske + Budrich.

Arthur, Lore, Elizabeth McNess, and Michael Crossley. 2016. "Positioning Insider-Outsider Research in the Contemporary Context." In *Revisiting Insider-Outsider Research in Comparative and International Education*, edited by Michael Crossley, Lore Arthur, and Elizabeth McNess, 11–20. Oxford: Symposium Books.

Artiles, Alfredo J., and Alan Dyson. 2005. "Inclusive Education in the Globalization Age: The Promise of Cultural-Historical Analysis." In *Contextualizing Inclusive Education: Evaluating Old and New Perspectives*, edited by David Mitchell, 37–62. London: Routledge.

Asiwe, C. C., and Odirin Omiegbe. 2014. "Legal and Ethical Issues of Persons with Special Needs in Nigeria." *Educational Research and Reviews* 9 (15): 516–22.

Assmann, Jan. 1992. "Frühe Formen politischer Mythomotorik." In *Revolution und Mythos*, edited by Dietrich Harth and Jan Assmann, 39–61. Frankfurt am Main: Fischer.

Autorengruppe Bildungsberichterstattung. 2014. *Bildung in Deutschland 2014*. Bielefeld: Bertelsmann. https://www.bildungsbericht.de/de/bildungsberichte -seit-2006/bildungsbericht-2014/pdf-bildungsbericht-2014/bb-2014.pdf

Autorengruppe Bildungsberichterstattung. 2016. *Bildung in Deutschland 2016*. Bielefeld: Bertelsmann. https://www.bildungsbericht.de/de/bildungsberichte -seit-2006/bildungsbericht-2016/pdf-bildungsbericht-2016/bildungsbericht -2016

Baker, David P., and Gearld K. LeTendre. 2005. *National Differences, Global Similarities*. Stanford: Stanford University Press.

Ball, Stephen J. 1998. "Big Policies / Small World: An Introduction to International Perspectives in Education Policy." *Comparative Education* 34 (2): 119–30. https://doi.org/10.1080/03050069828225

Barton, Len, ed. 1988. *The Politics of Special Educational Needs*. London: Falmer Press.

Barton, Len, and Sally Tomlinson, eds. 2014. *Special Education and Social Interests*. London: Routledge.

Bäumer-Schleinkofer, Änne. 1995. *Nazi Biology and Schools*. Frankfurt am Main: Peter Lang.

Beauftragter der Bundesregierung für die Belange behinderter Menschen. 2021. "English Information." Accessed October 26, 2021. https://www.behindertenb eauftragter.de/Languages/EN/english-node.html#doc41780bodyText1

Beauvoir, Simone de. (1968) 2000. *Das andere Geschlecht*. Reinbek: Rowohlt.

Becker-Ritterspach, Florian A. A., and Jutta C. E. Becker-Ritterspach. 2006. "Isomorphie und Entkopplung im Neo-Institutionalismus." In *Einführung in den Neo-Institutionalismus*, edited by Konstanze Senge and Kai-Uwe Hellmann, 102–17. Wiesbaden: VS Verlag für Sozialwissenschaften.

Beco, Gauthier de. 2014. "The Right to Inclusive Education According to Article 24 of the UN Convention on the Rights of Persons with Disabilities: Background, Requirements and (Remaining) Questions." *Netherlands Quarterly of Human Rights* 32 (3): 263–87. https://doi.org/10.1177/016934411403200304

Beco, Gauthier de. 2016. "Transition to Inclusive Education Systems According to the Convention on the Rights of Persons with Disabilities." *Nordic Journal of Human Rights* 34 (1): 40–59. https://doi.org/10.1080/18918131.2016.1153183

Beco, Gauthier de. 2018. "The Right to Inclusive Education: Why is there so much Opposition to its Implementation?" *International Journal of Law in Context* 14 (3): 396–415. https://doi.org/10.1017/S1744552317000532

Beech, Jason. 2009. "Who Is Strolling through the Global Garden? International Agencies and Educational Transfer." In *International Handbook of Comparative Education*, edited by Robert Cowen and Andreas M. Kazamias, 341–57. Dordrecht: Springer Science and Business Media.

Beech, Jason. 2011. *Global Panaceas, Local Realities*. Frankfurt am Main: Peter Lang.

Benzecry, Claudio E., and Monika Krause. 2010. "How Do They Know? Practicing Knowledge in Comparative Perspective." *Qualitative Sociology* 33 (4): 415–22. https://doi.org/10.1007/s11133-010-9159-8

Berger, Peter, and Thomas Luckmann. (1966) 1984. *The Social Construction of Reality*. Harmondsworth: Penguin.

Berg-Schlosser, Dirk, and Gisèle Meur. 2009. "Comparative Research Design." In *Configurational Comparative Methods. Qualitative Comparative Analysis (QCA) and Related Techniques*, edited by Benoit Rihoux and Charles C. Ragin, 19–32. Thousand Oaks: Sage.

Berhanu, Girma, and Alan Dyson. 2012. "Special Education in Europe, Overrepresentation of Minority Students." In *Encyclopedia of Diversity in Education*, edited by James A. Bank, 4:2070–73. London: Sage.

Bickenbach, Jerome E. 2009. "Disability, Culture and the UN Convention." *Disability and Rehabilitation* 31 (14): 1111–24. https://doi.org/10.1080/096382809 02773729

Biermann, Julia, and Justin J. W. Powell. 2014. "Institutionelle Dimensionen inklusiver Schulbildung—Herausforderungen der UN-Behindertenrechtskonvention für Deutschland, Island und Schweden im Vergleich." *Zeitschrift für Erziehungswissenschaft* 17 (4): 679–700. https://doi.org/10.1007/s11618-014-0588-0

Blanck, Jonna M. 2014. *Organisationsformen schulischer Integration und Inklusion: Eine vergleichende Betrachtung der 16 Bundesländer. Discussion Paper SP I 2014–501*. Berlin: Wissenschaftszentrum Berlin (WZB).

Blanck, Jonna M. 2015. "Schulische Integration und Inklusion in Deutschland." In *Inklusion von Schülerinnen und Schülern mit sonderpädagogischem Förderbedarf in Schulleistungserhebungen*, edited by Poldi Kuhl, Petra Stanat, Birgit Lütje-Klose, Cornelia Gresch, Hans Anand Pant, and Manfred Prenzel, 153–77. Wiesbaden: Springer. https://doi.org/10.1007/978-3-658-06604-8_6

Blanck, Jonna M., Benjamin Edelstein, and Justin J. W. Powell. 2013. "Persistente schulische Segregation oder Wandel zur inklusiven Bildung?" *Swiss Journal of Sociology* 39 (2): 267–92.

Blanck, Jonna M., Benjamin Edelstein, and Justin J. W. Powell. 2014. "Auf dem Pfad zur inklusiven Bildung?" In *Inklusion und Chancengleichheit: Diversity im Spiegel von Bildung und Didaktik*, edited by Saskia Schuppener, Nora Bernhardt, Mandy Hauser, and Frederik Poppe, 97–104. Bad Heilbrunn: Klinkhardt.

BMAS (Bundesministerium für Arbeit und Soziales). 2011a. *Unser Weg in eine inklusive Gesellschaft: Der Nationale Aktionsplan der Bundesregierung zur Umsetzung der UN-Behindertenrechtskonvention*. Berlin: BMAS. https://www.bmas.de /DE/Service/Publikationen/a740-aktionsplan-bundesregierung.html

BMAS (Bundesministerium für Arbeit und Soziales). 2011b. "Übereinkommen der Vereinten Nationen über Rechte von Menschen mit Behinderungen: Erster Staatenbericht der Bundesrepublik Deutschland. Vom Bundeskabinett beschlossen am 3. August 2011." https://www.bmas.de/SharedDocs/Downloa ds/DE/staatenbericht-2011.pdf?__blob=publicationFile&v=1

BMAS (Bundesministerium für Arbeit und Soziales). 2016. *Nationaler Aktionsplan 2.0 der Bundesregierung zur UN-Behindertenrechtskonvention (UN-BRK)*. Berlin: BMAS. https://www.bmas.de/DE/Service/Publikationen/a750-nationaler-akti onsplan-2-0.html

BMZ (Bundesministerium für wirtschaftliche Zusammenarbeit und Entwicklung). 2013. *Aktionsplan zur Inklusion von Menschen mit Behinderungen (Laufzeit 2013–2015): Strategiepapier 1/2013*. Bonn: BMZ. https://www.gemeinsam-einfach -machen.de/SharedDocs/Downloads/DE/AS/Aktionsplaene/aktionsplan_bmz .pdf?__blob=publicationFile&v=6

BMZ (Bundesministerium für wirtschaftliche Zusammenarbeit und Entwicklung). 2019. *Inklusion von Menschen mit Behinderungen in der deutschen Entwicklungszusammenarbeit: Strategiepapier 12/2019*. Bonn: BMZ. https://www.bmz.de/re source/blob/23582/1b38a51a083cf2ba585e099516d0a80d/strategiepapier495 -12-2019-data.pdf

Boa, Fraser. 1994. *The Way of Myth*. Boston: Shambhala.

Boli, John, Francisco O. Ramirez, and John W. Meyer. 1985. "Explaining the Origins and Expansion of Mass Education." *Comparative Education Review* 29 (2): 145–70.

Boxenbaum, Eva, and Stefan Jonsson. 2008. "Isomorphism, Diffusion and Decoupling." In *The Sage Handbook of Organizational Institutionalism*, edited by Royston Greenwood, Christine Oliver, Kerstin Sahlin, and Roy Suddaby, 78–98. London: Sage.

BRK-Allianz (Alliance of German Non-Governmental Organizations Regarding the UN Convention on the Rights of Persons with Disabilities). 2013. "For Independent Living, Equal Rights, Accessibility and Inclusion! First Civil Society Report on the Implementation of the UN Convention on the Rights of Persons with Disabilities in Germany." Accessed October 27, 2021. http://www.brk-allianz.de/attachments/article/93/Alternative_Report_German_CRPD_Alliance_final.pdf

Brock-Utne, Birgit. 2000. *Whose Education for All?* New York: Falmer Press.

Bruce, Susan Marie, and Kavita Venkatesh. 2014. "Special Education Disproportionality in the United States, Germany, Kenya, and India." *Disability & Society* 29 (6): 908–21. https://doi.org/10.1080/09687599.2014.880330

Bundestag, and Bundesrat. 2008. "Gesetz zu dem Übereinkommen der Vereinten Nationen vom 13. Dezember 2006 über die Rechte von Menschen mit Behinderungen sowie zu dem Fakultativprotokoll vom 13. Dezember 2006 zum Übereinkommen der Vereinten Nationen über die Rechte von Menschen mit Behinderungen vom 21. Dezember 2008." Bundesgesetzesblatt Teil II Nr. 35 vom 31.12.2008. http://www.bgbl.de/xaver/bgbl/start.xav?startbk=Bundesanzeiger_BGBl&jumpTo=bgbl208s1419.pdf

BuReg (Bundesregierung). 2008. "Denkschrift zum Übereinkommen der VN über die Rechte von Menschen mit Behinderungen." Bundestags-Drucksache 16/10808. https://dserver.bundestag.de/btd/16/108/1610808.pdf

BuReg (Bundesregierung). 2014a. "Unterrichtung durch die Bundesregierung: Nationaler Bildungsbericht—Bildung in Deutschland 2014 und Stellungnahme der Bundesregierung." Bundestags-Drucksache 18/2990. http://dipbt.bundestag.de/doc/btd/18/029/1802990.pdf

BuReg (Bundesregierung). 2014b. "Antwort der Bundesregierung auf die Kleine Anfrage der Abgeordneten Özcan Mutlu, Kai Gehring, Corinna Rüffer, weiterer Abgeordneter und der Fraktion BÜNDNIS90/DIEGRÜNEN—Drucksache 18/2886–Stand und Perspektiven schulischer Inklusion." Bundestags-Drucksache 18/3101. http://dipbt.bundestag.de/dip21/btd/18/031/1803101.pdf

BuReg (Bundesregierung). 2020. *Deutsche Nachhaltigkeitsstrategie: Weiterentwicklung 2021.* Berlin: BuReg. www.bundesregierung.de/publikationen

Caerus Capital. 2017. "The Business of Education in Africa." Washington, DC: Caerus Capital.

Campbell, Fiona. 2009. Contours of Ableism. Basingstoke: Palgrave Macmillan.

CESCR (Committee on Economic, Social and Cultural Rights). 1999. "Implementation of the International Covenant on Economic, Social and Cultural Rights: General Comment No. 13. The Right to Education." UN Document E/C.12/1999/10.

Chabott, Colette. 2003. *Constructing Education for Development: International Organizations and Education for All.* New York: Routledge.

Charlton, James L. 1998. *Nothing about Us without Us.* Berkeley: University of California Press.

Charmaz, Kathy. 2013. "Grounded Theory Methods in Social Justice Research." In *Strategies of Qualitative Inquiry,* edited by Norman K. Denzin and Yvonna S. Lincoln, 4th ed., 291–336. Thousand Oaks: Sage.

Charmaz, Kathy. 2014. *Constructing Grounded Theory.* 2nd ed. London: Sage.

Chataika, Tsitsi, Judith Anne McKenzie, Estelle Swart, and Marcia Lyner-Cleophas. 2012. "Access to Education in Africa: Responding to the United Nations Convention on the Rights of Persons with Disabilities." *Disability & Society* 27 (3): 385–98. https://doi.org/10.1080/09687599.2012.654989

Cheng, Sealing. 2011. "The Paradox of Vernacularization: Women's Human Rights and the Gendering of Nationhood." *Anthropological Quarterly* 84 (2): 475–505.

Chua, Lynette J. 2018. *The Politics of Love in Myanmar: LGBT Mobilization and Human Rights as a Way of Life.* Stanford: Stanford University Press.

Clarke, Adele. 2012. *Situationsanalyse: Grounded Theory nach dem Postmodern Turn.* Wiesbaden: VS Verlag für Sozialwissenschaften.

Corbett, Jenny, and Roger Slee. 2016. "An International Conversation on Inclusive Education." In *Inclusive Education: Policy, Context and Comparative Perspectives,* edited by Felicity Armstrong, Derrick Armstrong, and Len Barton. London: Routledge [Ebook].

Corbin, Juliette, and Anselm Strauss. 2008. *Basics of Qualitative Research.* Thousand Oaks: Sage.

CRPD (Committee on the Rights of Persons with Disabilities). 2013. "Concluding Observations on the Initial Report of Australia." UN Document CRPD/C/AUS/CO/1.

CRPD (Committee on the Rights of Persons with Disabilities). 2014a. "Concluding Observations on the Initial Report of Sweden." UN Document CRPD/C/SWE/CO/1.

CRPD (Committee on the Rights of Persons with Disabilities). 2014b. "Concluding Observations on the Initial Report of the Republic of Korea." UN Document CRPD/C/KOR/CO/1.

CRPD (Committee on the Rights of Persons with Disabilities). 2015a. "Concluding Observations on the Initial Report of Germany." UN Document CRPD/C/DEU/CO/1.

CRPD (Committee on the Rights of Persons with Disabilities). 2015b. "Concluding Observations on the Initial Report of Gabon." UN Document CRPD/C/GAB/CO/1.CRPD (Committee on the Rights of Persons with Disabilities).

2015c. "Concluding Observations on the Initial Report of Kenya." UN-Document CRPD/C/KEN/CO/1.

CRPD (Committee on the Rights of Persons with Disabilities). 2016. "General Comment on Article 24 UN CRPD." UN Document CRPD/C/GC/4.

CRPD (Committee on the Rights of Persons with Disabilities). 2017. "Concluding Observations on the Initial Report of the United Kingdom of Great Britain and Northern Ireland." UN Document CRPD/C/GBR/CO/1.

CRPD (Committee on the Rights of Persons with Disabilities). 2018a. "Concluding Observations on the Initial Report of South Africa." UN Document CRPD/C/ZAF/CO/1.

CRPD (Committee on the Rights of Persons with Disabilities). 2018b. "Concluding Observations on the Initial Report of the Russian Federation." UN Document CRPD/C/RUS/CO/1.

CRPD (Committee on the Rights of Persons with Disabilities). 2019a. "Concluding Observations on the Initial Report of India." UN-Doc. CRPD/C/IND/CO/1.

CRPD (Committee on the Rights of Persons with Disabilities). 2019b. "Concluding Observations on the Combined Second and Third Periodic Reports of Spain." UN Document CRPD/C/ESP/CO/2–3.

CSACEFA (Civil Society Action Coalition on Education for All). 2010. "Millennium Development Goals: Nigeria Struggles to Meet Target to Educate over 10m Out of School Children." Leaflet.

CSACEFA (Civil Society Action Coalition on Education for All). n.d. "About Us—Civil Society Action Coalition on Education for All (CSACEFA)." Accessed October 26, 2021. https://www.csacefa.org/index.php/about-us/

Czarniawska, Barbara. 2012. "Operational Risk, Translation, and Globalization." *Contemporary Economics* 6 (2): 26–39. https://doi.org/10.5709/ce.1897-9254.40

Czarniawska, Barbara, and Bernward Joerges. 1996. "Travel of Ideas." In *Translating Organizational Change*, edited by Barbara Czarniawska and Guje Sevón, 13–48. Berlin: Walter de Gruyter.

Czarniawska, Barbara, and Guje Sevón, eds. 1996. *Translating Organizational Change*. Berlin: Walter de Gruyter.

Czarniawska, Barbara, and Guje Sevón, eds. 2005a. *Global Ideas. How Ideas, Objects and Practices Travel in the Global Economy*. Frederiksberg: Liber & Copenhagen Business School Press.

Czarniawska, Barbara, and Guje Sevón. 2005b. "Translation is a Vehicle, Imitations its Motor, and Fashion sits at the Wheel." In *Global Ideas: How Ideas, Objects and Practices Travel in the Global Economy*, edited by Barbara Czarniawska and Guje Sevón, 7–12. Frederiksberg: Liber & Copenhagen Business School Press.

D'Alessio, Simona, and Steven Cowan. 2013. "Cross-Cultural Approaches to the Study of 'Inclusive' and 'Special Needs' Education." In *Annual Review of Comparative and International Education 2013*, 227–61. International Perspectives on

Education and Society 20. Bingley: Emerald Group Publishing. https://doi.org/10.1108/S1479-3679(2013)0000020021

D'Alessio, Simona, Verity Donnelly, and Amanda Watkins. 2010. "Inclusive Education across Europe." *Revista de Psicologia y Educación* 1 (5): 109–26.

D'Alessio, Simona, and Amanda Watkins. 2009. "International Comparisons of Inclusive Policy and Practice: Are We Talking about the Same Thing?" *Research in Comparative and International Education* 4 (3): 233–49. http://dx.doi.org/10.2304/rcie.2009.4.3.233

Daniels, Susanne von. 1983. *Krüppel-Tribunal: Menschenrechtsverletzungen im Sozialstaat*. Cologne: Pahl-Rugenstein.

Deephouse, David L., and Mark Suchman. 2008. "Legitimacy in Organizational Institutionalism." In *The Sage Handbook of Organizational Institutionalism*, edited by Royston Greenwood, Christine Oliver, Kerstin Sahlin, and Roy Suddaby, 49–77. London: Sage.

Degener, Theresia. 1995. "Disabled Persons and Human Rights." In *Human Rights and Disabled Persons: Essays and Relevant Human Rights Instruments*, edited by Theresia Degener and Yolan Koster-Dreese, 9–39. Dordrecht: Martinus Nijhoff.

Degener, Theresia. 2009. "Die UN-Behindertenrechtskonvention als Inklusionsmotor." *Recht der Jugend und des Bildungswesens*, 57 (2): 200–219.

Degener, Theresia. 2012. "Das Recht auf inklusive Bildung als Menschenrecht." *Kritische Justiz* 45 (4): 405–19. https://doi.org/10.5771/0023-4834-2012-4-405

Degener, Theresia. 2017. "A New Human Rights Model of Disability." In *The United Nations Convention on the Rights of Persons with Disabilities*, edited by Valentina Della Fina, Rachele Cera, and Giuseppe Palmisano, 41–59. Cham: Springer International Publishing. https://doi.org/10.1007/978-3-319-43790-3_2

Degener, Theresia, and Andrew Begg. 2019. "Disability Policy in the United Nations: The Road to the Convention on the Rights of Persons with Disabilities." In *Aufbrüche und Umbrüche: Behindertenpolitik und Behindertenrecht in Deutschland und Europa seit den 1970er-Jahren*, edited by Theresia Degener and Marc von Miquel, 43–77. Bielefeld: Transcript.

Dei, George J. Sefa, Alireza Asgharzadeh, Sharon Eblaghie Bahador, and Riyad Ahmed Shahjahan. 2006. *Schooling and Difference in Africa*. Toronto: University of Toronto Press.

Della Fina, Valentina. 2017. "Article 24 [Education]." In *The United Nations Convention on the Rights of Persons with Disabilities: A Commentary*, edited by Valentina Della Fina, Rachele Cera, and Giuseppe Palmisano, 439–70. Cham: Springer International. https://doi.org/10.1007/978-3-319-43790-3_28

Depaepe, Marc, and Paul Smeyers. 2008. "Educationalization as an Ongoing Modernization Process." *Educational Theory* 58 (4): 379–89.

DGB (Deutscher Gewerkschaftsbund). 2015. "Gemeinsam statt getrennt—gewerkschaftliche Kriterien für die Entwicklung inklusiver Schulen." Berlin: DGB. https://schule.dgb.de/++co++1e6920ce-adf5-11e4-99de-52540023ef1a

DiMaggio, Paul, and Walter W. Powell. 1983. "The Iron Cage Revisited." *American Sociological Review* 48 (2): 147–60.

DIMR (Deutsches Institut für Menschenrechte). 2015. *Parallelbericht an den UN-Fachausschuss für die Rechte von Menschen mit Behinderungen anlässlich der Prüfung des ersten Staatenberichts Deutschlands gemäß Artikel 35 der UN-Behindertenrechtskonvention.* Berlin: DIMR. https://www.institut-fuer-mensch enrechte.de/fileadmin/Redaktion/Publikationen/Parallelbericht/Parallelberic ht_an_den_UN-Fachausschuss_fuer_Rechte_Menschen_mit_Behinderungen _Pruefung_1_Staatenbericht.pdf

DIMR (Deutsches Institut für Menschenrechte). 2021. "Rechte von Menschen mit Behinderungen." Accessed October 26, 2021. https://www.institut-fuer-mensc henrechte.de/themen/rechte-von-menschen-mit-behinderungen

DIPF (Leibniz-Institut für Bildungsforschung und Bildungsinformation). 2020. "Education in Germany." Last modified June 23, 2020. https://www.bildungsb ericht.de/en/the-national-report-on-education/education-in-germany

Dixon, Pauline. 2013. *International Aid and Private Schools for the Poor.* Cheltenham: Edward Elgar.

Dörschner, Dörte. 2014. *Die Rechtswirkungen der UN-Behindertenrechtskonvention in Deutschland am Beispiel des Rechts auf inklusive Bildung.* Münster: LIT.

DPhV (Deutscher Philologenverband). 2010. "Position des Deutschen Philologenverbands zum Thema 'Inklusion.'" Accessed October 27, 2021. https:// www.dphv.de/wp-content/uploads/2020/08/2010-Positionspapier_Inklusion _Bildungspoltische-Forderungen.pdf

DPhV (Deutscher Philologenverband). 2011. "8 Thesen des DPhV zur Struktur und Qualität von Schulen und Abschlüssen." Accessed October 27, 2021. https://www.dphv.de/wp-content/uploads/2020/08/2011-Schule-und-Schulstr uktur.pdf

DPOs (Disabled Persons Organizations). 2010. "Positionierung der Verbände zum Entwurf der KMK-Empfehlungen 'Kinder und Jugendliche mit Behinderungen in Schulen' (Stand 6. August 2010)." Accessed October 27, 2021. https:// www.vdk.de/deutscher-behindertenrat/mime/00064313D1308307730.pdf

DPOs (Disabled Persons Organizations). 2011a. "Stellungnahme der Verbände zu den KMK-Empfehlungen 'Inklusive Bildung von Kindern und Jugendlichen mit Behinderungen in Schulen' vom 3.12.2010." Accessed October 27, 2021. https://www.vdk.de/deutscher-behindertenrat/mime/00064313D1308307730 .pdf

DPOs (Disabled Persons Organizations). 2011b. "Verbändeübergreifende Positionierung anlässlich der KMK-Amtschefkonferenz am 15. September 2011 zu den KMK-Empfehlungen 'Inklusive Bildung von Kindern und Jugendlichen mit Behinderungen in Schulen' (Stand 17. Juni 2011)." Accessed April 6, 2021. http://www.sovd.de/fileadmin/downloads/pdf/stellungnahmen/TTTTStN _Verbaende_zur_Amtschefkonferenz__mit_Logos_2011-8-31.pdf

Egede, Edwin. 2007. "Bringing Human Rights Home." *Journal of African Law* 51 (2): 249–84.

Ejiogu, Aloy M. 1986. *Landmarks in Educational Development in Nigeria: An Appraisal.* Lagos: Joja Educational Research and Publishers.

Ellger-Rüttgardt, Sieglind. 1995. "Special Education in Germany." *European Journal of Special Needs Education* 10 (1): 75–91. https://doi.org/10.1080/08856259 50100108

Ellger-Rüttgardt, Sieglind Luise. 2016. "Historicher Überblick." In *Handbuch Inklusion und Sonderpädagogik,* edited by Ingeborg Hedderich, Gottfried Biewer, Judith Hollenweger, and Reinhard Markowetz, 17–27. Bad Heilbrunn: Klinkhardt.

ESSPIN (Education Sector Support Programme in Nigeria). 2013. "Inclusive Education Approach Paper." Doc No. ESSPIN 064. https://www.esspin.org/re sources/reports/programme/esspin-programme-management

ESSPIN (Education Sector Support Programme in Nigeria). 2017. "Education Sector Support Programme in Nigeria (ESSPIN)." Accessed October 26, 2021. http://www.esspin.org/

European Agency. 2017. *European Agency Statistics on Inclusive Education: 2014 Dataset Cross-Country Report.* Odense: European Agency for Special Needs and Inclusive Education.

Ewang, Anietie. 2019. "Nigeria Passes Disability Rights Law." Human Rights Watch, January 25. https://www.hrw.org/news/2019/01/25/nigeria-passes-dis ability-rights-law

Fabunmi, Martins. 2005. "Historical Analysis of Educational Policy Formulation in Nigeria." *International Journal of African & African American Studies* 4 (2): 1–7.

Fafunwa, A. Babs. (1974) 2018. *History of Education in Nigeria.* Abingdon: Routledge.

Falola, Toyin. 1999. *The History of Nigeria.* Westport: Greenwood.

Falola, Toyin. 2009. *Colonialism and Violence in Nigeria.* Bloomington: Indiana University Press.

Falola, Toyin, and Matthew M. Heaton. 2008. *A History of Nigeria.* Cambridge: Cambridge University Press.

Feller, Barbara, and Wolfgang Feller. 2001. *Die Adolf-Hitler-Schulen: Pädagogische Provinz versus ideologische Zuchtanstalt.* Weinheim: Juventa.

Florian, Lani. 2007. "Reimagining Special Education." In *The Sage Handbook of Special Education,* edited by Lani Florian, 7–20. London: Sage.

FME (Federal Ministry of Education). 2003. "Education Sector Status Report." https://planipolis.iiep.unesco.org/sites/default/files/ressources/nigeria_ed_sect or_status_may_2003.pdf

FME (Federal Ministry of Education). 2005. "Nigeria Education Sector Diagnosis." https://planipolis.iiep.unesco.org/sites/default/files/ressources/nigeria_ed ucation_sector_diagnosis.pdf

FME (Federal Ministry of Education). 2007. *Federal Ministry of Education 10 Year*

Strategic Plan, Draft 8 05 March 2007. https://planipolis.iiep.unesco.org/sites
/default/files/ressources/nigeria_10_year_federal_education_plan_draft.pdf

FME (Federal Ministry of Education). 2008. "The Development of Education.
National Report of Nigeria by the Federal Ministry of Education for the Forty-
Eighth Session of the International Conference on Education (ICE), Theme:
Inclusive Education—the Way Forward." http://www.ibe.unesco.org/fileadm
in/user_upload/archive/National_Reports/ICE_2008/nigeria_NR08.pdf

FME (Federal Ministry of Education). 2010. *Training Manual on Adaptation and
Implementation of Inclusive Education in Nigeria.* Abuja: FME.

FME (Federal Ministry of Education). 2012a. *4-Year Strategic Plan for the Development of the Education Sector: 2011-2015.* Abuja: FME.

FME (Federal Ministry of Education). 2012b. *2012 Implementation Report of the
4-Year Strategic Development Plan for the Education Sector.* Abuja: FME.

FME (Federal Ministry of Education). 2015. "*Education for All—a Collective Responsibility: Nigeria EFA Review Report 2000–2014 Strides and Milestones.*" http://une
sdoc.unesco.org/images/0023/002310/231081e.pdf

FME (Federal Ministry of Education). 2016. "National Policy on Inclusive Education in Nigeria (Draft)." Softcopy.

FME (Federal Ministry of Education). n.d. "Implementation Plan for Special
Needs Education Strategy." Hardcopy.

FMWA (Federal Ministry of Women Affairs and Social Development). 2011.
"Report of the National Baseline Survey in Persons with Disabilities (PWDs)
in Nigeria, Funded by the Millennium Development Goals (MDGs) Office,
with Statistical Support from the National Bureau of Statistics (NBS)." Softcopy.

Foucault, Michel. (1969) 2002. *The Archaeology of Knowledge.* London: Routledge.

Foucault, Michel. 1980. *Power/Knowledge. Selected Interviews and Other Writings,
1972–1977.* Edited by Colin Gordon. New York: Pantheon.

Friedland, Roger, and R. Robert Alford. 1991. "Bringing Society Back In." In *The
New Institutionalism in Organizational Analysis,* edited by Walter W. Powell and
Paul J. DiMaggio, 232–63. Chicago: University of Chicago Press.

FRN (Federal Republic of Nigeria). 2004a. "Compulsory, Free Universal Basic
Education Act." http://www.unesco.org/education/edurights/media/docs/7bd
bc8b2a9a9188909f3ed44baf5392c3b68f844.pdf

FRN (Federal Republic of Nigeria). 2004b. *National Policy on Education.* 4th ed.
Lagos: Nigerian Educational Research and Development Council Press.

FRN (Federal Republic of Nigeria). 2009. "National Report Submitted in Accordance with Paragraph 15 (A) of the Annex to Human Rights Council Resolution 5/1. Nigeria." UN Document A/HRC/WG.6/4/NGA/1.

FRN (Federal Republic of Nigeria). 2013a. *National Policy on Education.* 6th ed.
Lagos: Nigerian Educational Research and Development Council Press.

FRN (Federal Republic of Nigeria). 2013b. "National Report Submitted in Accordance with Paragraph 5 of the Annex to Human Rights Council Resolution 16/21. Nigeria." UN Document A/HRC/WG.6/17/NGA/1.

FRN (Federal Republic of Nigeria). 2015. *Nigeria 2015 Millennium Development Goals End-Point Report.* Abuja: Office of the Senior Special Assistant to the President on Millennium Development Goals (MDGs). https://planipolis.iiep.une sco.org/sites/default/files/ressources/nigeria_mdgs_report_2015_abridged_ve rsion.pdf

FRN (Federal Republic of Nigeria). 2017a. *Economic Recovery and Growth Plan, 2017–2020.* Abuja: Ministry of Budget and National Planning. https://nation alplanning.gov.ng/wp-content/uploads/2021/02/ERGP-CLEAN-COPY.pdf

FRN (Federal Republic of Nigeria). 2017b. *Implementation of the SDGs: A National Voluntary Review.* Abuja: FRN. https://sustainabledevelopment.un.org/content /documents/16029Nigeria.pdf

FRN (Federal Republic of Nigeria). 2018. "Discrimination Against Persons with Disabilities (Prohibition) Act, 2018." Softcopy.

FRN (Federal Republic of Nigeria). n.d. *National Action Plan (NAP) for Implementation of the UBE Programme to Achieve Education for All (EFA) and the Millennium Development Goals by 2015.* Abuja: FRN.

Füssel, Hans-Peter, and Rudolf Kretschmann. 1993. *Gemeinsamer Unterricht für behinderte und nicht-behinderte Kinder.* Bonn: M. Wehle.

Gabel, Susan, ed. 2005. *Disability Studies in Education: Readings in Theory and Method.* New York: Peter Lang.

Gabel, Susan, Svjetlana Curcic, Justin J. W. Powell, Khalid Kader, and Lynn Albee. 2009. "Migration and Ethnic Group Disproportionality in Special Education." *Disability & Society* 24 (5): 625–39.

Garuba, Ayo. 1996. *Basics of Special Education.* Oyo: Educational and Management Services EMS.

Gebhardt, Markus, Christine Sälzer, Julia Mang, Katharina Müller, and Manfred Prenzel. 2015. "Performance of Students with Special Educational Needs in Germany." *Journal of Cognitive Education and Psychology* 14 (3): 343–56. https:// doi.org/10.1891/1945-8959.14.3.343

Geißler, Gert. 2011. *Schulgeschichte in Deutschland: Von den Anfängen bis in die Gegenwart.* Frankfurt am Main: Peter Lang.

Gelhaus, Dirk, and Jörn O. Hülter. 2003. *Die Ausleseschulen als Grundpfeiler des NS-Regimes.* Würzburg: Königshausen & Neumann.

Gemeinsam Leben Gemeinsam Lernen. 2015. "Eingabe an den UN Fachausschuss Bildung." Accessed November 6, 2016. http://www.gemeinsamleben-ge meinsamlernen.de/sites/all/themes/skeletontheme/css//UN%20Fachausschu ss%20M%C3%A4rz%202015.pdf

George, Alexander L., and Andrew Bennett. 2005. *Case Studies and Theory Development in the Social Sciences.* Cambridge: MIT Press.

Germany. 2015. "German Statement Concerning the Draft General Comment on

Article 24 CRPD." Accessed October 27, 2021. http://www.ohchr.org/Docum ents/HRBodies/CRPD/GC/RighttoEducation/Germany.pdf

Giesecke, Hermann. 1999. *Hitlers Pädagogen*. 2nd ed. Munich: Juventa.

Globale Bildungskampagne. 2013. *Gleiche Rechte, gleiche Chancen. Inklusive Bildung für Kinder mit Behinderungen*. Berlin: Globale Bildungskampagne. https://www .bildungskampagne.org/sites/default/files/download/Gleiche%20Rechte%2C %20gleiche%20Chancen_barrierefrei.pdf

GPE (Global Partnership for Education). 2013. "Federal Republic of Nigeria. Appraisal of Education Sector Plans of Five States of the North West Region." http://www.globalpartnership.org/content/appraisal-education-sector-plans -5-states-nigeria

GPE (Global Partnership for Education). 2021. "About GPE." Accessed October 26, 2021. https://www.globalpartnership.org/who-we-are/about-gpe

Greenwood, Royston, Christine Oliver, Kerstin Sahlin, and Roy Suddaby. 2008. "Introduction." In *The Sage Handbook of Organizational Institutionalism*, edited by Royston Greenwood, Christine Oliver, Kerstin Sahlin, and Roy Suddaby, 1–46. London: Sage.

Guar, N., and D. Ivom. 2010. *Ability in DisABILITY: A Handbook on Understanding Disability*. Abuja: Yaliam Press.

Hafner-Burton, Emilie M., and Kiyoteru Tsutsui. 2005. "Human Rights in a Globalizing World: The Paradox of Empty Promises." *American Journal of Sociology* 110 (5): 1373–411. https://doi.org/10.1086/428442

Hall, Jacquelyn Dowd. 2005. "The Long Civil Rights Movement and the Political Uses of the Past." *Journal of American History* 91 (4): 1233–63. https://doi.org /10.2307/3660172

Hamelink, Cees J. 2012. "Human Rights." *Journal of International Communication* 18 (2): 245–65. https://doi.org/10.1080/13216597.2012.709929

Hänsel, Dagmar. 2003. "Die Sonderschule—ein blinder Fleck in der Schulsystemforschung." *Zeitschrift für Pädagogik* 48 (4): 591–609.

Hänsel, Dagmar. 2005. "Die Historiographie der Sonderschule: Eine kritische Analyse." *Zeitschrift für Pädagogik* 51 (1): 101–15.

Hänsel, Dagmar. 2006. *Die NS-Zeit als Gewinn für Hilfsschullehrer*. Bad Heilbrunn: Klinkhardt.

Hänsel, Dagmar. 2014. "Die nationalsozialistische Hilfsschullehrerausbildung in ihren Kontinuitäten zu vorangegangenen und nachfolgenden Entwicklungen." *International Journal for the Historiography of Education* 4 (2): 29–50.

Härmä, Joanna. 2013. "Access or Quality? Why Do Families Living in Slums Choose Low-Cost Private Schools in Lagos, Nigeria?" *Oxford Review of Education* 39 (4): 548–66. https://doi.org/10.1080/03054985.2013.825984

Harry, Beth. 2014. "The Disproportionate Placement of Ethnic Minorities in Special Education." In *The Sage Handbook of Special Education*, edited by Lani Florian, 2nd ed., 1:73–95. London: Sage.

Helbig, Marcel, and Rita Nikolai. 2015. *Die Unvergleichbaren: Der Wandel der Schulsysteme in den deutschen Bundesländern seit 1949*. Bad Heilbrunn: Klinkhardt.

Helfferich, Cornelia. 2014. "Leitfaden- und Experteninterviews." In *Handbuch Methoden der empirischen Sozialforschung*, edited by Nina Baur and Jörg Blasius, 559–74. Wiesbaden: Springer Fachmedien. https://doi.org/10.1007/978-3-531 -18939-0_39

Heyer, Katharina. 2015. *Rights Enabled: The Disability Revolution, from the US, to Germany and Japan, to the United Nations*. Ann Arbor: University of Michigan Press.

Heyer, Katharina. 2021. "What is a Human Right to Inclusive Education? The Promises and Limitations of the CRPD's Inclusion Mandate." In *Handbuch Inklusion international / International Handbook of Inclusive Education*, edited by Andreas Köpfer, Justin J. W. Powell, and Raphael Zahnd, 45–58. Opladen, Berlin, Toronto: Verlag Barbara Budrich. https://doi.org/10.2307/j.ctv1f70kvj.5

Hildeschmidt, Anne, and Irmtraud Schnell. 1998. *Integrationspädagogik: Auf dem Weg zu einer Schule für Alle*. Weinheim: Juventa.

Horkheimer, Max, and Theodor W. Adorno. (1944) 1969. *Dialektik der Aufklärung: Philosophische Fragmente*. Frankfurt am Main: Fischer.

House of Representatives. 2008. "A Bill for an Act to Ensure Full Integration of Nigerians with Disability into the Society and to Establish a National Commission for Persons with Disability and Vest it with the Responsibilities for their Education, Health Care and the Protection of their Social, Economic, Civil and Political Rights. Sponsors: Hon. Abike Dabiri and 17 Other Hon." Softcopy.

Hutcheon, Emily, and Gregor Wolbring. 2012. "Voices of 'Disabled' Post Secondary Students." *Journal of Diversity in Higher Education* 5 (1): 39–49.

IOM (International Organization for Migration). 2014. *Needs Assessment of Nigerian Education Sector*. Abuja: IOM. http://publications.iom.int/system/files/pdf /needs_assessment_nigerianeducsector.pdf

IQB (Institut zur Qualitätsentwicklung im Bildungswesen). n.d. "Bildungsstandards." Accessed October 26, 2021. https://www.iqb.hu-berlin.de/bista

Jakobi, Anja P., Janna Teltemann, and Michael Windzio. 2010. "The Internationalization of Education Policy in a Cross-National Perspective." In *Transformation of Education Policy*, edited by Kerstin Martens, Alexander-Kenneth Nagel, Michael Windzio, and Ansgar Weymann, 227–58. London: Palgrave Macmillan.

Jay, Jason. 2013. "Navigating Paradox as a Mechanism of Change and Innovation in Hybrid Organizations." *Academy of Management Journal* 56 (1): 137–59. https://doi.org/10.5465/amj.2010.0772

Jepperson, Ronald L. 1991. "Institutions, Institutional Effects, and Institutionalism." In *The New Institutionalism in Organizational Analysis*, edited by Walter W. Powell and Paul DiMaggio, 143–63. Chicago: University of Chicago Press.

JONAPWD (Joint National Association of Persons with Disabilities). 2012. "Memorandum Submitted to the National Assembly on Review of the 1999 Constitution of the Federal Republic of Nigeria." Softcopy.

JONAPWD (Joint National Association of Persons with Disabilities). 2015. "Joint National Association of Persons with Disabilities at a Glance." Accessed October 26, 2021. http://www.jonapwd.org/about.html

Keller, Reiner. 2008. *Wissenssoziologische Diskursanalyse: Grundlegung eines Forschungsprogramms.* Wiesbaden: VS Verlag für Sozialwissenschaften.

Keller, Reiner. 2011. "The Sociology of Knowledge Approach to Discourse (SKAD)." *Human Studies* 34 (1): 43–65. https://doi.org/10.1007/s10746-011 -9175-z

Keller, Reiner. 2013a. *Doing Discourse Research: An Introduction for Social Scientists.* London: Sage.

Keller, Reiner. 2013b. "Zur Praxis der Wissenssoziologischen Diskursanalyse." In *Methodologie und Praxis der Wissenssoziologischen Diskursanalyse*, edited by Reiner Keller and Inga Truschkat, 27–68. Wiesbaden: VS Verlag für Sozialwissenschaften.

Keller, Reiner, Andreas Hirseland, Werner Schneider, and Willy Viehöver. 2005. "Die diskursive Konstruktion von Wirklichkeit: Einleitende Bemerkungen zum Verhältnis von Wissenssoziologie und Diskursforschung." In *Die diskursive Konstruktion der Wirklichkeit*, edited by Reiner Keller, Andreas Hirseland, Werner Schneider, and Willy Viehöver, 7–21. Konstanz: UVK.

Kiuppis, Florian. 2016. "From Special Education, via Integration, to Inclusion." *ZEP—Zeitschrift für Internationale Bildungsforschung und Entwicklungspädagogik* 39 (3): 28–33.

Klemm, Klaus, and Jutta Roitsch. 2015. *Hauptsache Bildung.* Münster: Waxmann.

KMK (Kultusministerkonferenz). 1994. "Empfehlungen zur sonderpädagogischen Förderung in den Schulen in der Bundesrepublik Deutschland. Beschluß der Kultusministerkonferenzvom06.05.1994." http://www.kmk.org/fileadmin/Dateien /veroeffentlichungen_beschluesse/1994/1994_05_06-Empfehl-Sonderpaedag ogische-Foerderung.pdf

KMK (Kultusministerkonferenz). 2010. "Pädagogische und rechtliche Aspekte der Umsetzung des Übereinkommens der Vereinten Nationen vom 13. Dezember 2006 über die Rechte von Menschen mit Behinderungen in der schulischen Bildung; Beschluss der Kultusministerkonferenz vom 18.11.2010." http://www .kmk.org/fileadmin/Dateien/veroeffentlichungen_beschluesse/2010/2010_11 _18-Behindertenrechtkonvention.pdf

KMK (Kultusministerkonferenz). 2011. "Inklusive Bildung von Kindern und Jugendlichen mit Behinderungen in Schulen; Beschluss der Kultusministerkonferenz vom 20.10.2011." http://www.kmk.org/fileadmin/Dateien/veroeffe ntlichungen_beschluesse/2011/2011_10_20-Inklusive-Bildung.pdf.

KMK (Kultusministerkonferenz). 2016. *Sonderpädagogische Förderung in Schulen 2005 bis 2014, Dokumentation 210.* Berlin: KMK. https://www.kmk.org/fileadm in/Dateien/pdf/Statistik/Dokumentationen/Dok_210_SoPae_2014.pdf

KMK (Kultusministerkonferenz). 2017. *"Basic Structure of the Education System in the Federal Republic of Germany."* https://www.kmk.org/fileadmin/Dateien/pdf /Dokumentation/en_2017.pdf

KMK (Kultusministerkonferenz). 2018. *Sonderpädagogische Förderung in Schulen 2007 bis 2016, Dokumentation 214*. Berlin: KMK. https://www.kmk.org/filead min/Dateien/pdf/Statistik/Dokumentationen/Dok_214_SoPaeFoe_2016.pdf

KMK (Kultusministerkonferenz). 2019. *The Education System in the Federal Republic of Germany 2016/2017: A Description of the Responsibilities, Structures and Development in Education Policy for the Exchange of Information in Europe*. Berlin: KMK. https://www.kmk.org/fileadmin/Dateien/pdf/Eurydice/Bildungswesen-engl -pdfs/dossier_en_ebook.pdf

KMK (Kultusministerkonferenz). 2020. *Sonderpädagogische Förderung in Schulen 2009 bis 2018: Statistische Veröffentlichungen der Kultusministerkonferenz, Dokumentation Nr. 223*. Berlin: KMK. https://www.kmk.org/fileadmin/Dateien/pdf /Statistik/Dokumentationen/Dok223_SoPae_2018.pdf

KMK (Kultusministerkonferenz). 2021. "Aufgaben der Kultusministerkonferenz." Accessed October 26, 2021. https://www.kmk.org/kmk/aufgaben.html

KMK (Kultusministerkonferenz), and HRK (Hochschulrektorenkonferenz). 2015. "Lehrerbildung für eine Schule der Vielfalt / Englisch Version: Educating Teachers to Embrace Diversity: Joint Recommendations by the German Rectors' Conference and the Standing Conference of the Ministers of Education and Cultural Affairs of the States in the Federal Republic of Germany." http:// www.kmk.org/fileadmin/Dateien/veroeffentlichungen_beschluesse/2015/2015 _03_12-KMK-HRK-Empfehlung-Vielfalt-englisch.pdf

Knoblauch, Hubert. 2001. "Diskurs, Kommunikation und Wissenssoziologie." In *Handbuch Sozialwissenschaftliche Diskursanalyse*, vol. 1: *Theorien und Methoden*, edited by Rainer Keller, Andreas Hirseland, Werner Schneider, and Willy Viehöver, 207–33. Wiesbaden: VS Verlag für Sozialwissenschaften. https://doi .org/10.1007/978-3-322-99906-1_8

Kocaj, Aleksander, Poldi Kuhl, Anna J. Kroth, Hans Anand Pant, and Petra Stanat. 2014. "Wo lernen Kinder mit sonderpädagogischem Förderbedarf besser?" *KZfSS Kölner Zeitschrift für Soziologie und Sozialpsychologie* 66 (2): 165–91. https://doi.org/10.1007/s11577-014-0253-x

Kocaj, Aleksander, Poldi Kuhl, Camilla Rjosk, Malte Jansen, Hans Anand Pant, and Petra Stanat. 2015. "Der Zusammenhang zwischen Beschulungsart, Klassenkomposition und schulischen Kompetenzen von Kindern mit sonderpädagogischem Förderbedarf." In *Inklusion von Schülerinnen und Schülern mit sonderpädagogischem Förderbedarf in Schulleistungserhebungen*, edited by Poldi Kuhl, Petra Stanat, Birgit Lütje-Klose, Cornelia Gresch, Hans Anand Pant, and Manfred Prenzel, 335–70. Wiesbaden: Springer Fachmedien. https://doi.org /10.1007/978-3-658-06604-8_12

Koch, Sascha. 2009. "Die Bausteine neo-institutionalistischer Organisationstheorie— Begriffe und Konzepte im Lauf der Zeit." In *Neo-Institutionalismus in der Erziehungswissenschaft: Grundlegende Texte und empirische Studien*, edited by Sascha Koch and Michael Schemmann, 110–31. Wiesbaden: VS Verlag für Sozialwissenschaften.

Koch, Sascha, and Michael Schemmann. 2009. "Neo-Institutionalismus und Erziehungswissenschaft—Eine einleitende Verhältnisbestimmung." In *Neo-Institutionalismus in der Erziehungswissenschaft: Grundlegende Texte und empirische Studien*, edited by Sascha Koch and Michael Schemmann, 7–18. Wiesbaden: VS Verlag für Sozialwissenschaften. https://doi.org/10.1007/978-3-531-91496-1_1

Konrad, Franz-Michael. 2012. *Geschichte der Schule*. Munich: Beck.

Köbsell, Swantje. 2006. "The Disability Rights Movement in Germany: History, Development, Present State." *Disability Studies Quarterly* 26 (2). http://dx.doi.org/10.18061/dsq.v26i2.692

Köpfer, Andreas, Justin J. W. Powell, and Raphael Zahnd, eds. 2021. *Handbuch Inklusion international / International Handbook of Inclusive Education*. Opladen, Berlin, Toronto: Verlag Barbara Budrich. https://doi.org/10.3224/84742446

Kottmann, Brigitte. 2006. *Selektion in die Sonderschule: Das Verfahren zur Feststellung von sonderpädagogischem Förderbedarf als Gegenstand empirischer Forschung*. Bad Heilbrunn: Klinkhardt.

Lang, Raymond. 2009. "The United Nations Convention on the Right and Dignities for Persons with Disability: A Panacea for Ending Disability Discrimination?" *Current Trends and Development in Global Disability Research / Mondialisation et Recherche sur le Handicap : Courants Actuels* 3 (3): 266–85. https://doi.org/10.1016/j.alter.2009.04.001

Latour, Bruno. 1986. "The Power of Association." In *Power, Action, and Belief: A New Sociology of Knowledge?*, edited by John Law, 264–80. London: Routledge & Kegan Paul.

Lawrence, Thomas B., Roy Suddaby, and Bernard Leca. 2009. "Introduction: Theorizing and Studying Institutional Work." In *Institutional Work: Actors and Agency in Institutional Studies of Organization*, edited by Thomas B. Lawrence, Roy Suddaby, and Bernard Leca, 1–28. Cambridge: Cambridge University Press.

Lendvai, Noémi, and Paul Stubbs. 2007. "Policies as Translation: Situating Transnational Social Policies." In *Policy Reconsidered: Meanings, Politics and Practices*, edited by Susan M. Hodgson and Zoë Irving, 173–89. Bristol: Policy Press.

Leschinsky, Achim. 2005. "Vom Bildungsrat (nach) zu PISA: Eine zeitgeschichtliche Studie zur deutschen Bildungspolitik." *Zeitschrift für Pädagogik* 56 (6): 818–39.

Levitt, Peggy, and Sally Merry. 2009. "Vernacularization on the Ground." *Global Networks* 9 (4): 441–61.

Ley, Astrid, and Annette Hinz-Wessels. 2012. *The "Euthanasia Institution" of Brandenburg an der Havel: Murder of the Ill and Handicapped during National Socialism*. Berlin: Metropol.

Locke, Richard, and Kathleen Thelen. 1998. "Problems of Equivalence in Comparative Politics." *Newsletter of the APSA Organized Section in Comparative Politics* 9 (1): 9–12.

Lütje-Klose, Birgit, Susanne Miller, Susanne Schwab, and Bettina Streese, eds. 2017. *Inklusion: Profile für die Schul- und Unterrichtsentwicklung in Deutschland, Österreich und der Schweiz. Theoretische Grundlagen—Empirische Befunde—Praxisbeispiele.* Münster: Waxmann.

Mahoney, James, and Kathleen Thelen. 2010. "A Theory of Gradual Institutional Change." In *Explaining Institutional Change. Ambiguity, Agency, and Power,* edited by James Mahoney and Kathleen Thelen, 1–37. New York: Cambridge University Press.

Martens, Kerstin, and Philipp Knodel. 2014. *Internationalization of Education Policy: A New Constellation of Statehood in Education?* Edited by Michael Windzio. London: Palgrave Macmillan.

Merry, Sally Engle. 2006. *Human Rights and Gender Violence: Translating International Law into Local Justice.* Chicago: University of Chicago Press.

Merry, Sally Engle, and Peggy Levitt. 2017. "The Vernacularization of Women's Human Rights." In *Human Rights Futures,* edited by Stephen Hopgood, Jack Snyder, and Leslie Vinjamuri, 213–36. Cambridge: Cambridge University Press. https://doi.org/10.1017/9781108147767.009

Meyer, John W. 1994. "Rationalized Environments." In *Institutional Environments and Organizations.: Structural Complexity and Individualism,* edited by W. Richard Scott and John W. Meyer, 28–54. Thousand Oaks: Sage.

Meyer, John W., John Boli, Georg M. Thomas, and Francisco O. Ramirez. 1997. "World Society and the Nation-State." *American Journal of Sociology* 103 (1): 144–81.

Meyer, John W., and Francisco O. Ramirez. 2000. "The World Institutionalization of Education." In *Discourse Formation in Comparative Education,* edited by Jürgen Schriewer, 111–32. Frankfurt am Main: Peter Lang.

Meyer, John W., and Brian Rowan. 1977. "Institutionalized Organizations: Formal Structure as Myth and Ceremony." *American Journal of Sociology* 83 (2): 340–63.

Meyer, John W., and W. Richard Scott. 1983. "Centralization and the Legitimacy Problems of Local Governments." In *Organizational Environments: Ritual and Rationality,* edited by John W. Meyer and W. Richard Scott, 199–215. Beverly Hills: Sage.

Meyer, John W., W. Richard Scott, and Terrence E. Deal. 1992. "Institutional and Technical Sources of Organizational Structure: Explaining the Structure of Educational Organizations." In *Organizational Environments: Ritual and Rationality,* edited by John W. Meyer and W. Richard Scott, 45–67. Newbury Park: Sage.

Meyer, Renate E. 2008. "New Sociology of Knowledge: Historical Legacy and Contributions to Current Debates in Institutional Research." In *The Sage Handbook of Organizational Institutionalism,* edited by Royston Greenwood, Christine Oliver, Kerstin Sahlin, and Roy Suddaby, 519–38. Thousand Oaks: Sage.

Miles, Susie, and Anupam Ahuja. 2007. "Learning from Difference: Sharing International Experiences of Developments in Inclusive Education." In *The Sage Handbook of Special Education*, edited by Lani Florian, 131–45. London: Sage.

Miles, Susie, and Nidhi Singal. 2010. "The Education for All and Inclusive Education Debate: Conflict, Contradiction or Opportunity?" *International Journal of Inclusive Education* 14 (1): 1–15. https://doi.org/10.1080/13603110802265125

Minello, Alessandra, and Hans-Peter Blossfeld. 2016. "From Parents to Children: The Impact of Mothers' and Fathers' Educational Attainments on Those of Their Sons and Daughters in West Germany." *British Journal of Sociology of Education* 38 (5): 686–704. https://doi.org/10.1080/01425692.2016.1150156

Ministerium für Gesundheitswesen, and Akademie für Ärztliche Fortbildung. 1978. *Schwerbeschädigtenbetreuung und Rehabilitation: Eine Zusammenstellung der wichtigsten gesetzlichen Bestimmungen und Arbeitsmaterialien mit Anmerkungen und Sachregister*. Berlin: Staatsverlag der Deutschen Demokratischen Republik.

Mißling, Sven, and Oliver Ückert. 2014. *Inklusive Bildung: Schulgesetz auf dem Prüfstand*. Berlin: Deutsches Institut für Menschenrechte. https://www.institut-fuer
-menschenrechte.de/fileadmin/Redaktion/Publikationen/Studie_Inklusive_Bil
dung_Schulgesetze_auf_dem_Pruefstand.pdf

Mizunoya, Suguru, Sopie Mitra, and Izumi Yamasaki. 2016. *Towards Inclusive Education: The Impact of Disability on School Attendance in Developing Countries. Innocenti Working Paper No.2016-03*. Florence: UNICEF. https://www.unicef-irc.org/pu
blications/pdf/IWP3%20-%20Towards%20Inclusive%20Education.pdf

Möckel, Andreas. 2007. *Geschichte der Heilpädagogik*. 2nd ed. Stuttgart: Klett-Cotta.

Moser, Vera. 2012. "Gründungsmythen der Heilpädagogik." *Zeitschrift für Pädagogik* 58 (2): 262–74.

Moser, Vera, and Ada Sasse. 2008. *Theorien der Behindertenpädagogik*. Munich: Ernst Reinhardt.

Mostert, Mark P. 2016. "Stigma as Barrier to the Implementation of the Convention on the Rights of Persons with Disabilities in Africa." In *The African Disability Rights Yearbook*, edited by Charles Ngewna, Ilze Grobbelaar-du Plessis, Helene Combrinck, and Serges Djoyou Kamga, 3–24. Pretoria: Pretoria University Law Press.

Motunrayo, Joel. 2019. "No New Data Shows that 10 Million Children are Out of School in Nigeria." Africa Check, June 13. https://africacheck.org/spot-check
/no-new-data-shows-that-10-million-children-are-out-of-school-in-nigeria/

Muhammad, Nafisatu, and Ahmed Modibbo Mohammed. 2005. *Improving the Quality of Nomadic Education in Nigeria*. African Experiences—Country Case Studies. Paris: Association for the Development of Education in Africa.

Müller, Katharina, Manfred Prenzel, Christine Sälzer, Julia Mang, Jörg-Henrik Heine, and Markus Gebhardt. 2017. "Wie schneiden Schülerinnen und Schüler an Förderschulen bei PISA ab?" *Unterrichtswissenschaft* 45 (2): 175–92.

Münch, Sybille. 2016. *Interpretative Policy-Analyse*. Wiesbaden: Springer Fachmedien.

Mundy, Karen, and Francine Menashy. 2014. "The World Bank and Private Provi-

sion of Schooling." *Comparative Education Review* 58 (3): 401–27. https://doi
.org/10.1086/676329

Mutua, Makau. 2001. "Savages, Victims, and Saviors: The Metaphor of Human
Rights." *Harvard International Law Journal* 42 (1): 201–45.

Naraian, Srikala. 2017. *Teaching for Inclusion: Eight Principles for Effective and Equitable Practice.* New York: Teachers College Press.

National Technical Working Group on Education Sector. 2009. "Report of the
Vision 2020 National Technical Working Group on Education." Softcopy.

NBS (National Bureau of Statistics Nigeria). 2015. *Nigerian Formal Education Sector, Summary Report: 2010–2012.* Abuja: NBS.

NESSE (Network of Experts in Social Sciences of Education and Training). 2012.
*Education and Disability/ Special Needs: Policies and Practices in Education, Training
and Employment for Students with Disability and Special Educational Needs in the
EU.* Brussels: European Union. http://www.nesse.fr/nesse/activities/reports/ac
tivities/reports/disability-special-needs-1

Netzwerk Artikel 3. 2010. "Schattenübersetzung des NETZWERK ARTIKEL
3 e.V. Korrigierte Fassung der zwischen Deutschland, Liechtenstein, Österreich und der Schweiz abgestimmten, Übersetzung Übereinkommen über die
Rechte von Menschen mit Behinderungen." Accessed October 27, 2021. http://
www.netzwerk-artikel-3.de/dokum/schattenuebersetzung-endgs.pdf

NHRC (National Human Rights Commission). n.d. "Response of the National
Human Rights Commission of Nigeria to the Implementation of Article 33 of
the Convention on the Rights of Persons with Disabilities." Accessed October
27, 2021. http://www2.ohchr.org/english/issues/disability/docs/NigeriaHuma
nRightsCommission.doc

Niven, Cecil Rex. 1967. *A Short History of Nigeria.* Ibadan: Longman Nigeria.

Nkechi, C. M. 2013. "Education of the Disabled in Nigeria." *Journal Plus Education*
10 (1): 133–42.

Nnamani, Sunday N. 2015. "Functional Local Government System in Nigeria." In
*Intcess 15: 2nd International Conference on Education and Social Sciences Abstracts &
Proceedings,* edited by Ferit Uslu, 1148–54. Istanbul: OCERINT International
Organization Center of Academic Research.

Nola, Robert. 1998. "Knowledge, Discourse, Power and Genealogy in Foucault."
In *Foucault,* edited by Robert Nola, 109–54. London: Frank Cass.

NPC (National Planning Commission). 2004. "National Economic Empowerment and Development Strategy NEEDS." Abuja: NPC. http://www.cbn.gov
.ng/out/Publications/communique/GUIDELINES/rd/2004/NEEDS.pdf

NPC (National Planning Commission). 2009. *Nigeria Vision 20: 2020.* Abuja:
NPC. https://nationalplanning.gov.ng/wp-content/uploads/2021/02/nigeria
-vision-20-20-20.pdf

NPopC (National Population Commission Nigeria), and RTI International. 2016a.
2015 Nigeria Education Data Survey (NEDS): National Report. Washington, DC:
United States Agency for International Development.

NPopC (National Population Commission Nigeria), and RTI International. 2016b. *2015 Nigeria Education Data Survey (NEDS): Education Profile.* Washington, DC: United States Agency for International Development.

Nyssen, Elke. 1979. *Schule im Nationalsozialismus.* Heidelberg: Quelle & Meyer.

Obanya, Pai. 2001. "UBE as a Necessary First Step." In *Universal Basic Education in Nigeria: Concepts, Issues and Prospects,* edited by P. O. Nwaokolo, G. C. Igborgbor, and G. C. Nduka, 1–8. Asaba: Federal College of Education (Technical) Asaba.

Obiakor, Festus E., Michael Eskay, and Michael O. Afolayan. 2012. "Special Education in Nigeria." In *Advances in Research and Praxis in Special Education in Africa, Caribbean, and the Middle East,* edited by Kagendo Mutua and Cynthia Szymanski Sunal, 23–36. Charlotte: Information Age.

Obiakor, Festus E., and Fr. MaxMary Tabugbo Offor. 2011. "Special Education Provision in Nigeria." *International Journal of Special Education* 26 (1): 13–19.

Obidi, S. S. 2005. *Culture and Education in Nigeria.* Ibadan: University Press PLC.

OHCHR (Office of the High Commissioner for Human Rights). 2013. "Thematic Study on the Right of Persons with Disabilities." UN Document A/HRC/25/29.

Okonkwo, Uche Uwaezuoke, and Mary-Noelle Ethel Ezeh. 2008. "Implications of Missionary Education for Women in Nigeria." *Journal of International Women's Studies* 10 (2): 186–97.

Olutoyin, Babatunde Isaac. 2014. "Treaty Making and Its Application under Nigerian Law." *International Journal of Business and Management Invention* 3 (3): 7–18.

Omenka, Nicholas Ibeawuchi. 1989. *The School in the Service of Evangelization.* Leiden: Brill.

Omoeva, Carina, Benjamin Sylla, Rachel Hatch, and Charles Gale. 2013. *Out of School Children. Data Challenges In Measuring Access to Education.* Washington, DC: Education Policy and Data Center.

Onogu, Sanni. 2016. "Disability Bill: A Legislation as a Phoenix." *Vanguard,* August 13, 2016. http://www.vanguardngr.com/2016/08/disability-bill-legislation-phoenix/

Opp, Günther. 1992. "A German Perspective on Learning Disabilities." *Journal of Learning Disabilities* 25 (6): 351–60. https://doi.org/10.1177/002221949202500603

Oyelade, A. F. 2017. "Aliu Babatunde Fafunwa's Philosophy of Education." *Makerere Journal of Higher Education* 9 (1): 87–96. https://doi.org/10.4314/majohe.v9i1.7

Peters, Susan. 2007. "Inclusion as a Strategy for Achieving Education for All." In *The Sage Handbook of Special Education,* edited by Lani Florian, 117–30. London: Sage.

Pfahl, Lisa. 2010. "Organisierte Armut: Soziale Ausgrenzung im gegliederten Schulsystem." *WZB Mitteilungen,* no. 128: 11–13.

Pfahl, Lisa. 2011. *Techniken der Behinderung: Der deutsche Lernbehinderungsdiskurs, die Sonderschule und ihre Auswirkungen auf Bildungsbiografien.* Bielefeld: Transcript.

Pfahl, Lisa, and Justin J. W. Powell. 2009. "Menschenrechtsverletzung im deutschen Schulsystem: behindert werden durch Sonderbeschulung." In *Grundrechtereport: Zur Lage der Bürger- und Menschenrechte in Deutschland*, edited by Till Müller-Heidelber, Ulrich Finckh, Elke Steven, Moritz Assall, Marai Pelzer, Andrea Würdinger, Martin Kutscha, Rolf Gössner, and Ulrich Engelfried, 95–99. Frankfurt am Main: Fischer.

Pfahl, Lisa, and Justin J. W. Powell. 2011. "Legitimating School Segregation: The Special Education Profession and the Discourse of Learning Disability in Germany." *Disability & Society* 26 (4): 449–62. https://doi.org/10.1080/09687599.2011.567796

PLAC (Policy and Legal Advocacy Centre). n.d. a. "SB 42: National Commission for the Eradication of Child Destitution (Establishment) Bill, 2019." Accessed October 27, 2021. https://placbillstrack.org/view.php?getid=6633

PLAC (Policy and Legal Advocacy Centre). n.d. b. "Bill Process." Accessed October 26, 2021. https://placbillstrack.org/index.php

Poore, Carol. 2009. *Disability in Twentieth-Century German Culture*. Ann Arbor: University of Michigan Press.

Powell, Justin J. W. 2007. "Behinderung in der Schule, behindert durch Schule?" In *Disability Studies, Kultursoziologie und Soziologie der Behinderung: Erkundungen in einem neuen Forschungsfeld*, edited by Anne Waldschmidt and Werner Schneider, 321–43. Bielefeld: Transcript.

Powell, Justin J. W. 2009. "Von schulischer Exklusion zur Inklusion?" In *Neo-Institutionalismus in der Erziehungswissenschaft: Grundlegende Texte und empirische Studien*, edited by Sascha Koch and Michael Schemann, 1:213–32. Wiesbaden: VS Verlag für Sozialwissenschaften.

Powell, Justin J. W. 2013. "Kulturen der sonderpädagogischen Förderung und 'schulische Behinderung.'" In *Kulturvergleich in der qualitativen Forschung*, edited by Merle Hummrich and Sandra Rademacher, 139–54. Wiesbaden: Springer Fachmedien Wiesbaden. https://doi.org/10.1007/978-3-531-18937-6_8

Powell, Justin J. W. (2011) 2016. *Barriers to Inclusion: Special Education in the United States and Germany*. London: Routledge.

Powell, Justin J. W., and Lisa Pfahl. 2012. "Sonderpädagogische Fördersysteme." In *Handbuch Bildungs- und Erziehungssoziologie*, edited by Ullrich Bauer, Uwe H. Bittlingmayer, and Albert Scherr, 721–39. Wiesbaden: VS Verlag für Sozialwissenschaften. https://doi.org/10.1007/978-3-531-18944-4_43

Powell, Justin J. W., and Lisa Pfahl. 2019. "Disability and Inequality in Educational Opportunities from a Life Course Perspective." In *Research Handbook on the Sociology of Education*, edited by Rolf Becker, 383–406. Cheltenham: Edward Elgar. https://doi.org/10.4337/9781788110426.00031

Powell, Justin J. W., and Sandra Wagner. 2014. "An der Schnittstelle Ethnie und Behinderung benachteiligt: Jugendliche mit Migrationshintergrund an deutschen Sonderschulen weiterhin überrepräsentiert." In *Behinderung und Migration: Interdisziplinäre Perspektiven*, edited by Gudrun Wansing and Manuela Westphal, 177–99. Wiesbaden: VS Verlag für Sozialwissenschaften.

Power, Colin. 2015. *The Power of Education*. Singapore: Springer Singapore. https://doi.org/10.1007/978-981-287-221-0_1

Prior, Lindsay. 2008. "Documents and Action." In *The Sage Handbook of Social Research Methods*, edited by Pertti Alasuutari, Leonard Bickmann, and Julia Brannen, 479–92. London: Sage.

Prognos AG. 2014. *Evaluation des Nationalen Aktionsplans der Bundesregierung zur Umsetzung der UNBehindertenrechtskonvention: Abschlussbericht*. Basel: Prognos AG.

Proske, Matthias. 2001. *Pädagogik und die Dritte Welt: Eine Fallstudie zur Pädagogisierung sozialer Probleme*. Frankfurter Beiträge zur Erziehungswissenschaft. Frankfurt am Main: Johann Wolfgang Goethe-Universität.

Proske, Matthias. 2002. "Pädagogisierung und Systembildung." *Zeitschrift für Erziehungswissenschaft* 5 (2): 279–98. https://doi.org/10.1007/s11618-002-0020-z

Przeworski, Adama, and Henry Teune. 1970. *The Logic of Comparative Social Inquiry*. New York: Wiley-Interscience.

Ragin, Charles C. 1992. "Introduction." In *What Is a Case? Exploring the Foundations of Social Inquiry*, edited by Charles C. Ragin and Howard S. Becker, 1–17. Cambridge: Cambridge University Press.

Ramirez, Francisco O., and John Boli. 1987. "The Political Construction of Mass Schooling: European Origins and Worldwide Institutionalization." *Sociology of Education* 60 (1): 2–17. https://doi.org/10.2307/2112615

Reilly, Rosemary C. 2010. "Process Tracing." In *Encyclopedia of Case Study Research*, edited by Albert J. Mills, Gabrielle Durepos, and Elden Wiebe, 2:734–36. Thousand Oaks: Sage.

Richardson, John G., and Justin J. W. Powell. 2011. *Comparing Special Education: Origins to Contemporary Paradoxes*. Stanford: Stanford University Press.

Rioux, Marcia. 2007. "Disability Rights in Education." In *The Sage Handbook of Special Education*, edited by Lani Florian, 107–16. London: Sage.

Roeder, Peter M. 2003. "TIMSS und PISA—Chancen eines neuen Anfangs in Bildungspolitik, -planung, -verwaltung und Unterricht: Endlich ein Schock mit Folgen?" *Zeitschrift für Pädagogik* 49 (2): 180–97.

Rottenburg, Richard. 2002. *Weit hergeholte Fakten: Eine Parabel der Entwicklungshilfe*. Stuttgart: Lucius & Lucius.

Ryan, Mark. 2020. *The Enduring Legacy: Structured Inequality in America's Public Schools*. Ann Arbor: University of Michigan Press.

Sächsische Landesschule. 2021. "Landesschule mit dem Förderschwerpunkt Hören, Förderzentrum Samuel Heinicke" Accessed October 27, 2021. http://www.landesschule-fuer-hoergeschaedigte.sachsen.de/

Sahlin, Kerstin, and Linda Wedlin. 2008. "Circulating Ideas." In *The Sage Hand-*

book of Organizational Institutionalism, edited by Royston Greenwood, Christine Oliver, Kerstin Sahlin, and Roy Suddaby, 218–42. London: Sage.

Salheiser, Axel. 2014. "Natürliche Daten." In *Handbuch Methoden der empirischen Sozialforschung*, edited by Nina Baur and Jörg Blasius, 813–27. Wiesbaden: Springer Fachmedien. https://doi.org/10.1007/978-3-531-18939-0_62

Sälzer, Christine, Markus Gebhardt, Katharina Müller, and Elena Pauly. 2015. "Der Prozess der Feststellung sonderpädagogischen Förderbedarfs in Deutschland." In *Inklusion von Schülerinnen und Schülern mit sonderpädagogischem Förderbedarf in Schulleistungserhebungen*, edited by Poldi Kuhl, Petra Stanat, Birgit Lütje-Klose, Cornelia Gresch, Hans Anand Pant, and Manfred Prenzel, 129–52. Wiesbaden: Springer Fachmedien. https://doi.org/10.1007/978-3-658-06604-8_5

Sander, Alfred. 1969. *Die Sonderschulen im geteilten Deutschland*. Berlin: Marhold.

Santos, Boaventura de Sousa. 2009. "Toward a Multicultural Conception of Human Rights." In *International Human Rights Law in a Global Context*, edited by Felipe Gomez Isa and Koen de Feyter, 97–121. Bilbao: University of Deusto.

Schmidt, Vivien A. 2008. "Discursive Institutionalism: The Explanatory Power of Ideas and Discourse." *Annual Review of Political Science* 11 (1): 303–26. https://doi.org/10.1146/annurev.polisci.11.060606.135342

Schmidt, Vivien A. 2010. "Taking Ideas and Discourse Seriously." *European Political Science Review* 2 (1): 1–25. https://doi.org/10.1017/S175577390999021X

Schmidt, Vivien A. 2011. "Reconciling Ideas and Institutions through Discursive Institutionalism." In *Ideas and Politics in Social Science Research*, edited by Daniel Béland and Robert Henry Cox, 47–64. Oxford: Oxford University Press.

Schmidt, Vivien A. 2015. "Discursive Institutionalism: Understanding Policy in Context." In *Handbook of Critical Policy Studies*, edited by Frank Fischer, Douglas Torgerson, Anna Durnová, and Michael Orsini, 171–89. Cheltenham: Edward Elgar.

Schneider, Christian, Cordelia Stillke, and Bernd Leinweber. 1996. *Das Erbe der NAPOLA: Versuch einer Generationengeschichte des Nationalsozialismus*. Hamburg: Hamburger Edition.

Schneider, Volker, and Frank Jannig. 2006. *Politikfeldanalyse: Akteure, Diskurse und Netzwerke in der öffentlichen Politik*. Wiesbaden: VS Verlag für Sozialwissenschaften.

Schnell, Irmtraud. 2016. "(Lern-)Behinderung und soziale Ungleichheit— Sonderpädagogik im Förderschwerpunkt Lernen als Sonderpädagogisierung unterprivilegierter Lebensverhältnisse." In *Handbuch Therapeutisierung und Soziale Arbeit*, edited by Roland Anhorn and Marcus Balzereit, 875–903. Wiesbaden: Springer Fachmedien. https://doi.org/10.1007/978-3-658-10870-0_33

Scott, W. Richard. 1994. "Institutions and Organizations." In *Institutional Environments and Organizations: Structural Complexity and Individualism*, edited by W. Richard Scott, John W. Meyer, and Associates, 55–80. Thousand Oaks: Sage.

Scott, W. Richard. 2003. "Institutional Carriers: Reviewing Modes of Transporting

Ideas over Time and Space and Considering Their Consequences." *Industrial and Corporate Change* 12 (4): 879–94.

Scott, W. Richard. 2008. *Institutions and Organizations*. 3rd ed. Thousand Oaks: Sage.

The Senate. 2013. "A Bill for an Act to Ensure Full Integration of Persons with Disabilities into the Society and to Establish a National Commission for Persons with Disabilities and Vest It with the Responsibilities for Their Education, Health Care and the Protection of Their Social, Economic, Civil Rights. Sponsored by Senator Nurudeen Abatemi-Usman." Softcopy.

Senge, Konstanze. 2011. *Das Neue am Neo-Institutionalismus: Der Neo-Institutionalismus im Kontext der Organisationswissenschaft*. Wiesbaden: VS Verlag für Sozialwissenschaften.

Slee, Roger. 1998. "High Reliability Organisations and Liability Students: The Politics of Recognition." In *School Effectiveness for Whom? Challenges to the School Effectiveness and School Improvement Movements*, edited by Roger Slee, Gaby Weiner, and Sally Tomlinson, 101–14. London: Falmer Press.

Slee, Roger. 2013. "How Do We Make Inclusive Education Happen When Exclusion is a Political Predisposition?" *International Journal of Inclusive Education* 17 (8): 895–907. https://doi.org/10.1080/13603116.2011.602534

Smith, Natalie. 2011. "The Face of Disability in Nigeria." *Disability, CBR and Inclusive Development* 22 (1): 35–47.

Smith, Wendy K., and Marianne W. Lewis. 2011. "Toward a Theory of Paradox: A Dynamic Equilibrium Model of Organizing." *Academy of Management Review* 36 (2): 381–403. https://journals.aom.org/doi/10.5465/amr.2009.0223

Special Interest Group for Persons with Disability. 2009. "Report of the Vision 2020 Special Interest Group for Persons with Disability." Hardcopy.

Special Rapporteur on Disability. 2007. "Report of the Special Rapporteur on Disability of the Commission for Social Development on Monitoring of the Implementation of the Standard Rules on the Equalization of Opportunities for Persons with Disabilities." UN Document E/CN.5/2007/4.

Steiner-Khamsi, Gita. 2010. "The Politics and Economics of Comparison." *Comparative Education Review* 54 (3): 323–42. https://doi.org/10.1086/653047

Steiner-Khamsi, Gita. 2012. "The Global/Local Nexus in Comparative Policy Studies." *Comparative Education* 48 (4): 455–71.

Steiner-Khamsi, Gita. 2014. "Cross-National Policy Borrowing: Understanding Reception and Translation." *Asia Pacific Journal of Education* 34 (2): 153–67. https://doi.org/10.1080/02188791.2013.875649

Steiner-Khamsi, Gita, and Ines Stolpe. 2006. *Educational Import: Local Encounters with Global Forces in Mongolia*. New York: Palgrave Macmillan.

Stone, Deborah. 2012. *Policy Paradox: The Art of Political Decision Making*. 3rd ed. New York: W. W. Norton.

Stone, Diane. 2012. "Transfer and Translation of Policy." *Policy Studies* 33 (6): 483–99. https://doi.org/10.1080/01442872.2012.695933

Stübig, Heinz. 2013. "Das Schulwesen in ausgewählten europäischen Ländern im 19. Jahrhundert." In *Aus der Geschichte Lernen, Zukunft zu gestalten: Inklusive Bildung und Erziehung in Vergangenheit, Gegenwart und Zukunft*, edited by Eckhard Rohrmann, 31–45. Marburg: Tectum.

Suchman, Mark C. 1995. "Managing Legitimacy: Strategic and Institutional Approaches." *The Academy of Management Review* 20 (3): 571–610. https://doi.org/10.2307/258788

Tacke, Veronika. 2006. "Rationalität im Neo-Institutionalismus." In *Einführung in den Neo-Institutionalismus*, edited by Konstanze Senge and Kai-Uwe Hellmann, 89–101. Wiesbaden: VS Verlag für Sozialwissenschaften.

Thakur, A. S., and A. N. Ezenne. 1980. *A Short History of Education in Nigeria*. New Delhi: National Publishing House.

Thornton, Patricia H., and William Ocasio. 1999. "Institutional Logics and the Historical Contingency of Power in Organizations." *American Journal of Sociology* 105 (3): 801–43. https://doi.org/10.1086/210361

Thornton, Patricia H., and William Ocasio. 2008. "Institutional Logics." In *The Sage Handbook of Organizational Institutionalism*, edited by Royston Greenwood, Christine Oliver, Roy Suddaby, and Kerstin Sahlin, 99–129. London: Sage.

Thornton, Patricia H., William Ocasio, and Michael Lounsbury. 2012. *The Institutional Logics Perspective*. Oxford: Oxford University Press.

Tomasevski, Katarina. 2004. *Manual on Rights-Based Education: Global Human Rights Requirements Made Simple*. Bangkok: UNESCO Bangkok. https://unesdoc.unesco.org/ark:/48223/pf0000135168

Tomlinson, Sally. 2012. "The Irresistible Rise of the SEN Industry." *Oxford Review of Education* 38 (3): 267–86. https://doi.org/10.1080/03054985.2012.692055

Tomlinson, Sally. (1982) 2014. "A Sociology of Special Education." In *The Politics of Race, Class and Special Education: The Selected Works of Sally Tomlinson*, edited by Sally Tomlinson, 15–31. London: Routledge.

Tomlinson, Sally. 2017. *A Sociology of Special and Inclusive Education: Exploring the Manufacturing of Inability*. London: Routledge.

Traue, Boris, Lisa Pfahl, and Lena Schürmann. 2014. "Diskursanalyse." In *Handbuch Methoden der empirischen Sozialforschung*, edited by Nina Baur and Jörg Blasius, 493–508. Wiesbaden: Springer Fachmedien. https://doi.org/10.1007/978-3-531-18939-0_34

Tröhler, Daniel. 2016. "Educationalization of Social Problems and the Educationalization of the Modern World." In *Encyclopedia of Educational Philosophy and Theory*, edited by Michael A. Peters, 1–6. Singapore: Springer Singapore. https://doi.org/10.1007/978-981-287-532-7_8-1

Truschkat, Inga. 2013. "Zwischen interpretativer Analytik und GTM—Zur Methodologie einer wissenssoziologischen Diskursanalyse." In *Methodologie und Praxis der Wissenssoziologischen Diskursanalyse*, vol. 1: *Interdisziplinäre Perspektiven*, edited by Reiner Keller and Inga Truschkat, 69–87. Wiesbaden: VS Verlag für Sozialwissenschaften. https://doi.org/10.1007/978-3-531-93340-5_3

UBEC (Universal Basic Education Commission). 2019. "Unaccessed Matching Grant Form 2005–2019, 22 July 2019." Accessed October 27, 2021. https://ub ec-static.s3.amazonaws.com/media/grant/UPDATE_OF_MATCHING_GR ANT_TO_STATES_AS_AT_22ND_JULY_2019_-_UNACCESSED.pdf

UBEC (Universal Basic Education Commission). 2021. "Who We Are." Accessed October 27, 2021. https://www.ubec.gov.ng/about/who-we-are/

UIS (UNESCO Institute for Statistics). 2015. "A Growing Number of Children and Adolescents Are out of School as Aid Fails to Meet the Mark." Policy Paper 22 Fact Sheet 31. Paris: UNESCO. http://uis.unesco.org/sites/default/files/do cuments/fs31-a-growing-number-of-children-and-adolescents-are-out-of-sch ool-as-aid-fails-to-meet-the-mark-2015-en.pdf

UIS (UNESCO Institute for Statistics). 2021. "Country Data Nigeria." Accessed October 27, 2021. http://uis.unesco.org/en/country/ng

Ukpor, C. O., Isaac Ofem Ubi, and Abigail E. Okon. 2012. "Assessment of Factors Determining Parents' Preference for Private Secondary Schools in Rural Communities of Cross River State." *Global Journal of Educational Research* 11 (2): 99–106.

Umeasiegbu, Veronica, and Debra Harley. 2014. "Education as a Tool for Social Justice and Psychological Wellbeing for Women with Disabilities in a Developing Country: The Challenges and Prospects in Nigeria." *The African Symposium* 14 (1–2): 119–31.

UN (United Nations). 2005. "UN Enable—Sixth Session of the Ad Hoc Committee—Daily Summary of Discussions." https://www.un.org/esa/socdev /enable/rights/ahc6summary.htm

UN (United Nations). 2015. *The Millennium Development Goals Report*. New York: UN.

UN (United Nations). 2021. "Status: Convention on the Rights of Persons with Disabilities." UN Treaty Collection. Accessed October 27, 2021. https://trea ties.un.org/Pages/ViewDetails.aspx?src=TREATY&mtdsg_no=IV-15&chapte r=4&clang=_en

UNESCO (United Nations Educational, Scientific and Cultural Organization). 2008. "UNESCO National Education Support Strategy (UNESS) for Nigeria 2006–2015." Abuja: UNESCO Office Nigeria. http://unesdoc.unesco.org/ima ges/0018/001831/183136e.pdf

UNESCO (United Nations Educational, Scientific and Cultural Organization). 2010. *Global Education Monitoring Report 2010*. Paris: UNESCO. http://unesd oc.unesco.org/images/0018/001866/186606E.pdf

UNESCO (United Nations Educational, Scientific and Cultural Organization). 2014. "How Long it Will Take to Complete Basic Education Depends on Which African Child You Are." https://en.unesco.org/gem-report/sites/defau lt/files/day_of_african_child_0.pdf

UNESCO (United Nations Educational, Scientific and Cultural Organization). 2020. *Global Education Monitoring Report 2020: Inclusion and Education: All Means All*. Paris: UNESCO. https://unesdoc.unesco.org/ark:/48223/pf0000373718

UNGA (United Nations General Assembly). 1948. "Universal Declaration of Human Rights." UN Document A/RES/217[III].

UNGA (United Nations General Assembly). 1966. "International Covenant on Civil and Political Rights and Optional Protocol." UN Document A/RES/21/2200.

UNGA (United Nations General Assembly). 1975. "Declaration on the Rights of Disabled Persons." UN Document A/RES/30/3447(XXX).

UNGA (United Nations General Assembly). 1976. "International Year of Disabled Persons." UN Document A/RES/31/123.

UNGA (United Nations General Assembly). 1989. "Convention on the Rights of the Child." UN Document A/RES/44/25.

UNGA (United Nations General Assembly). 1993. "Standard Rules on the Equalization of Opportunities for Persons with Disabilities." UN Document A/RES/48/96.

UNGA (United Nations General Assembly). 2006. "Convention on the Rights of Persons with Disabilities." UN Document A/RES/61/106.

UNGA (United Nations General Assembly). 2015. "Transforming Our World: The 2030 Agenda for Sustainable Development." UN Document A/RES/70/1.

UNHRC (United Nations Human Rights Council). 2007. "Report of the Special Rapporteur on the Right to Education, Vernor Muñoz. Addendum Mission to Germany." UN Document A/HRC/4/29/Add.3.

UNICEF (United Nations Children's Fund). 2013. *The State of the World's Children 2013: Children with Disabilities*. New York: UNICEF. https://data.unicef.org/resources/the-state-of-the-worlds-children-2013-children-with-disabilities/

UNICEF (United Nations Children's Fund). 2015. "Nigeria Conflict Forces More Than 1 Million Children from School. Press Release 22 December 2015." Accessed November 12, 2020. https://www.unicef.org/media/media_86621.html

UNICEF (United Nations Children's Fund). 2017. "More than Half of All Schools Remain Closed in Borno State, Epicentre of the Boko Haram Crisis in Northeast Nigeria." Accessed October 27, 2021. https://www.unicef.org/media/media_100953.html

UNICEF (United Nations Children's Fund), and FME (Federal Ministry of Education). 2012. *All Children in School By 2015, Global Initiative on Out-of-School Children, Nigeria Country Study*. Abuja: UNICEF Nigeria Country Office. https://unesdoc.unesco.org/ark:/48223/pf0000225788

UNICEF Nigeria (United Nations Children's Fund Nigeria). 2021. "Education." Accessed October 27, 2021. https://www.unicef.org/nigeria/education

VENRO (Verband Entwicklungspolitik deutscher Nichtregierungsorganisationen). 2010. *Gewusst wie—Menschen mit Behinderung in Projekte der Entwicklungszusammenarbeit einbeziehen*. Bonn: VENRO. https://venro.org/fileadmin/user_upload/Dateien/Daten/Publikationen/VENRO-Dokumente/Gewusst Wie_v06_WEB.pdf

Wæraas, Arild, and Jeppe Agger Nielsen. 2016. "Translation Theory 'Translated.'" *International Journal of Management Reviews* 18 (3): 236–70. https://doi.org/10 .1111/ijmr.12092

Waterkamp, Dietmar. 2006. *Vergleichende Erziehungswissenschaft: Ein Lehrbuch.* Münster: Waxmann.

Weigt, Michael. 1998. "25 Jahre Empfehlungen des Deutschen Bildungsrates und was davon schulpolitisch übrigblieb." *Gemeinsam leben—Zeitschrift für integrative Erziehung,* no. 2. http://bidok.uibk.ac.at/library/gl2-98-empfehlungen .html

Weisser, Jan. 2005. *Behinderung, Ungleichheit und Bildung. Eine Theorie der Behinderung.* Bielefeld: Transcript.

Weisser, Jan. 2007. "Für eine anti-essentialistische Theorie der Behinderung." *Behindertenpädagogik* 46 (3–4): 237–49.

Werning, Rolf, Alfredo J. Artiles, Petra Engelbrecht, Myriam Hummel, Marta Caballeros, and Antje Rothe, eds. 2016. *Keeping the Promise? Contextualizing Inclusive Education in Developing Countries.* Bad Heilbrunn: Klinkhardt.

Weymann, A. 2010. "The Educating State—Historical Developments and Current Trends." In *Transformation of Education Policy,* edited by K. Martens, A. Nagel, M. Windzio, and A. Weymann, 53–73. Basingstoke: Palgrave Macmillan.

WHO (World Health Organization), and World Bank. 2011. *World Report on Disability.* Geneva: WHO.

Wiborg, Susanne. 2010. "Why is There No Comprehensive Education in Germany?" *History of Education* 39 (4): 539–56. https://doi.org/10.1080/00467601 003685733

Wiseman, Alexander Q., James Pilton, and J. Courtney Lowe. 2010. "International Educational Governance Models and National Policy Convergence." In *International Educational Governance,* edited by S. Karin Amos, 12:3–18. Bingley: Emerald.

Wittmütz, Volkmar. 2007. "Die preußische Elementarschule im 19. Jahrhundert." In *Lernen und Lehren in Frankreich und Deutschland: Apprendre et enseigner en Allemagne et en France,* edited by Stefan Fisch, Florence Gauzy, and Chantal Metzger, 15–32. Stuttgart: Franz Steiner. http://www.europa.clio-online.de/es say/id/artikel-3406

Wolbring, Gregor. 2008. "The Politics of Ableism." *Development* 51 (2): 252–58. https://doi.org/10.1057/dev.2008.17

Wolfsteller, René. 2017. "The Institutionalisation of Human Rights Reconceived." *International Journal of Human Rights* 21 (3): 230–51. https://doi.org/10.1080 /13642987.2017.1298730

World Bank. 2015. "Governance and Finance Analysis of the Basic Education Sector in Nigeria. Report No. ACS14245." Washington, DC: World Bank Group Education. https://openknowledge.worldbank.org/bitstream/handle/10986/23 683/Governance0and0on0sector0in0Nigeria.pdf?sequence=1

World Conference on Special Needs Education. 1994. "The Salamanca Statement and Framework for Action on Special Needs Education." Paris: UNESCO. http://www.unesco.org/education/pdf/SALAMA_E.PDF

World Education Forum. 2000. *The Dakar Framework for Action. Education for All: Meeting Our Collective Commitments*. Paris: UNESCO. http://unesdoc.unesco.org/images/0012/001211/121147e.pdf

Zeune Schule. 2021. "Lernen Sie uns kennen." Accessed October 27, 2021. https://www.zeune-schule.de/lernen-sie-uns-kennen/

Ziemen, Kerstin, Anke Langner, Andreas Köpfer, and Saskia Erbring, eds. 2011. *Inklusion: Herausforderungen, Chancen und Perspektiven*. Hamburg: Dr. Kovač.

Index

Note: Page numbers in *italics* refer to the illustrations and tables; 'n' indicates chapter notes.

unions. *See* teachers' unions
United Kingdom (UK), 20, 40, 125. *See also* colonial education
United Nations Committee on the Rights of Persons with Disabilities, 13, 16, 18, 19, 21, 111, 129–130; General Comment on Article 24 (2016), 1, 14, 16, 83, 105, 110–111
United Nations Convention on the Rights of Persons with Disabilities (UN CRPD), 3–4, 11–13; Article 2, 15; Article 4, 40; Article 33, 7, 12, 40, 74; Article 34, 13; domestication of, 7, 22, 39, 40, 55, 74, 97, 103; ratification of, 22, 39, 54–55, 64, 69, 74, 76, 78, 87, 91, 97, 127. *See also* Article 24 United Nations Convention on the Rights of Persons with Disabilities (UN CRPD)
United Nations Special Rapporteur on Disability, 15
United Nations Special Rapporteur on the Right to Education, 69, 76

United States of America (USA), 11, 18–19, 126
universal basic education (UBE), 34–35, 38–42, 63, 96–98, 102, 104, 122, 148n5, 148n9; Nigerian implementation discourse, 41–61, *43, 44, 46, 50, 59*
universal primary education (UPE), 18, 33, 35, 42, 63

vernacularization of human rights, 11–12, 121, 126–129
Vision 20:2020 (Nigeria), 35, 49–51

Western model of education, 30, 32, 60, 124–126, 148n2. *See also* mass schooling
World Education Forum in Dakar (2000), 5, 40

Zimbabwe, 18